SEX

—— AND ——

GOD

—— AT ——

YALE

NATHAN HARDEN

SEX

— AND —

GOD

— AT —

YALE

PORN, POLITICAL CORRECTNESS,
AND A GOOD EDUCATION GONE BAD

THOMAS DUNNE BOOKS
ST. MARTIN'S PRESS
NEW YORK

THOMAS DUNNE BOOKS.
An imprint of St. Martin's Press.

SEX AND GOD AT YALE. Copyright © 2012 by Nathan Harden. Foreword
copyright © 2012 by Christopher Buckley. All rights reserved.
Printed in the United States of America. For information, address
St. Martin's Press, 175 Fifth Avenue, New York, N.Y. 10010.

www.thomasdunnebooks.com
www.stmartins.com

Library of Congress Cataloging-in-Publication Data

Harden, Nathan.
    Sex and God at Yale : porn, political correctness, and a good
education gone bad / Nathan Harden.
        p. cm.
    Includes bibliographical references and index.
    ISBN 978-0-312-61790-5 (hardcover)
    ISBN 978-1-250-01354-5 (e-book)
    1. Yale University—Students.   2. Education, Higher—Moral
and ethical aspects—United States.   3. College students—Sexual
behavior—United States.   4. Political correctness—United States.
I. Title.
    LD6343.H26 2012
    378.746'8—dc23

                                                        2012024226

First Edition: September 2012

10 9 8 7 6 5 4 3 2 1

To J. Dyess, whose faith, patience, and daring support
helped make this book possible

CONTENTS

CONTENTS

CONTENTS

FOREWORD

Why a foreword by me—or given the context, should I say, foreplay? Could it be that Nathan Harden asked me because I share a surname with the author of *God and Man at Yale*? I wonder. At any rate, I was beguiled—seduced?—by the early pages that he sent me months ago, along with the request that I provide a few words by way of curtain-raising. Having now read the whole book, let me assert a few caveats before plunging in.

First, Mr. Harden says some nice things about a talk I gave at a Yale commencement some years ago. I was unaware that there would be any mention of it in his book, and now find myself in the awkward position of appearing to say nice things about him by way of payback. This is not the case. Second, he says nice things about the author of *God and Man at Yale*. This much I anticipated, but for the record, I am not here out of reciprocity. Third, though I genuinely share Mr. Harden's pain at the administration-sanctioned riot of carnality he witnessed on Yale property, something arrests my inner Captain Renault from declaring that I'm shocked—*shocked*. My capacity to be appalled by Yale has long since gone numb, just as my affection for Yale increases with every passing year. More and more I feel like Mrs. Patrick Campbell, who, upon being told what Oscar Wilde and his boyfriends' friends were up to, remarked, "I don't care what they do, as long as they don't do it in the street and frighten the horses."

During my time in New Haven in the early 1970s, I saw things that . . . well, let me just quote one of my professors, the late Julian Hartt, a marvelous theologian who, confronted with the latest resplendent hypocrisy the administration was frantically trying to peddle as high-mindedness, remarked with a sly, knowing smile, "Anyone who has been at Yale as long as I have has witnessed the lowest absurdity carried out with the highest degree of solemnity."

Further shushing my inner Renault is the fact that—c'mon, now—we live in coarse, brutish times. Pandora's box was a potpourri compared with the filth that springs out at us from the Internet and cable TV. (Did I say "springs out at us"? Didn't we do the Googling and the channel selecting?) Is it realistic to be expected that Yale should be an island of civility in an ocean of sewage? In one of those same auditoria that Yale now apparently provides to porn "stars" and—groan—porn peddlers during "Sex Week," I once listened to a professor analyze a poem on the theme "No man is an island." No, Mr. Harden, we are all part of the main, alas. Even Yalies.

That said, I admit to reading his reportage with arching eyebrow and occasional dropped jaw. How-to lectures on—cover your ears, Muffy—masturbation? Oral sex? Anal sex? Labial piercing? Vibrating cock rings? Dental dams? What's a dental—oh, never mind. And this, from the same platforms on which stood—and stand, still—world-class great scholars, brimming with insight into Plato, Thucydides, Virgil, Locke, Descartes, Cervantes, Melville, Joyce, and all those other dead white males? Say it ain't so.

Mr. Harden describes one lecture by a creature named Katharine Gates on the topic of "Four Levels of Fetishism" ("leather, feet, fat, and goo," in case you were wondering). The climactic moment is worth quoting in its entirety:

> Standing there behind a Yale lectern, atop the platform she had been given that evening, Gates said something that I can guarantee no one other teacher has ever said in a Yale classroom. I heard a faint, collective gasp in the room afterward. In that moment, she made clear the totality of her belief in the acceptability of any and all desire. She said, "As far as I'm concerned, you can fantasize about beheading babies and fucking them in the neck."

Well, Toto, I don't think we're in Kansas anymore. This charming vignette appears about two-thirds of the way through the book, by which time my eyebrows had long since reached the point of arching-fatigue. One is grateful, at least, for that "faint, collective gasp," reassuring evidence that Yalies still number baby beheading for sexual purposes on the list of dwindling taboos. Boola, boola.

I confess to reading about the less repugnant aspects of Sex Week at Yale with a tinge of envy. When I was there, our saying—or mantra—was, "Sex at Yale is like a game of bridge: if you have a good hand, you're really better off playing with yourself." And to think that sounded so—risqué then!

What came as most surprising to this Old Blue was Mr. Harden's assertion that many young women now actually *hope* that the sexual encounter will be transacted briskly—maybe with a bit of kink thrown in—without any emotional strings attached. I guess one of the least-heard exchanges on campus these days is, *But will you respect me in the morning? Yeah, sure, whatever. Ow! Uh, could you like remove those titanium bolts from your clitoris?* I confess that at points while reading this book the thought went through my mind: *Why wasn't this going on while I was there?*

But as anyone who's had even a fleeting experience of porn knows: porn is to Eros what crack is to joy: an industrial-quality stimulant, an attaching of jumper cables to the libido. It is *not* sexy, never mind romantic; it dehumanizes and reduces its participants to the level of mechanics. What it leaves behind—other than sticky residue, much discussed during Sex Week—is a grim scrim of guilty satiation. *Post coitum omne animal triste est.* After coitus, every animal is sad. How then do the animals feel after the modern transaction known as "hooking up"? Or does such straightforward commerce inoculate against *tristesse*?

In the end, tempted as I might be by all this unfettered rumpy-pumpy, I think I'm happy to have been there in more reticent, demure times. (We managed to have fun.) If the Satyricon described herein is truly an accurate depiction of sensuality at Yale today, one yearns for the days when, as a member of the Class of 1913 put it, a glimpse of stocking was looked on as something shocking. Forty years ago, if someone had traveled all the way from the outside world to stand up onstage in SSS 114 to offer us pointers on how to spank the old monkey, it would have been an occasion of comedy, not higher education. What strikes one, in the end, is how utterly *preposterous* sex—whatever orifices are involved—becomes when it is treated with such ludicrous seriousness. The impotence of being earnest, if you will.

The gravamen of Mr. Harden's *J'accuse* is that by tacitly sanctioning this carnival of genitalia, and tut-tutting that "kids will be kids," Yale has lost its sense of moral purpose and is adrift, anchorless, in a sea of political correctness, relativism, and diversity.

In Yale's defense, I can't for the life of me recall any statement by which Yale publicly aspired to stake claim to a moral high ground. Which might be just as well. If, say, you admit a member of the Taliban as a student, or hire an advocate of suicide bombing as member of the faculty, what corporate moral claim, really, are you in a position to make? That "academic freedom" dictates that you have no choice but to admit a member of a fanatical death cult that stones women to death, buries homosexuals alive, cuts off hands and feet, blows up stone Buddhas, detonates suicide bombs, and provides safe haven to affiliated terrorists who fly commercial airliners into skyscrapers? That's diversity. Would Yale invite a member of the Aryan Nations or a neo-Nazi party with a briefcase full of lectures on the subject of "What Holocaust?" I like to think not. But then I used to think it wouldn't welcome the Taliban, or provide an apologist for Hezbollah with a lectern.

It is Mr. Harden's assertion here that feminism has, ironically, brought about an environment in which women willingly—even proudly—allow themselves to become what they once adamantly rejected: objects of debasement and degradation. Betty Freidan, thou shouldst be living at this hour. This is not to say that some of the Yale men depicted here could be mistaken for Dink Stover. If feminism has empowered women to regard sex as a matter of mere engineering, then it has, finally, achieved its goal: moral equivalence with the male of the species, who, for all his shortcomings, never had many illusions on that score. You've come a long way, baby.

But there are real consequences to this new sexual contract. In Mr. Harden's telling, sexual harassment and nonconsensual sex— what we used to call "rape"—have now reached alarming levels. Surprise. Eliminate basic standards of decency and rules of comportment, and inherit the whirlwind.

But never mind the quote-unquote moral question—no, for Yale a concrete danger looms. As Mr. Harden relates, the U.S. Department of Education's Office for Civil Rights has launched an investigation to determine whether Yale's policies on sexual harassment and assault constitute a violation of women's rights under Title IX. In my relatively halcyon days, Title IX was generally just shorthand for the issue of women's athletics. Life was simpler then. According to Mr. Harden, if Yale were found to be in violation of those Title IX statutes, "it could lose all federal funding, currently more than half a billion dollars per year. Financially, it would bring the university to its knees almost overnight." Moola, moola.

So—lots to chew on in this thoughtful and important book. Dental dam optional.

—Christopher Buckley

Bright college years, with pleasure rife,
The shortest, gladdest years of life;
How swiftly are ye gliding by!
Oh, why does time so quickly fly?
The seasons come, the seasons go,
The earth is green or white with snow,
But time and change shall not avail
To break the friendships formed at Yale.

In after years, should trouble rise
To cloud the blue of sunny skies,
How bright will seem, through mem'ry's haze
Those happy, golden, bygone days!
Oh, let us strive that ever we
May let these words our watch cry be,
Where'er upon life's sea we sail:
"For God, for country, and for Yale!"

—H. S. Durand, 1881

INTRODUCTION

What you are about to read is my story. But, for a moment, imagine what it might be like if this story were your own. Imagine you are an eighteen-year-old freshman girl arriving at Yale for the first time. You are bright, poised, excited, nervous about making new friends, and still, if truth be told, a bit naïve. On the day you arrive at Yale, your parents drive you up to the main entrance to the university, an arched Gothic corridor known as Phelps Gate. Your dad hasn't said much during the entire trip. Your mother, on the other hand, is in the throes of empty-nest syndrome and has been crying pretty much nonstop since you pulled out of the driveway the day before.

Your parents help you unload a trunk full of overstuffed suitcases, duct-taped cardboard boxes, bags full of Costco-sized bottles of laundry detergent, granola bars, and an electric blanket your mother insisted you bring along. A pile of clutter is now all you have left of home. You look at that pile and it reminds you that you are leaving home forever. What a shocking thought.

Mom is standing there wiping her eyes. Dad keeps clearing his throat and staring down at the ground. You swallow hard. Your eyes are watering. You know if you stand there much longer, you are going to lose it. One last kiss and "I love you" and a deep breath, and you take your first and final step away from them.

"Call me," your mother shouts. You don't dare look back, because you really are crying now.

Walking through those Yale gates, you think about all it took to get here: all those nights studying and all those AP exams (you took seven of them), the constant pressure not to fail.

Back in high school, there was a continuous demand to excel in everything. You did homework until late every night and got basically no sleep for four years. You edited the school paper, led the debate team to a state championship, participated in model UN, and, on your own initiative, organized a food drive for a local homeless shelter during senior year. You speak French and read Latin. You played the flute in the school band, and you even ran three years on the track team because you knew being an athlete could give you an edge on your college application (even though you hated the 6 a.m. practices and were slower than a two-legged turtle). You had basically no social life. When you were named valedictorian of your high school, it came as a relief rather than a thrill.

You suffered through all this because you knew that elite colleges are looking for "well-rounded" candidates. Yale rejects almost 95 percent of its applicants. It isn't good enough to be smart; you have to make yourself look truly, almost painfully, interesting if you want to stand out. For the last four years, your life has been devoted to the single purpose of building up a truly awesome college application.

You've worked hard, desperately hard, to get into the college of your dreams. Somehow you made it. Now you are here. As you step into the main quad, you are engulfed by the buzz of swarming students, and mesmerized by the massive spectacle of Yale's Gothic grounds. You experience a moment of sublime validation: You are a Yale student.

Yeah, okay. But among thousands of equally accomplished Yale students, how are you now going to forge an identity?

In the past, you have always been the Smart Girl—the articulate, poised, confident pride of Your Town, USA. Now, at Yale, you are just one more smart girl among many. And even in high school, if you wanted to fit in socially, or be noticed by the opposite sex, being the smartest was never enough. You also needed to be desirable. On top of the crushing academic pressures you faced, and in the midst of your frantically overloaded schedule, you felt, every day, the pressure to be eye-catching and effortlessly hot.

You think of yourself as an attractive person, cute even. You take care of yourself. You had a serious boyfriend for two years in high school. Somehow though, the little devil of insecurity still manages to whisper in your ear from time to time. You roll your eyes at the girls who spend all their time reading *Cosmo*. On a moment's notice you can offer a five-point lecture on the unjust and unhealthy body-image standards imposed by all the Photoshopped toothpicks-with-breasts on the cover of women's fashion magazines. You know better. Still, you aren't immune to the normal pressures of a teenage girl. And no matter how many perfect report cards you get, and no matter how many times you pick up *The Economist* instead of *Glamour* magazine, the nagging self-doubt about who you are and what makes you valuable never really goes away.

You still want guys to notice you. Now that you are at Yale, you are no longer the smartest girl in school—not even close. Everywhere around you there seem to be people who have accomplished more, scored higher, won bigger prizes, and just been all-around wonderful. On the very first evening you find out that there is a gold medal–winning Olympic figure skater on the floor below. Then you learn that the girl in the dorm room across the hall was actually named one of *Glamour* magazine's ten most inspiring young women of the year after she built some kind of orphanage in Tanzania at the age of seventeen. Nice. How are you supposed to compete with that? How are you going to stand out? What are you going to have to do to get the boys' attention?

Let me give you a clue. There is a party coming up soon, known at Yale as the "Freshman Screw." Everyone will be there. And you had better throw any ideas you have about self-respect and women's equality out the window. You are in Yale's domain now, an elite culture with its own set of rules and expectations. If you expect to have any romantic life at all in the next four years, you will soon learn what it takes. You are about to be surrounded by thousands of young men who expect sex with no relationship or commitment involved. Time to get with the program, sister.

The chapters of this book fall into two categories. The first category presents a detailed and more or less chronological journey through an event called "Sex Week" that has been held every other year over the last decade. In those chapters I expose Yale's relationship with the for-profit sex industry, and catalog examples of the sexual culture at its most extreme. The second category consists of topical chapters, which draw from a wide range of my experiences as a student at Yale, and together paint a picture of the major moral, political, and intellectual forces at work on campus. In these chapters it becomes clear that the depravity of "Sex Week" is no aberration. Rather, it is symptomatic of deeper and more widespread dysfunction.

This is a story of a great institution in decline—an institution of tremendous power and influence that is no longer aware of why it exists or for what purpose. On a more personal level, this is the story of a student who falls in love with a truly great university— who enters feeling utterly in awe of the place—but who soon becomes aware that, when it comes to living up to its lofty reputation, Yale is failing in an extravagant fashion. At Yale, there is definitely a low side to higher ed. And because it is such a culturally and politically influential place, the consequences are potentially far-reaching.

Today, there is a war being waged on the minds of America's

brightest young people—especially its young women. I've been in the middle of it, and what I discovered was truly shocking. It is my intention, with this book, to shed light on things at Yale that others would like to remain secret. While the material is at times scandalous and salacious, it is not my intention to merely titillate. Likewise, while the material I cover is frequently absurd to the point of being humorous, it is not my intention to merely poke fun. However controversial the material, and however absurd the details may seem, this book is ultimately an account of how America's most influential university is shaping the lives of future political and cultural leaders. Therefore, my story has implications for the nation as a whole—and the world beyond.

PART ONE

Yale for Sale: *How I*

received an elite Yale education

with a little help from

the for-profit sex industry

1

SEX WEEK

No matter how far I have traveled, something from Yale has always followed with me.
                    —Gerald Ford, L.L.B., class of 1941

My very first class as a Yale student told me much more, in hindsight, about the education I was about to receive than all the glossy brochures and guided tours I had been given before I arrived. It was a literature class called Heroes and the Mock-Heroic, taught by an eminent professor of English, Dr. Claude Rawson. Fresh from summer break, half a dozen students and I, along with Dr. Rawson, were seated around a seminar table in a small classroom. Rawson was dressed rather sloppily in an oversized, untucked polo shirt. He wore white socks and flip-flops with the thong wedged between his toes. He lacked couture, perhaps, but he had an impressive British accent to make up for it.

The room was only about half full, and there were plenty of empty seats left around the table. I glanced around at the other students, and waited silently for class to begin. It was all still very new to me, and I was simply trying to soak in the experience. Out the window I could see the stately stone-clad buildings of Yale's Old Campus, the earliest of which dates back more than 250 years. I felt an incredible sense of belonging. I was at Yale! That's all I could think about in that moment.

The reading that day was from Homer's *Iliad*. It was the famous climactic scene in which Achilles chases Hector around the city of Troy, catches him, and savagely cuts him down. We read a brief passage aloud in which Hector pleads for an honorable burial and begs Achilles not to feed him to the dogs. The professor then paused and asked the class to analyze the passage.

A few of us offered interpretations, none of which seemed to be what the professor was looking for. Then a girl seated directly across the table from me spoke up. She had dark hair with severe, short-cropped bangs. She half smiled while she talked, as if she were pleased with the insight she was about to impart to the rest of us. She began to describe—with plenty of impressive theoretical language—how all of the bloody battle imagery of the *Iliad*'s climactic scene was really an elaborate metaphor for sex.

That girl turned out to be Aliza Shvarts, an art major who would, later that school year, initiate a media firestorm and provoke national outrage over her senior art project, which she claimed consisted of blood and tissue from numerous self-induced abortions. (More on that later.)

For my part, I was unimpressed by Aliza's interpretation of the *Iliad,* and my furrowed brow must have shown it. I couldn't see what the battle of Achilles and Hector had to do with sex. But, as a new Yale student, I guess I had a lot to learn. Dr. Rawson, while still appearing not to find the exact answer he was looking for, seemed to acquiesce: "Well yes, of course," he said, glancing down at the text, "everything is sexual."

A few years before my arrival, Yale University had begun hosting a veritable marathon of sex-related seminars and special events every other year, known collectively as "Sex Week at Yale." At no other time do those words of my professor, "everything is sexual," appear more probably correct. It happens during the spring semester. The campus is flooded with banners and posters announcing, Sex Week! Sex Week! Sex Week! Students are barraged with e-mails announcing each day's proceedings, and encouraged to attend the week's "educational" programs. Sex Week is everywhere you turn.

No fewer than seventeen official events were held during Sex Week 2008—ranging from a porn-star look-alike contest (judged by a real-life porn film director), to safe-sex workshops, to lectures on the female orgasm. The event was so chock-full of goodies that organizers were forced to stretch Sex "Week" into eleven continuous days of nonstop sex, sexuality, sexiness, and sexsationalism.

Somehow during those eleven days, amid all the sex, students are supposed to go to class. No one is forced to attend Sex Week events, of course, but you cannot escape the storm of sex-related activity. National media descend upon the campus to chronicle the strange mix of lewdness and Ivy League snob appeal. There are news vans in the quad with big satellite dishes bolted on top. And reporters with press badges roam the hallways, trailed by camera crews. The university's student-run paper, the *Yale Daily News,* recounts each day's highlights to the entire student body. As one of my classmates put it: You can hardly understand what it is like to walk into the dining hall, grab some eggs and coffee and the morning paper, then try to maintain your appetite after glimpsing a front page full-color photo of a smiling freshman clutching a pair of anal beads.[1]

In February of my junior year, Sex Week was due to be held at Yale for the fourth time. I received an e-mail detailing the schedule of events. The first few items on the list seemed relatively harmless:

TONIGHT!! FRIDAY, FEBRUARY 8
Speed Dating—Give Some, Get Some! SM Dining Hall: Doors Open 9:15 p.m.

SUNDAY, FEBRUARY 10
Stevie Jay   8 p.m., SSS 114
**Life, Love, Sex, Death, and Other Works in Progress . . .
a Multi-Chakra Extravaganza**

MONDAY, FEBRUARY 11
Pepper Schwartz, Ph.D.   4:30 p.m., LC 101
Myths & Misconceptions About Sex and Relationships

Dr. Ruth Westheimer   7:30 p.m., Slifka Center
Sexually Speaking

By Tuesday, however, things started to look dicey:

TUESDAY, FEBRUARY 12
Logan Levkoff   4 p.m., LC 102
The Female Orgasm

Patty Brisben   7:30 p.m., Davies Auditorium
**Everything You've Always Wanted to Know About Sex
(and Sex Toys!)**
Pure Romance Product Giveaways!

Girls' Night Out   9–11 p.m., Center St. Lounge
OPEN BAR w/ Patty Brisben. First 100 Women Get a Free
Pure Romance Gift Bag. $5 Cover at the Door.

I suppose Tuesday was intended mainly for the ladies, since the focus seemed to be on their own particular . . . uh, physiology. I was fairly shocked by the items on the schedule. So I decided to go and see for myself what was about to be peddled within the hallowed halls of Yale University.

One day that week, after class, I attended Ms. Levkoff's homily on *la petite mort*. I found Logan Levkoff to be an attractive woman, with long, flowing blond locks. When I arrived, she was dressed in a climate-clashing style, wearing shorts and, below them, Eskimo boots. She introduced herself as a certified sex educator, the author of a dating guide, and, last but not least, an official spokesperson for Trojan® brand condoms.

The chief point of her lecture was that our sexual culture is overly focused on the desires of men, rather than women. She complained, in particular, that when it comes to oral sex, "women are doing most of the servicing." As a result of the focus on men, she said, women aren't comfortable enough with their own sexuality and, consequently, often have difficulty achieving orgasm. Ms. Levkoff apparently had less trouble than most. She informed us that she had her first orgasm at the age of seven while watching the Playboy Channel on her parents' television. It was a touching personal story. But I lost track of her point when she started tossing Trojan® condoms into the audience and one almost hit me in the head. I ducked out and headed to the next event on the schedule.

Snow was falling steadily as I made my way across campus. Steam drifted up from the pavement and I heard church bells calling people in for the evening mass. But I wasn't on my way to church. I was on my way to see Patty Brisben, the founder and CEO of a company called Pure Romance. Brisben is the world's leading entrepreneurial purveyor of female sex toys. Her presentation packs a lot of heat. And contrary to what her company name suggests, neither purity nor romance seems to be her primary concern. She brings out all the stuff they never told you about in high school sex-ed class.

The auditorium sits on the lower floor of a building that houses the Engineering Department—not altogether inappropriate considering all the robotic contraptions Brisben brought along to promote. It is a great gray rectangular auditorium with windowless concrete walls, like a bomb shelter with theater-style seating for seven hundred. It feels vaguely Orwellian. I suppose the university administration was glad to have this particular presentation confined to a windowless room, much better to keep it out of public view.

As I entered, there was a long line leading up the front of the room. In front of the chalkboards the Pure Romance people had set up a series of long tables loaded down with the company's products. There were dildos and vibrators, various lotions, oils and scented candles. They managed to include a couple of euphemistically titled how-to books including *Tickle Your Fancy* and another, *Tickle His Pickle*. Brisben once stated in a media interview that Yale students seemed more reserved and less clued-in about sex than students she had encountered elsewhere.[2] All those sex toys were, I suppose, her way of trying to loosen us up.

Once we all found seats, they passed out sales catalogs to everyone in the auditorium. The Pure Romance catalog looks much different than you would imagine, considering what's inside. It features lots of smiling, mostly middle-aged women who seem to be sharing innocent secrets and good laughs with friends. The color palette is not lipstick red, but rather soft pink and pastel blue. It looks more like *Better Homes and Gardens* than *Playgirl*. It manages to present a lot of very kinky materials in a format that feels tame, sociable, and normal. It really is an ingenious bit of marketing.

Page 1 contains a dozen "Foreplay & Games" products, ranging from "Spicy Dice" to "Tickle & Whip." Next comes a host of massage aids and bath lotions. On pages 4 and 5 one can find lubricants, arousal creams, and liquid "Performance Enhancers." On page 6 are the bondage toys. On page 7, clitoral vibrators. I had received hundreds of paper handouts in college, but never one like this.

There was the "Mr. Big" cock ring on page 8, male stimulators on page 9, followed by five pages full of assorted faux phalluses and battery-powered vibrators, including the "Wave Rider," the "Humdinger," and the "Shake & Shimmy" models. There was a page of products toward the end under the category of "Anal Play," which I prefer not to describe in detail. Finally, an assortment of novelty lingerie (worn by paper-thin models) including the "Midnight Fetish" outfit and, of course, the ubiquitous "French Maid" costume.

As I finished glancing through the catalog, the speaker, Ms. Brisben, neared the table of gizmos and reached down to turn on her wireless microphone. She had barely taken the stage, and already I was struggling to avoid unpleasant visualizations. This woman, I guessed, was in her fifties, and she was about to give a sex toy demonstration to an audience full of eighteen- to twenty-two-year-olds—kids young enough, undoubtedly, to be her children, maybe even grandchildren. How is she going to pull this off? I wondered. The age differential was awkward, not to mention a little creepy, a bit like having your mom's best friend over for a chat about kinky sex.

Patty Brisben's personal story is a compelling one. She started Pure Romance out of her garage in 1993. Twice divorced, she built the company into a $100-million-a-year business largely on her own wits. Her sales model capitalizes on social connections among women. Customers can become "consultants," hosting house parties and selling Pure Romance products to other women. It's like a Tupperware club for desperate housewives. Brisben's business acumen is admirable, to be sure. But what was she doing at Yale? I wondered.

While I observed, the MC took the stage in order to introduce Brisben, gratefully proclaiming to us all: "Pure Romance makes Sex Week possible!" I later learned that Brisben had paid the organizing committee $30,000 to fund Sex Week at Yale.[3] In fact, her money provided almost the entire budget for the week's proceedings. All of the sudden, the strange and freaky event was beginning to make sense to me.

Funding Sex Week is a shrewd business decision on Brisben's part. She gets a platform from which to promote her products to Yale students directly, hopefully hooking some long-term customers along the way. She also gets her company's name in the national news once the media report the juicy details of her visit to a prestigious university, which they inevitably do. That equals a lot more PR than she could buy with such money directly. And she gets to do it all in the name of "educating" the youth of America. Pure Romance conducts this kind of "education" at about fifteen different universities across the country.

The easy compatibility of corporate interests and "education" is a notable feature of Sex Week at Yale. It can be observed not only in the case of Pure Romance, but also with the participation of other official sponsors like Vivid Entertainment, the world's largest producer of pornographic films, and Trojan brand condoms. All three of these companies hosted events during Sex Week and distributed their products to students for free in Yale classrooms. (Yes, even porn films.) All the while, neither the university administration nor the organizers of Sex Week seemed to worry about whether the goals of these for-profit companies were compatible with the purported educational goals of the university itself. Trojan exists to sell condoms. Vivid Entertainment exists to sell porn. And Pure Romance exists to sell its various kinky bedroom accessories. Why such companies should be given a prominent platform—an entire week, no less—to promote their corporate agendas in Yale classrooms is, I think, a question without a good answer.

Brisben is a stout yet attractive woman with short bleached blond hair. Once she begins to speak, I am impressed by her charisma and rapport with the twenty-five-and-under crowd. She shows no sign of the awkwardness I feel as a listener. The adult retail industry, she explains, is something about which the public is tragically uninformed. "I want you to have a better understanding of how these products can benefit your life," she passionately declares. Meanwhile, an entourage of assistants begins to move products out for demonstration.

"How many of you have been in an adult-book store or shopped online?" she asks. Many, many hands go up in the audience. She gestures toward her table of lurid merchandise. "Do you want to see some of these?" she says. "Yes!" my fellow students scream in unison. What follows is like a live QVC program. Brisben pitches one vibrator and arousal cream after the next, tag-teaming with a younger assistant. The program is well choreographed and well rehearsed, with lots of humorous punch lines at just the right moments. Things move along quickly as, one by one, she extols the merits of her favorite products.

First, she instructs us on various methods of foreplay. She calls for volunteers. Two students, one girl and one guy, come forward. As they stand before her, she initiates a kind of role-playing game. "You're going to go home and get your guy butt naked," she tells the girl. Brisben then puts a blindfold on the male student, puts some scented oil on the back of his hand, and begins to rub him with the "Hot Heart Massager" ($13 not including shipping and handling).

After returning the volunteers to their seats, she begins to demonstrate the ins and outs of personal lubricants. You've got your water-based lubricants, which "do not stain." You've got your silicon lubricants, which, she adds, are "great for anal play." Finally, you've got your playful lubricants, which feature various scents and heating actions.

She calls for more volunteers. Another guy and girl come forward, this time even younger looking than the first pair. I squirm in my seat as Brisben rubs lubricant onto a plastic penis, puts it up to her mouth, then starts breathing heavily onto it in order to initiate the heating action—all of this while flanked by a guy and a girl who may well be teenagers.

"I really feel that we are a nation of low libido," Brisben declares ruefully. In order to fix this problem, she recommends various arousal creams, including one called "Ex-T-Cee" that she jokes "pretty much does everything that the street drug does." If all else fails, there is the mega-powered "X-Scream." "Please don't purchase this for your first time," she warns slyly. "You will be running around butt-naked, sitting in the snow, screaming your own name." By the way, she adds, there will be free samples of "X-Scream" awaiting us when we exit the auditorium.

Next come the sound effects. She puts a microphone up against a clitoral vibrator known as "the silver bullet." Amplified buzzing and pulsing noises fill the room. It sounds like a mule in heat. Then she turns the device up until it's roaring like a Harley-Davidson.

There are laughs all over the room. You have to hand it to her. She knows how to work a crowd.

"Girls, do you ever get tired of doing this?" She begins to move her fist up and down in a furious pantomime, simulating manual stimulation of the male member. There are more laughs all over the room. Luckily, she has a fix for those times when a hand just won't do the job. She asks a male student to hold out his middle and index fingers. Showing no limit to her brazenness, she begins to slide a flexible silicon tube up and down his fingers, which serve, in this case, as a stand-in for the phallus. She is simulating sex with the guy.

I am amazed that this simulated sexual activity with a young student gives her no pause. I doubt that a male of her age could get away with working such hands-on demonstrations on a young female. The next day a picture of this very incident appeared in the national news.[4] Not the most tasteful image for a school like Yale to project. However, it seems speaker-to-student simulated sexual activity has become just another part of the Yale education.

Admittedly, students themselves appear, for the most part, quite comfortable with Brisben's hands-on style. She begins to give away various dildos and vibrators. Girls publicly clamor for the handouts. One particular model is called the "B.O.B." (short for battery-operated boyfriend). Brisben claims to have designed it herself, naming it, so she says, after an ex-husband.

She pauses briefly to pitch her "Come Clean" sanitation gel. I feel that I may need some even though I haven't actually touched any of her products directly. She finishes with an extended demonstration of how to use anal beads during intercourse, promising that they will produce "an unbelievable orgasm for the male." They're not for everybody, she warns us.

In general, her tone is one of good cheer and calm assurance. Her presentation is punctuated by statements about the relativity of human sexual experience (it's all about what works for you). She also speaks frequently of her products in terms of self-empowerment (they offer variety, choices, self-knowledge, etc.). But probably the only real empowerment that came out of it was the eventual boost to Ms. Brisben's bank account.

A special six-digit code appears on the PowerPoint screen as Brisben closes her presentation. Students are told they may use the code to obtain a discount on their next purchase from the company's Web site. Her presentation is to be followed by a "Girls' Night Out" party at a local nightclub. Female students who attend are promised an open bar and a gift bag full of Pure Romance products.

"If you've taught your children what you believe to be the right morals in life, I don't think that just having a Sex Week is going to corrupt them," Brisben later told a reporter.[5]

After leaving the Pure Romance event, I crossed the street and passed through Woolsey Hall, a colossal neoclassical building with a large rotunda and massive limestone columns. I have always found it to be one of the most impressive sights on campus. It was erected in 1902 and dedicated to the numerous Yale veterans who have died in America's wars. Their names, ranks, and class years are carved by the thousands onto the building's marble walls. The dates range across the entire breadth of American history, all the way back to the Revolutionary War. Each name testifies to the long-established commitment of the university and its students to public service. I had just spent an hour with the bawdy Ms. Brisben; and, as I passed by all those hallowed names, I began to think about how much the school had changed in the course of the last century.

I thought about how, back in 1969, during the height of the Vietnam-era antiwar movement, Yale's faculty voted to revoke credit for military ROTC courses. The ban stood for more than forty years. During that time, Yale students were forced to drive an hour and a half to the University of Connecticut in order to attend required ROTC classes. The ban was implemented, largely, as a reaction against the Vietnam War. However, over the last two decades, the university cited the military's discrimination against gays and lesbians through its "don't ask, don't tell" policy as a reason to continue the ban. Yet, tellingly, Yale never had any problem accepting money from the military on behalf of students who held ROTC scholarships.

Now that the "don't ask, don't tell" policy has been revoked, the ROTC is finally returning to Yale. It is a welcome change. But I am struck by a nagging question: Why, for so many years, did the ROTC fall below clitoral stimulators on the list of things worthy of the university's sanction?

Most political liberals have long since abandoned the reflexive antimilitarism of the late 1960s. Americans have learned that one can oppose war and still support the troops. But the folks who run Yale remain stuck in 1969. In reality, I doubt the ROTC ban at Yale ever had much to do with the military's policy on gays in the first place. Instead, I think "don't ask, don't tell" was a convenient excuse for Yale to stick its nose up at the military.

Regardless of one's personal political views, military men and women are worthy of admiration and support. Often, ROTC students put their lives on the line for us all by becoming active-duty military officers after graduation. You would think that the university administrators would have gone out of their way to accommodate these young men and women. But for more than forty years they chose to play the hypocrite in their quest to keep the military at arm's length. They took ROTC students' scholarship money, then shoved them out the back door—forcing them to do their actual military training at another university sixty miles away.

Yale banned the military on the pretext of its moral objections to "don't ask, don't tell." But, in view of Yale's collaboration with the for-profit sex industry, I find such moral posturing disingenuous. Why should university administrators allow a dildo peddler into Yale's classrooms when for forty years they forbade the ROTC the same privilege? Yale's leaders made space in the classroom for Patty Brisben and her traveling sex toy pageant, but no room for those who risk their lives in service of our country.

Today Yale would never build a military memorial like Woolsey

Hall. As I passed through the building, I noticed a faded inscription on the marble floor beneath my feet. It was some sort of poetic tribute to Yale's fallen soldiers. The gold letters had been worn away by a hundred years and by tens of thousands of footsteps. Now those letters are almost indecipherable. I am sure there are many at Yale who wouldn't mind if they disappeared altogether. The university continues to enjoy the prestige of an intellectual and spiritual legacy it long ago abandoned. The grand old buildings remain, but all too often, there is nothing grand going on within them. Through architecture, Yale's past testifies against its present.

At a fundamental level, there is a connection between Patty Brisben and the ROTC ban. It centers on the question of purpose. Yale was once animated by a sense of service to the nation. Now it is plagued by a void of moral purpose. And where no clear purpose is evident, hosting a sex toy exhibition may serve as well as any other reason for a university's existence. The public-spiritedness that, for most of its history, infused Yale with a sense of purpose, and gave it its greatness, is now all but gone. What remains is a how-to lecture on the Hot Heart Massager and the "battery-operated boyfriend."

2

THE GREAT PORN DEBATE

*Great things have happened and luck came my way, and I
want to say that whatever credit is due of a personal character in the honor that came to me, I believe is due to Yale.*
— William Howard Taft, B.A., class of 1878

The most hyped event of Sex Week 2008 was something billed as
the "Great Porn Debate." Seating was limited and students clam-
ored to get tickets, which were handed out to early arrivers at
events throughout the week. Competition was tough, and it took
me about four attempts showing up early to various presentations
to finally get a ticket. There was a buzz on campus all week in the
lead-up to the Friday night debate.

Yale students are pathologically addicted to debate. The Yale
Political Union, which constitutes the largest student organization
on campus, bills itself as "the oldest and most respected student
debating society in America." The YPU serves as the umbrella organization for seven individual "parties," covering the entire spectrum of political ideologies. Currently, these include the Liberal
Party, the Party of the Left, the Independent Party, the Federal-
ist Party, the Conservative Party, the Tory Party, and the Party of

the Right. The YPU sponsors a weekly debate, which is held in a large lecture hall and is open to members of all parties. Normally, a famous politician or journalist is invited to speak on some hot-button political issue such as gay marriage or health-care reform. After the speech, students are allowed to speak and ask questions.

The YPU attracts big names from the right and left; a recent fall term included both John Kerry and Karl Rove on the guest list. Senator Kerry is a Yale graduate and, famously, along with George W. Bush, a member of Skull and Bones. And while Kerry came up just short in his quest to become the president of the United States, he did manage to get himself elected president of the YPU in 1964.

In addition to the weekly YPU meetings, each individual party holds its own weekly debate. These gatherings are generally more casual. Students gather in the evenings, often in the college common rooms. There is usually some drinking involved, and sometimes a makeshift bar is erected. Cocktails are mixed. Then the fun begins. One by one, students stand before their classmates to give impromptu speeches in voices of practiced authority, all the while attempting to make themselves heard over the constant cheers and jeers of their alcoholically compromised classmates. No, I'm not making this up; this is what Yale students do for fun.

At these smaller gatherings, students are surrounded for the most part by classmates with similar political ideologies. The point is less about debating a particular issue, and more about cultivating the art of a fine argument. Yalies take this business seriously; it's rhetorical warfare. Yet they want, first and foremost, to have a blast. It's a competitive, yet friendly and supportive, environment. Students focus on one-upping each other by making the most persuasive speeches. It has the lively feel of a debate in the British Parliament. The applause or vocal disapproval of the group serves to measure each student's performance. The wilder the arguments are, the more entertaining the evening is. What you say is not as important as how well you say it. Students do not necessarily even believe the arguments they are making. You can see, therefore, why the YPU has produced so many successful American politicians over the years.

The topics of debate are often tongue-in-cheek, or even downright zany. For example, during the year of the "Great Porn Debate," the Party of the Right hosted debates on the following topics, to name a few:

- *Resolved:* You can have this gun when you pry it from my cold dead hands.
- *Resolved:* Christianity gives Eros poison to drink.
- *Resolved:* Art is a waste of talent.
- *Resolved:* Patriotism is glorified brand loyalty.

And, my personal favorite:

- *Resolved:* Smash the state.

Good friends. Good drink. Good speeches. Good times. If there is one thing that best captures the essence of the Yale experience, it would be a YPU party debate. With a culture that so relishes good argument, you can see why the Great Porn Debate was popular. But I suppose the biggest reason the Great Porn Debate stimulated so much interest during Sex Week is, quite simply, this: It was about porn.

The Great Porn Debate was held in a vast ballroom above a nightclub called Hula Hank's, a gaudy sexual meat market widely considered to be the worst nightspot in New Haven (and that's quite a put-down). There is a swing above the bar, where drunken kids can fly through the air and vomit on the crowd below. There is even a Wheel of Fortune in the corner, which produces fits of bleeps and flashing lights whenever it is spun around. One online reviewer endorsed the establishment thusly: "If you're looking for some stupid fun, look no further." He goes on to recommend it as a place "where you can act a fool with no shame."[1] Above this very establishment the Great Porn Debate was set to take place.

It was brutally cold that night. Arriving at the scene, I found hundreds of Yalies lined up inside the building and spilling out onto the street. The turnout was huge and there was a buzz of excitement in the air. With me in line was a young freshman English major named Constance, who, when asked by a reporter why she had decided to attend, replied quite simply: "I'm just here 'cause I love porn. And I'm not ashamed to say it at all."[2] In so doing, she captured what I suppose were the prevailing sentiments among students in attendance.

Adding to student excitement was the fact that the debate was going to be televised on ABC's *Nightline* news program. I later learned from one of the student organizers of Sex Week that Yale officials got nervous about how the Great Porn Debate might affect Yale's public image, due to the fact that it was going to be nationally televised. For this reason, they would not allow the event to take place on campus, even though they had provided free use of Yale classrooms and lecture halls for every other Sex Week event. In hindsight, the porn debate turned out to be mild compared with most of the other events on the schedule. I thought back to Patty Brisben's dildo presentation earlier in the week. Yale was lucky that ABC hadn't tried to televise that one.

Set to make the case against porn was Donny Pauling, a former porn producer turned antiporn activist, and a fellow named Craig Gross, a young, earring-wearing fellow with a stylish hairdo, who runs a religious ministry for porn addicts and recovering porn stars called XXXChurch.com. Gross has been called "the pastor of porn."

There to argue the pro-porn side were two porn stars: Monique Alexander, aged twenty-five, and Ron Jeremy, aged fifty-four. Alexander, like many female porn actresses, got into the business when she was only eighteen. Ron Jeremy—in addition to being the living embodiment of the porn mustache—is easily the most recognized male porn actor in the world. He is listed in the *Guinness World Records* under "most appearances in adult films." He has appeared in more than 1,800 over the last thirty years, and has managed to become something of a pop-culture icon along the way. Some students began shouting, "We love Ron," while waiting for the program to start.

The room was almost entirely full by the time I got in. So I sat toward the back. I had come to think of myself as something of a "concerned observer" rather than just a regular student attending Sex Week. It had become increasingly clear to me that the point of Sex Week was not to educate but to titillate—not to inform students, but to market sex toys and sell porn. I took my seat and soaked in the noise and excitement of the room. The parliamentary debater's equivalent of a rock concert was about to begin. Soon the stars of the broadcast took the stage. There to moderate the debate was the impressively articulate Martin Bashir of ABC News. Lights when down. Spotlights up. One thousand students fell silent.

The debate itself was fairly predictable. Ron Jeremy and the pro-porn side argued that pornography is basically harmless. It's fun and entertaining, and shouldn't be taken too seriously. It can even be seen as a healthy outlet for sexual fantasy. Ultimately, people who want to restrict pornography are sticking their nose in other people's business and are trying to impose their values on others. It's a free country, and anyone, so long as he or she is at least eighteen, should be allowed to make porn or view porn if he or she wants to. Sure, it's not for everyone. But if you don't like it, no one is forcing you to watch—so the argument goes.

Craig Gross, the porn pastor, along with his associate on the antiporn side, argued that porn harms everyone involved—both the person who consumes it and the person who makes it. He made the case that, in particular, porn harms and exploits the young women who appear in it. Jeremy and Alexander, both of whom had become wealthy and well known in the business, represent the extremely rare exception. Most porn actors are from poor or disadvantaged backgrounds. They have little education. The girls in porn are usually no more than eighteen or nineteen when they start in the business. They dream of fame and fast money. But their careers usually last no more than a year, after which they either leave the business or are cast aside by the industry. They are filmed performing risky unprotected intercourse with multiple partners. Sexually transmitted diseases, including chlamydia, gonorrhea, and HIV, are a constant worry. The acts they perform are physically punishing. And once the images are made, they are out there forever. Girls who hope to move on—have careers, get married, have children—may find that they can never escape their past. Those images will be floating around on the Internet decades from now, waiting to be discovered by co-workers, parents, sons, and daughters.

More broadly, Gross argued that porn negatively affects the way women are viewed in society. Men may start to view women as mere sex objects, whose value on the magazine page or video screen rises no higher than being a tool of male pleasure. He claimed that this ultimately shapes how men treat women in the real world. Porn, he argued, doesn't simply remain in the world of fantasy; it enters actual relationships, actual marriages. It hinders love and sexual intimacy. While a small number of corporations who produce porn are growing fantastically rich, the porn actors, the consumers of porn, and society as a whole are getting nothing but a dysfunctional sexual culture—so went his argument.

Looking back, the whole thing was a bit of a circus. Most students seemed to treat it as an amusing distraction, a little break from the normal solemnity of college work, maybe nothing more than a chance to see Ron Jeremy, a B-list celebrity, in person. During the Q&A, no serious questions arose. The only question I can recall was one audience member asking Jeremy if he ever had a problem with erectile dysfunction. Ultimately, I doubt the Great Porn Debate changed anyone's mind. As students got up to head for the exits, I heard a guy in the row behind say to his friends, "Hey, let's go watch some porn."

The panelists stayed around to mingle after the event. I hung around awhile too. A mighty throng of students surrounded Monique Alexander and Ron Jeremy. From across the large room I could see a steady flash of camera bulbs as students collected images of themselves arm-in-arm with the porn stars, images that I assumed they would not be taking home to show Grandma.

Around the less-celebrated Mr. Gross and Mr. Pauling, there was no throng. No flashing bulbs. Up close I noticed they were both wearing makeup. Actually, they both looked like they had done nine rounds at the Clinique counter at Macy's. Someone had plastered their faces with a pancake of glare-reducing foundation. And was that rouge? Oh yes, it was. The pastor of porn and his antiporn sidekick looked like they had just stepped off the stage at the local tranny bar. They had changed into their street clothes but forgot to wipe off their Cover Girl concealer. Of course, I'm being ridiculous. Everyone wears makeup on TV. But watching them stand around after the show, talking to a handful of students about the dangers of porn while looking like burlesque twins from the neck up, was enough to make me crack a smile.

I found out later the Craig Gross and Ron Jeremy are something like old pals. They do similar debates at colleges all over the country, and occasionally even in churches. Gross pays Ron Jeremy a fee for each debate. And, apparently, they do pretty much the same debate over and over, and Jeremy is happy to show up and take the money. On Gross's Web site there are pictures of him and Jeremy chumming around and posing for the camera. Gross claims that his kids call Jeremy "Uncle Ronny." It strikes me that one of the appealing things about Gross is that, unlike some antiporn activists, he seems to treat the people in the porn business with genuine care and respect, even if he strongly disapproves of what they are doing. He actually passes out to people in the industry Bibles emblazoned with the slogan "Jesus Loves Porn Stars" on the cover. It is an odd sort of ministry, amusingly subversive, the guiding philosophy of which seems to be "Hate the sin, love the sinner."

I don't know how many porn stars Gross has managed to convert in the course of his pastoral career; but I do know that there is an overwhelming consensus at Yale that porn is completely healthy and harmless, and Gross was just about the only person I had heard during all of Sex Week who had challenged that consensus. He was the only one who had called attention to the ways in which porn might harm the way we view women or how it might damage our sexual culture. College is supposed to be a place where opposing views are freely debated, where students' ideas and prejudices can be challenged, where minds can be changed. But that doesn't happen when students hear only one point of view. For that reason alone, I was glad that the porn pastor had been man enough to put on his TV makeup and provide some perspective other than the one Playboy® Enterprises Inc. would have us all buy into.

In order to help students keep track of which porn star was appearing in what classroom and when, Sex Week organizers had designed a postcard-sized calendar of events. Looking over the schedule, I noticed that each day had a theme, such as "Seduction," "Foreplay," or one titled "What a Girl Wants." Like most guys, I've spent much of my life wondering what a girl wants, and hoping that it would turn out to be me. But Sex Week seemed to be sending a different kind of message about what girls want, or what they should aspire to. In fact, what a girl really wants, if you were to believe the schedule of events, is to be a porn star.

Girls would soon get their chance to audition for the part. Saturday night featured a porn star look-alike contest at a local nightclub, to be judged by two real-life female porn stars and one male director. Yale students, used to being tested on the basis of their intelligence, hard work, and creativity, would now face the playful equivalent of a porn film casting call.

Printed in red ink across the face of the official Sex Week schedule was a silhouette of a nude woman, crouched on her knees, legs apart, with one hand draped over her head and the other reaching down toward her crotch. I suppose girls looking for instruction on how to pose during the porn star look-alike contest could use this as an instructive model. The week's events were printed in black ink right over the nude silhouette. There was the AIDS awareness benefit above her head at 5 p.m. on Friday, the "Skull & Boned" party right across her chest for 10:30 on Saturday. Listed right above her genitals was Sunday evening's event, called "Sex & Spirituality: A

Panel Discussion." Below that was Monday's 7:30 event sponsored by Trojan® brand condoms, which, the schedule informed me, included "vibrating ring giveaways."

While looking over the schedule, I begin to think: Sex Week is billed as an open-minded exploration of sexual topics. It is, supposedly, a forum for serious intellectual debate. It is, supposedly, a forum where assumptions about sex and gender roles are boldly broken down, deconstructed, and debated. But you can't "break down" gender assumptions by heedlessly adopting the aesthetics of those same assumptions. The naked silhouette across the face of the schedule of events reinforces graphically what I had learned by actually attending the events: *Sex Week promotes a particular image of the ideal woman.* This ideal woman is the porn star. She exists for one purpose—to serve male pleasure. She is valued and measured on the basis of her ability to fulfill that one purpose. Her level of intelligence doesn't matter. Her talents and abilities are irrelevant, as are her feelings. All that matters is whether she has a trim waist and big boobs, and can strike a good porn star pose. Just as she literally hovers in the background on the printed schedule, she looms over every event like a piece of propaganda that no one even bothers to question.

In pornography, women are normally portrayed as passive objects of aggressive male sexuality. They are often made to submit to degrading acts on camera. A woman who is passive, and not respected by men—this is not the kind of person Yale girls aspire to be *outside* the bedroom. So why should they be taught that this is what they should aspire to *inside* the bedroom?

If Yale girls are being trained to take leadership roles in government, business, and society, how can it be that they are—all the while—being trained to assume subservient sexual identities? Likewise, how can young men respect women as future co-workers or spouses, when—all the while—Yale is training them to view women sexually as subservient and subhuman? I get the feeling that the administrative leaders at Yale view sex as something completely unrelated to the rest of life, as though images and events that degrade women are acceptable simply because they have something to do with sex and are, therefore, private. But I think promoting a porn actress as the ideal kind of sexual partner does affect how young men measure and treat women, both in the bedroom and—eventually—in the boardroom. Worse yet, it might even affect how some Yale women measure and view themselves.

Earlier in the week, a D-list celebrity from the cable channel VH1 had been invited to give a lecture entitled "Seduction: How to Get the Girl You Always Wanted." He called himself "Matador: The Pickup Artist." Matador is a tanned, muscular fellow with long dark hair, prone to wearing leather vests with no shirt underneath. His entire career, so far as I can tell, is based on teaching young men an elaborate system of smooth moves, signals, and pickup lines, all designed to manipulate women and, ultimately, get them in the sack. On his Web site Matador claims to be an expert in the "Venusian arts." I like the highbrow sound of "Venusian." The term has a certain classical ring to it. Such a term elevates the seemingly bestial act of chasing tail, endowing it with a learned, Latinate air.

There are a couple of books for sale on the Venusian arts Web site, including *The Mystery Method: How to Get Beautiful Women into Bed,* and another with the quasi-biblical title of *Revelation,* a book, according to the Web site, that is "rich in power and subtlety, deep and high in content." It will teach you what to say to women, how to generate attraction, and "the solution to inner game."

Deep and high indeed.

The only thing deep here, so far as I can tell, is the bodily waste of a bull. The only thing high is, perhaps, the guy who wrote the book. However, I should not fail to mention that the companion *Revelation* DVD set is available for those who find reading a bore, but who still wish to study the Venusian arts.

Yale students were sent an e-mail encouraging them to attend Matador's seduction lecture. As a teaser, we were promised a special opportunity, which read as follows: "Come see Matador this evening in [classroom] SSS 114 and find out where he'll be 'peacocking' tonight."

Teaching students how to party seems to have become an academic priority at Yale lately. For example, the university now offers a full-credit seminar course in the American Studies Department called "Dance Music and Nightlife Culture in New York City." The course includes lectures from disc jockeys and a late-night field trip to a Manhattan club called the "Boom Boom Room."[3] Bumping and grinding at a nightclub has now become a form of classwork. However, other than Matador, I don't think any other lecturer in the history of Yale University has invited students out to a nightclub specifically in order to watch him go "peacocking" on the local female population.

Professor Matador from VH1 was bound to bring some original ideas to Yale. But there was something else about Matador that was not at all original, and that was his portrayal of women as basically reactive beings, who can be manipulated by the right formula of words and tricks into doing whatever a man wants them to do. I had begun to suspect that this view of women was completely conventional at Yale.

3

THE BUSINESS OF SEX ED

Yale was different, and I felt the difference in my bones: I was among the elite, and I knew that no amount of striving would make me one of them.

—Clarence Thomas, J.D., class of 1974

Currently, Yale has an endowment that totals somewhere around $20 billion. That's *billion* with a *b*. Not bad for a "nonprofit" institution. Not that I'm complaining. There are many benefits to attending a school that has so much money. They give you maid service in the dorms and fancy organic food in the dining halls. Maybe next they will start wallpapering the classrooms with $100 bills. Best of all, if you happen to be one of those rare students who lacks a trust fund, they give you a hefty scholarship based on your financial need. That's important because Yale costs more than $50,000 a year—considerably more than my family's annual income while I was growing up. In my family, McDonald's was a rare extravagance. But, as a college student, I was on the receiving end of enough scholarship dollars to buy about 100,000 Big Macs.

The Yale financial aid office was my personal equivalent of a rich uncle. When I imagine Yale officials looking over my application, I picture it like a scene out of a Dickens novel. With his last breath a dying British plutocrat utters the name of some dirty-faced orphan, making the poor kid fantastically rich and changing his life forever. Yale was the dying plutocrat. I was the dirty-faced orphan.

Because Yale has so much money, the university can afford to invite many distinguished cultural and political leaders to campus. The calendar of events is always chock-full of performances, readings, and speeches by notable artists and public figures. I met poets, academics, filmmakers, and journalists of the highest caliber—each invited to campus merely for the extracurricular benefit of Yale students. Prestigious names like Henry Kissinger, Gloria Steinem, and Tom Wolfe are regularly on the itinerary. During my time, I heard one talk by Hu Jintao and two by Tony Blair, the reigning president of China and the recent prime minister of Great Britain, respectively. But of all the high and mighty scholars, artists, and heads of state who visited Yale in my time—Guggenheim fellows, Grammy winners, Nobel laureates, leaders of the free and unfree worlds—there is one estimable individual who rises above them all.

You probably don't know his name. But, if you've seen much porn at all, odds are, you've seen his work.

It was the ninth day of Yale's never-ending Sex "Week" when porn king Steven Hirsch arrived on campus. His aim: to lecture Yale's budding student moguls on the business of porn. I was weary by this time, trying to maintain my regular class schedule while keeping up with the relentless calendar of Sex Week events. But I dared not miss the chance to soak up every drop of wisdom from this legendary entrepreneur, whose visit Yale had so graciously made possible.

Yale has played host to a lot of CEOs over the years. But few of them could top Hirsch in the *dinero* department. Hirsch is cofounder and CEO of Vivid Entertainment, the world's largest porn production company, which boasts annual revenues in excess of $100 million. I suppose if Sex Week organizers had simply wanted us to learn from a legendary businessman, they could have invited Warren Buffett. But I understand that, unlike Hirsch, Buffett normally travels without an entourage of porn star babes. So maybe they figured Hirsch would be more exciting. Hirsch was scheduled to speak in one of the undergraduate classrooms, room WLH 119.

Classrooms at Yale are full of memories for me. I remember one particularly grueling three-hour exam I took in WLH 119 on the history of the Roman Empire. Whenever I picture WLH 119 in my mind, I feel that old exam-time feeling. Exams have always felt like a blur to me, so much so that sometimes I am hardly aware of time as it passes. I get "in the zone." My nerves are on edge and my heart races. I sweat. I remember Livy, Virgil, Gregorovius, and Gibbon all muddled together in a heap of concentration, aching eyes, stiff knuckles, and the smell of ballpoint ink. I see the hunched backs of all my classmates as they hover over their blue books. We are all in it together—tackling intellectual challenges, looking at deep questions, and writing as fast as we can with all the excellence we can muster. I see the blurry presence of our professor as she paces across the front of the room. There is a kind of thrill in being surrounded by some of the smartest people in the world.

But sometimes, when I picture myself in WLH 119, the image of my professor standing beside the lectern is replaced by the bright smile and suntanned complexion of Steven Hirsch—the biggest smut peddler on the face of the earth.

Hirsch is already standing behind the podium when I arrive. He's got the image down pat. Copiously applied hair gel? Check. Tailored sport coat? Check. Open collar with one too many unfastened buttons? Check. All that's missing is the braided gold necklace. As I make my way into the room, I see my friend Cyrus sitting near the window. Cyrus cracks a sheepish hint of a smile, as if to say: *Hee-hee. Why are you here, you dirty dog?*

Hirsch begins by taking us on a nostalgic journey through his childhood. His father was a stockbroker, but suddenly left the world of finance when Hirsch was eleven for a career in the porn biz. Hirsch's father ended up working for Reuben Sturman, a Cleveland-based pornographer who made hundreds of millions of dollars in the porn business but, apparently, never paid taxes on any of it. (Sturman was convicted of tax evasion in 1989, and died in federal prison in 1997.) "Reuben was the one who invented the peep show," Hirsch proudly informs us. He doesn't bother to mention the criminal history of his dad's former boss. Instead, Hirsch continues with his own biography, telling us how, at the age of twenty-three, he set out to make Daddy proud by joining the family business. He started his own porn operation in 1983.

The loving son follows in his father's footsteps. It's an inspirational family tale. And Hirsch's autobiography is gearing up to be the feel-good story of the year.

Hirsch grips both sides of the podium as he moves into the stirring, rags-to-riches part of the narrative. He and a friend started their porn business with only $5,000. Within a few years, they were making millions. "We went after our dream," he declares. I now begin to realize that I am standing before the Horatio Alger of pornography. This man isn't promoting the exploitation of women for profit; he's promoting the American Dream.

Hirsch goes on to catalog all of his amazing contributions to American culture.

- On family values: "The first thing we would do is find a wholesome, all-American girl. If people liked her, they would come back for more."
- On the artistic front: "We changed the packaging side of the business, introduced retouched photos, and produced a unique box. We wanted our movies to reflect other movies that people wanted to see, with stories, plots, and character development."
- As a management genius: "We were the first one to sign girls to an exclusive contract." Unlike others, Hirsch didn't

want to fly under the radar. He got a real marketing person from New York, put together a media kit, and got himself profiled in *Forbes,* the *Wall Street Journal,* and the *Los Angeles Times.* He even rented a billboard on Sunset Boulevard. "Twenty years later"—he pauses for effect— "our competitors are long gone."

Hirsch boasts that he has produced 1,200 movies in the last twenty years. In addition, he sold several TV networks to Playboy for $100 million. He was the "first to adopt Blu-Ray technology," and the "first to really look at the wireless business." Hirsch is clearly a legend in his own mind—it is Hirsch's dream to bring on-demand porn to everyone's cell phone. Ten years from tomorrow, America, all of this will be yours. But there is a problem. "Phone companies are not yet comfortable with age verification," he explains. "When they are ready, we'll be there with the content." Nice to know he's putting the kids first.

Mobile porn, sending images straight into people's cell phones, has lately become a huge part of the porn industry. So I guess Hirsch's dream has come to pass.

Of all Hirsch's groundbreaking achievements and admirable qualities I am most impressed by his concern for children. Apparently, lots of people are taking Vivid Entertainment's cinematic masterworks and posting clips of them online for people to view for free. It's true: The porn industry is suffering financially from online piracy. But Hirsch's primary concern isn't about money. Every time an online pirate rips off a Vivid film, a child is put in harm's way, he says. This is the case because pirated porn is much easier for minors to access. "This issue is important to me not just as a producer, but as a parent. Any kid is two clicks away from the hardest of hard core. This is not a First Amendment issue. This is about our children."

I'm touched.

Hirsch is a smooth spokesperson for what he euphemistically refers to as "the business." He hits all of the right political buttons in his speech—kids, education, etc. He even tells us that he is interested in leaving behind an educational legacy. A new branch of his company, called VividEd (don't laugh), will feature porn films with how-to voice-overs. It will be an entirely new twist on sex education.

I think Hirsch should talk to some of my professors, since they are already successfully integrating porn into the educational experience. In fact, maybe Yale could sign on as an official sponsor of the new VividEd films. Never say never.

Once the Q&A starts up, I realize that the audience is taking Hirsch quite seriously. His smooth talk has worked its magic. Yale's budding corporate masters begin to quiz Hirsch as they would any other CEO. "Do you have plans to expand internationally? . . . Have you ever considered an IPO? . . . What do you estimate is the market value of your business?"

One diversity-conscious audience member asks Hirsch why he doesn't produce more gay porn. Not wanting to appear homophobic, Hirsch assures us that he tried gay porn, but found that he couldn't do it as well as gay producers can.

Just when I think the questions can get no more awkward, Cyrus speaks up from the row behind me with the question that no one else wanted to ask: "How many girls have you slept with?"

"Thousands, thousands," Hirsch responds in a dismissively sarcastic tone.

My head sinks into my hands. And I think the world can get no more absurd. I have to keep reminding myself: *I am at Yale. I am at Yale.* But, actually, I think I have died and been reborn into some freakish new world where this kind of banality passes for Yale-worthy education. Steven Hirsch has become my professor. And there is actually a bleached blond porn star sitting a few rows in front of me. I pinch myself. No, it's real.

Thankfully, it's almost over. Just as things are winding down, some blessed girl in the audience speaks up with a question that cuts straight to the heart of Hirsch's insincere claim that he dearly wants to protect children. Hirsch, you see, is perfectly willing to put someone else's eighteen-year-old daughter in one of his films. But what about his own daughter? "What would you do," the girl asks, "if one of your own children wanted to appear in one of your films?"

Hirsch stammers for a moment, "Uhhhh." He looks down at the podium, then back up. "I'm going to support my kids in whatever they choose to do."

You know, I almost believe him.

If Hirsch's daughter actually were to become a porn performer, what would that look like exactly? Take the following example as a clue: On March 23, 2004, a young French Canadian girl going by the assumed name "Lara Roxx" arrived in Los Angeles with hopes of making some quick money in the porn business. Prior to her arrival in California, Roxx's life had followed the trajectory of a stereotypical troubled youth.[1] Her parents divorced when she was sixteen. She rebelled, got into drugs, and eventually landed in a home for delinquents. By age eighteen she was working as a stripper in a Montreal nightclub. But nothing could have prepared her for what she was about to encounter in L.A.

Her first job took place the day after her arrival. When she showed up at the studio, she was shocked to learn what the director wanted her to do. It was not a conventional sex scene. Instead, the scene called for what is known as "double anal penetration"—a dangerous and frequently harmful act during which two males penetrate the anus of the female simultaneously. The potential for tearing, bleeding, and other tissue damage is high, as is the risk of infection. A frightened Roxx initially protested. But the producer told her she would lose the job if she did not agree to do as he directed.[2] She was to be paid $1,500 for the scene.

She took the money.

The men in the scene, Marc Anthony and Darren James, were veteran porn actors. Each has a long history of performing in racially charged porn films with titles like *Little White Slave Girls* and *Black Thai Affair*, as well as films that glamorize sex with underage girls such as *I Fucked My Daughter's Best Friend*. They were thirty-three and forty years of age, respectively. Roxx was only twenty-one at the time.

The two men performed the painful double anal penetration on Roxx, causing her serious injury, while the director and crew rolled tape. Both men ejaculated inside her. By the time the scene was done, Roxx's dream of getting rich in the porn business had already crumbled. Although she didn't know it yet, Lara Roxx would soon learn that she had contracted the HIV virus. She had been in L.A. for less than twenty-four hours.

James had tested negative for HIV on March 17, just one week before shooting the scene with Roxx.[3] James then had sex with fourteen women in the three weeks that followed. Many of those women also had multiple partners. Ultimately, more than fifty actors were quarantined as a result of the outbreak. And three of James's on-screen partners tested positive for HIV.

Roxx's story is important for the following reason: If, as I was, you happen to be naïve about some of the more extreme and risky behavior that goes on in the world of hard-core porn, then you cannot fully appreciate the absurdity of Steven Hirsch standing there and lecturing me in a Yale classroom. Hirsch is in a business in which performers like Roxx are put at risk of HIV and other diseases. He glamorizes potentially deadly behavior. And he makes a lot of money doing it.

In Los Angeles County alone, more than three dozen adult film performers are known to have tested positive for the HIV virus since 1998.[4] In addition, the Adult Industry Medical Health Care Foundation, based in the San Fernando Valley, has reported an average of fifteen new cases of gonorrhea, chlamydia, hepatitis, and other sexually transmitted diseases every single week.[5] That adds up to about four thousand infections in the last five years. And it doesn't count the cases that go unreported.

It's true, porn performers willingly put themselves in harm's way. And it was Roxx's own greed that led her to take the risks she took. But producers are still culpable for their part of the bargain. Think about it: The law protects even the lowest-paid workers in America, such as fast-food workers and supermarket cashiers. Employers are required to provide basic safety gear such as rubber gloves and first-aid kits in order to prevent illness or infection. Meanwhile, porn companies go around ordering their workers to exchange diseased bodily fluids.

To me, one of the saddest things about Lara Roxx's story is that the porn flick in which she likely contracted the HIV virus is still for sale. You might think that if an actor or actress contracts HIV while filming, the production would be scrapped. But in Roxx's case, the company went on to release the film. To this day, men around the world are debauching themselves over a scene in which Roxx likely contracted the virus that will one day kill her. As for her and the others who contracted the virus during the outbreak, porn producers are profiting from their damaged lives and, in all likelihood, early deaths.

In all, five actors contracted the virus during the 2004 outbreak. The industry's reaction was predictable: a lot of hand-wringing at first, followed by business as usual. Initially, several studios enacted policies requiring condom use. But the new safe-sex policies didn't last long. As it turns out, customers prefer porn without condoms. Porn is about fantasy, after all. And nasty realities like deadly STDs just don't make for good entertainment.

Hirsch's Vivid Entertainment was among those companies that committed to a policy of mandatory condom use: "Hey, we'll bite the bullet," Hirsch told the press. "We'll make a little bit less money, but we'll be sure that nobody contracts anything on our sets."[6] But Hirsch's commitment unfortunately did not last long. Vivid actors soon resumed the practice of performing without protection.

It's an unfortunate fact that for perhaps a majority of teenagers these days, porn functions as a crude form of sex education. Hirsch's movies promote sexual practices that, if imitated, put the lives of the young people who view them at risk. So my question is: *Why would Yale want to honor Hirsch by hosting his lecture?*

If Hirsch's own daughter were to become a porn star, it might entail unprotected sex on camera with ten different men per week. Astonishingly, Hirsch claims he would support this kind of life for his daughter. He is making great money, after all. And isn't that what matters in the end?

Clearly, Hirsh is an ideal role model for Yale's future business leaders. But why stop at simply inviting this man to instruct Yale students? Yale hasn't gone far enough. Steven Hirsch, a man of many hats—Vivid CEO, porn king, public health advocate, protector of children, and Yale guest lecturer—explained his company's ultimate response in the wake of the HIV outbreak: "We decided to go condom optional."[7]

Yale's School of Public Health should give this man an honorary degree.

The French revolutionaries thought they were innovative when they attempted to stretch the calendar week into ten days. But as Sex Week continues, I realize that Yale has outdone them. On the eleventh and final day of Sex Week 2008, Yale's erotic Reign of Terror is finally nearing its end. The agenda for the final day looks like this:

MONDAY, FEBRUARY 18
Peer Health Educators   4 p.m., LC 101
Eroticizing Safe Sex: Make It Fun!

Trojan Condoms   7:30 p.m., WLH 119
Evolve: America's Sexual Health Problem and What Trojan's Doing About It*
*Featuring Trojan condom and vibrating ring giveaways

Even though Steven Hirsch is reluctant to join America's great condom crusade, rest assured, Trojan® is completely committed to the cause. Actually, organizers have been hurling Trojans at us all week, throwing them out like peanuts at a ballpark during event after event. The entire campus is a sea of latex. We are swimming in personal lubricant.

I have no need for another lap full of Trojan vibrating rings, and no real interest in Trojan's remedy for America's sexual health problems. (I think it entails buying their products.) So I decide to skip the evening finale. Instead, I decide that, for me, Sex Week will climax at 4 p.m. That afternoon I make my way down to room LC 101 for the Peer Health Educators' forum. The happy snappy title of the event, "Eroticizing Safe Sex: Make It Fun!" suggests a roaring good time.

The Peer Health Educators group consists of Yale students who volunteer their time to distribute condoms to other students. Throughout the year, they keep Ziplok Baggies taped to the walls in every dorm hallway, each loaded with a colorful rainbow of condoms that are free for the taking. I'm not sure what motivates the Peer Educators to volunteer. Maybe the program functions as a résumé builder for aspiring gynecologists.

I enter the room and take a seat near the back of LC 101. Other than the Eroticizing Safe Sex presentation, my other chief memory of this room consists of a class on Dante that met there senior year. While studying Dante, of course, we read a lot about hell. I don't remember reading about it in the *Divine Comedy*, but there might be a circle of hell in which one is forced to watch bespectacled Yalies nervously talk about sex while rolling condoms onto wooden penises.

"What do you all associate with safe sex?" asks the first Peer Educator. He is holding a stack of condoms, and throws one to each student who offers a response.

"Condoms." (A condom flies through the air.)

"Dental dams." (Another condom flies.)

"No babies." (Condom sets altitude record.)

"No STIs." (Duck! Here comes a condom.)

STI, in case you haven't heard, stands for sexually transmitted infection. It's the new politically correct term for "sexually trans-mitted disease" because the word "disease" just sounds so—you know—judgmental and negative. Sex educators don't like to be negative unless they are talking about abstinence. Get your lingo straight: "STI" is the term for those in the know. And "STD" is just so 1990s.

Keeping it safe doesn't have to be boring. Mr. Peer Health Educator has lots of great ideas for us. "Try role play," he suggests.

I was actually hoping for a vegetable demonstration. In addition to teaching students how to handle latex, vegetable demonstrations are very useful for sexually active salads. Instead, the guy pulls out a wooden penis and begins to roll on a condom. Since porn makers have largely kept condoms out of their movies and, therefore, kept everyone in the dark about how to apply them, we are fortunate to have such real-world demonstrations at Yale.

"What do you say," the speaker continues, "if your sexual partner says, 'We don't need a condom. I know I don't have an STI.'"

"I don't trust you!" a fellow near the front blurts out, betraying a little too much enthusiasm. As a reward for his enthusiastic answer, the Peer Educators give the guy a pornographic film on DVD, courtesy of Hirsch & Co. Several other eager audience members are awarded Vivid® brand DVDs in return for their active participation in the presentation. Vivid benevolently donated these films in support of Sex Week at Yale. Anything for education.

The presentation takes on the look and feel of a science experiment. The speaker blows a condom up like a balloon. Quickly, I learn that silicon lubricant makes an inflated condom go POP! Water-based is the way to go, we are told. Clearly, when your lubricant starts eating holes in your condom, that's a bad thing.

"It's very hard to eliminate all risks in any sexual activity," he says. Actually, it's impossible to eliminate all risks. But never mind.

Mr. Peer Health closes out his portion of the talk with additional advice on lubrication and mutual masturbation.

The next Peer Health speaker is female. She's a short brunette who seems a bit nervous. "I'm so excited to be here," she begins. She is here to show us all the special items for ladies. She starts with a demonstration of the furtive female condom, followed by the elusive dental dam. The dental dam comes in a variety of fun colors and flavors. She passes out samples for us to taste. There are grape, mint, and vanilla. And zero calories—that's a new feature. Finally, she distributes a handout to the audience on how to perform cunnilingus.

A second girl gets up to speak. She seems more self-assured. And it's a good thing too, because this girl has been assigned the kinkiest subject matter of the day. I wish Patty Brisben and the Pure Romance folks could see her in action! This fair-faced Peer Educator delves without hesitation into battery-powered sex. What's the difference between a dildo and a dong? She has the answer. On the overhead projector she shows a photo of a topless porn star holding the largest dildo known to man. It's the size of a Louisville Slugger. The speaker offers a prize to any audience member who knows the porn star's name. Wouldn't you know it? One of my fellow Yale men is ready with the answer. I wish his mom were able to witness this proud moment.

The speaker goes on to elucidate the world of anal plugs, the G-spot, and female ejaculation. She tells us about special tools for lesbian couples, and shows us instruments that allow simultaneous vaginal and rectal stimulation. There are contraptions you strap on, some you can wear all day, and others that can be controlled by remote. Pictures of items from the Paris Sex Museum include a chair with a built-on dong and, most innovatively, a glass dildo filled with toy pigs and laced with spikes.

At this point, it has long ceased to be funny, and it just feels sad. I won't go into the male masturbatory devices or the graphic demonstrations of oral sex technique.

Fun, fun, fun! Safe sex is so much fun! And Yale utilizes super-large vaginas on PowerPoint to prove the point. The overhead projector fills the wall with a giant photograph of some woman's bikini-waxed genitalia. But we haven't seen enough. Amazingly, the speaker feels the need to teach us how to find erotic images on the Internet. She actually puts several Web addresses up on the screen for us to copy down. Any ten-year-old can find porn online, probably without even looking for it. *Does Yale really need to teach this to its students?*

The student next to me passes me a dental dam in case I'd like to taste one. My mind sinks into a blur as the girl up front finishes her talk. Something about sex with food objects and the erotica section at Barnes & Noble.

Finally, it's over. The ensemble cast of Peer Health Educators begins to shower the audience with door prizes. There is the usual fare: condoms, dental dams, and the like, and more porn films on DVD.

One of the girls up front is waving a Vivid® brand movie above her head, shouting: "Who wants porn? Who wants porn?"

Most Yale parents don't realize that $50,000 a year includes free porn as a bonus. I'm sure those parents who have taken out second mortgages in order to pay tuition would be glad to know the full value of their sacrifice. Moreover, it is ironic that porn is handed out at Yale's safe-sex seminars, since nearly all American porn is filmed "bareback." Yale's Peer Health Educators spent an hour telling us how important it is to practice safe sex "every time," then offered us glamorized portrayals of condom-free sex on our way out the door.

As I leave, I can still hear the girl shouting.

"Porn! Free porn for anyone who wants it!"

PART TWO

The Intellectual Void: *How I came to see Yale's lewd classroom material as just one symptom of an overall decline in academic standards*

4

ABORTION AS ART

When the sons of Eli
Break through the line
That is the sign we hail. . . .

> —Cole Porter, B.A., class of 1913

Nearly an entire academic year had passed since I had learned the secret to modern literary interpretation in my first English class at Yale. I had decided to drop that class. And I had all but forgotten the girl with the severe bangs and the hypersyllabic vocabulary—she who first clued me in to the fact that the *Iliad*, properly understood, should be read as an elaborate metaphor for sex, maybe nothing more than high-styled erotica. Horny old Homer was the Larry Flynt of his time, only with slightly more literary pretense. The deathly struggle between Achilles and Hector was not a metaphor for a larger civilizational struggle between ancient Greeks and non-Greeks, as I had once thought. Instead, it was to be understood as a metaphor for the horizontal mambo, the roll in the hay, the connubial congress. With all that thrusting of the spears and so forth, the blind ole bard was simply indulging his bawdy imagination. On the day Aliza Shvarts had explained it to me, she had used more lofty and impenetrable language, but that was the gist of it.

One day, the next spring, I opened the *Yale Daily News* to find a short article about Shvarts's senior art project. All of the sudden, the all-but-forgotten Ms. Shvarts came stampeding back into my consciousness, and not just mine. In fact, within hours of the article's appearance, she became famous around the world.

This is how the article began:

For senior, abortion a medium for art, political discourse

Thursday, April 17, 2008

Art major Aliza Shvarts '08 wants to make a statement.

Beginning next Tuesday, Shvarts will be displaying her senior art project, a documentation of a nine-month process during which she artificially inseminated herself "as often as possible" while periodically taking abortifacient drugs to induce miscarriages. Her exhibition will feature video recordings of these forced miscarriages as well as preserved collections of the blood from the process.

The goal in creating the art exhibition, Shvarts said, was to spark conversation and debate on the relationship between art and the human body. . . .[1]

The article continued with a detailed interview with Shvarts about her project. She assured the reporter that it wasn't her intention to scandalize anyone. Who, after all, would be offended by the idea of using aborted fetuses to make art? Shvarts said that she felt art should be a medium for political ideas, and that she was living up to the high standard of what art was truly meant to be. In one fell swoop, abortion became the latest innovation in modern art—thanks to the unprecedented intellectual barrenness of the Yale Art Department.

The article described how Shvarts's project would consist of a big cube hanging from the ceiling of the art gallery. Shvarts would mix the material from her multiple self-induced miscarriages with Vaseline, and then spread the bloody mixture out over long sheets of plastic. She would then drape the plastic from the cube. Shvarts said she planned to project video recordings onto the sides of the blood-drenched cube. These recordings, which she had made on her own video recorder, showed actual footage of Shvarts standing naked in her bathtub, bleeding, and collecting the discharged fluid. "I hope it inspires some sort of discourse," Shvarts said.

She made it clear in the interview that she was not ashamed of her exhibition and that she had become quite comfortable talking about her self-induced abortion experiences. She made sure to point out that she hadn't been carrying out the project in secret but had been working in coordination with various faculty members in the Yale School of Art. The article closed by helpfully providing the date and location of the art show, so everyone could be sure to go down and see her bloody opus in person.

In addition to the print edition, the *Yale Daily News* posted the Shvarts article on its Web site. Within hours, the article exploded across the Internet, with television news outlets, major newspapers, and countless blogs picking up the story, most heaping condemnation on Shvarts for pioneering the academic frontier of abortion as art. Others criticized the university for allowing such a project to be done in the first place. By that afternoon, accounts of Shvarts's art project could be read everywhere from the *Washington Post* Web site to London's *Daily Telegraph*.

Shvarts's project provoked a firestorm of condemnation from activist organizations on both sides of the abortion debate. Wanda Franz of the National Right to Life Committee called Shvarts "deranged" and "a serial killer." On the other side, NARAL Pro-Choice America issued a statement calling the project "offensive and insensitive to women who have suffered the heartbreak of miscarriage."

Despite the general disapproval from mainstream abortions rights activists, the students at the Yale Women's Center issued a statement of support, sufficient to inspire future abortion-blood artists the world over: "Whether it is a question of reproductive rights or of artistic expression," the center declared, "Aliza Shvarts' body is an instrument over which she should be free to exercise full discretion."[2]

In the midst of all the controversy, Shvarts was not content to let others defend her. The day after the initial story broke, she published an article of her own in the *Yale Daily News,* offering a lengthy explanation of her actions, full of intimate biological detail, and written in the recognizably opaque academic code language I had first heard from her in class eight months before. It began like this:

By Aliza Shvarts

Friday, April 18, 2008

> For the past year, I performed repeated self-induced miscarriages. . . . Using a needleless syringe, I would inject the sperm near my cervix within 30 minutes of its collection, so as to insure the possibility of fertilization. On the 28th day of my cycle, I would ingest an abortifacient, after which I would experience cramps and heavy bleeding. . . .[3]

The article quickly moved on from describing the details of the project to describing what it was all supposed to "mean." At that point Shvarts's writing devolved into dense and lengthy gymnastic academic doublespeak. She wrote that she wanted to call into question the relationship between "form and function" in the human body. She said the artwork would exist as a "verbal narrative" as well as an "independent concept." She said her work created "an ambiguity," which, in turn, "isolate[d] the locus of ontology" by means of "an intentional ambiguity." The most meaningful aspect of the piece, in her mind, she wrote, was that "the reality of the pregnancy" for herself and for her audience remained "a matter of reading."

Shvarts clarified her point further by explaining that the act of naming something, or "ascribing a word to something physical," is an act that "literally has the power to construct bodies." Furthermore, she wished to "destabilize the locus of the authorial act" and to "reclaim it from the heteronormative structures that seek to naturalize it." She then went on to write how she hoped to intervene in "the real" as it is commonly understood. The common understanding of "the real" that she so wanted to challenge was this: Most people think that certain body parts are meant to serve certain "natural" functions. But that idea is simply a myth, she believed—a myth that creates "the sexist, racist, ableist, nationalist and homophobic perspective." She intended to dispel that myth. Shvarts wrote that it is a myth that men are meant to be masculine and women feminine, a myth that penises and vaginas are meant for heterosexual intercourse, "or that mouths, anuses, breasts, feet or leather, silicone, vinyl, rubber, or metal implements" are not meant for sex. Furthermore, she wrote that it is a myth that the ovaries and the uterus are "meant" to birth a child.

After thoughtfully considering the form of her own body, Shvarts explained, she was able to conceive of all the other capabilities just waiting to be tapped. She discovered that her reproductive organs were capable of extending beyond the narrative chain of reproduction. She wrote that it is "the prerogative of every individual" to acknowledge and explore the full range of capabilities. In this case, exploring her body's full capabilities led her to the idea of turning abortion into art.

Perhaps Shvarts really did want to open my mind to her ideas regarding the purpose of ovaries, wombs, and menstrual blood. But, ultimately, I think the real purpose of the article was simply to win attention and notoriety for an "artist" who may or may not have any actual artistic talent.

I think the greatest talent Shvarts's article displayed was the ability to say in five hundred words what she might have said in fifty. Shvarts's essay, in my mind, is a powerful example of the intellectual posturing behind much of what passes for art in our elite universities these days. Shvarts has mastered the skill of saying a lot without saying much of anything.

I have had quite a bit of experience in these loquacious academic circles, so let me provide a few examples for those readers who aren't initiated in the language of hollow academic-speak. In one line from the article she writes:

> This piece—in its textual and sculptural forms—is meant to call into question the relationship between form and function as they converge on the body.

If you want your art to be seen as important, then "calling things into question" is great because it shows that you are bold enough to challenge fundamental truths that the more simple-minded would never dare to challenge. Elsewhere she writes:

> It creates an ambiguity that isolates the locus of ontology to an act of readership.

Sometimes the less thought there is behind the writing, the more complex the writing is. The term "the locus of ontology" sounds much more intellectual than simply writing about "the meaning" of a piece of art.

> This ambivalence makes obvious how the act of identification or naming—the act of ascribing a word to something physical—is at its heart an ideological act, an act that literally has the power to construct bodies.

You may have heard that God created the universe out of nothing by merely speaking it into existence. I believe Shvarts, in this passage, is claiming the same power for herself.

> It is the intention of this piece to destabilize the locus of that authorial act, and in doing so, reclaim it from the heteronormative structures that seek to naturalize it.

Sorry, I have no idea what that means.

> Often, normative understandings of biological function are a mythology imposed on form. It is this mythology that creates the sexist, racist, ableist, nationalist and homophobic perspective.

In general, you get better grades in the Yale Art Department if you pad every essay with a few politically correct stabs against racism, sexism, etc. But it doesn't really take any moral courage to take a stand for something that nearly everyone else in the university already believes.

> Just as it is a myth that women are "meant" to be feminine and men masculine, that penises and vaginas are "meant" for penetrative heterosexual sex (or that mouths, anuses, breasts, feet or leather, silicone, vinyl, rubber, or metal implements are not "meant" for sex at all), it is a myth that ovaries and a uterus are "meant" to birth a child.

If you have gone through most of your life thinking that ovaries were meant for reproduction, you now stand corrected. As for the "anuses, breasts, feet," etc.—graphic sexual language and imagery is very hip in the modern art world. During my senior year at Yale I went on a class trip to an art gallery in New York. The gallery was full of blown-up images from porno magazines attached to giant, wall-sized canvases. I think each piece was for sale for about $40,000.

The Art Department at Yale is one of the most prestigious in the world. But among the faculty, you will find almost no one who draws, paints, or sculpts with representational skill that approaches even the least of the masters from the Renaissance era. Instead, you will find many people who are busy making political statements. I appreciate contemporary art, including the abstract and the avant-garde, as well as anyone. My favorite painter happens to be from the twentieth century. But I'd like to know that the avant-garde is not simply a cover-up for a shortage of skill and talent. I'd like to know that dense academic doublespeak is not a cover-up for simply having nothing to say.

The charmers, the long-winded hoodwinkers, the expert self-promoters and shock artists, these are the new proprietors of fine art in our age. They urinate in a cup and put a crucifix in it; they videotape themselves standing around naked and project it onto a gallery wall. The museums buy it; the galleries sell it.

The first person to hang a blank canvas on a gallery wall was proclaimed a real genius. But our art world has gleaned the fields of rebellious innovation and shock value for so long that those fields are now barren. Modern art has moved so far beyond the constraints of traditionalism that antitraditionalism has now become just another form of stifling orthodoxy. Art that requires high levels of technical skill just isn't cool anymore, and it certainly won't make the headlines. Shvarts knows this. In this sense, her abortion art project was a highly successful attempt at the kind of meaningless shock art that prevails at Yale and most other universities nowadays.

Shvarts, after all, acted in full concert with her adviser and academic dean. Her project adviser, Pia Lindman, is best known for creating a bathhouse on the grounds of a former public school in Brooklyn, where her goal was to challenge American sensitivities to public nudity. How profound! Another of her best-known projects consists of photographs of herself confined in a weird, home-made torture device. Yale's leaders thought these projects were so innovative and wonderful that they offered her a teaching position.

Professors often have a tremendous influence on students. Hiring bad art teachers inevitably leads to bad student art. Aliza Shvarts is a very intelligent young woman, with a lot of potential. She graduated as the valedictorian of a prestigious prep school in southern California. A picture published on that occasion showed Shvarts looking clean-cut and preppy in a pleated skirt. After four years at Yale, she was photographed at a "performance art" event in New York organized by her Yale adviser, Lindman. The goal of this event was for people to gather in Federal Hall in New York City and stand on a "soapbox" while they aired their grievances to the gathered throng. A photograph of that event shows Shvarts standing on top of a wooden crate wearing frilly white boots, a black leotard, and bulbous leopard-print shorts, shouting at passersby at the top of her lungs. Yale obviously had quite a transformative effect on the young Shvarts. And it's easy to trace the influence back to her academic adviser.

Presently, Shvarts is working on a Ph.D. at NYU, and one day, presumably, she will be teaching other artists how to find "the locus of ontology" in all kinds of lowbrow, publicity-seeking stunts. NYU was a fitting place for Shvarts to do her graduate work. A few years ago, an undergraduate there attempted an art project that consisted of filming various student couples having sex in front of the class. Her professor actually approved the plan. However, senior administrators at NYU stepped in to stop the live classroom sex before it began.

Once the Shvarts story became a media sensation, senior Yale administrators went into emergency damage-control mode. They were getting thousands of media inquiries and messages from outraged alumni, some threatening to withhold donations. Within hours, the university issued a statement denying Shvarts's claims, calling her work a "creative fiction," while, at the same time, defending the theme of her project: "She is an artist and has the right to express herself through performance art," the university declared in an official statement.[4]

Doubts began circulating about the authenticity of Shvarts's claims. Yale's public affairs office continued assuring the public that Shvarts's project was nothing more than an elaborate put-up job. Tests had shown there was no human blood in Shvarts's art studio. However, in an interview, Shvarts called the university's claims "ultimately inaccurate." Shvarts was brought in and grilled by senior administrators. She was told that she would not be allowed to display her senior art project—and thus wouldn't be able to graduate—unless she publicly confessed that her project was a hoax, and that it contained no actual abortion blood.

Shvarts pushed back against the university, noting that her project was "university sanctioned," and saying in an interview:

> I'm not going to absolve them by saying it was some sort of hoax when it wasn't. I started out with the University on board with what I was doing, and because of the media frenzy they've been trying to dissociate with me. Ultimately I want to get back to a point where they renew their support because ultimately this was something they supported.[5]

In this instance, I think Shvarts did have a point. The university wasn't taking full responsibility for its faculty's prior complicity. Having previously witnessed so much extreme behavior in Yale classrooms without so much as a peep from the administration, I was amazed to see the university's swift, concerted action against Shvarts. It seems academic freedom has no bounds at Yale unless the university is facing a public relations crisis.

When it comes to Shvarts's project, "our normative understanding of 'the real'" (to use her words) is still a bit hazy. Some found it hard to believe that she really spent her entire senior year injecting herself with sperm and downing morning-after pills like they were M&Ms. Many suspected the entire thing was a fabrication. But, in an attempt to prove she had actually done what she claimed, Shvarts showed reporters videos she had made of herself standing naked in a shower, moaning, and leaking menstrual blood into containers. At least that much of the project was, frighteningly, real.

Eventually Shvarts backed down in the face of the university's demands. She withdrew her project and substituted another in its place. She was awarded her degree, but I heard she didn't even show up at the graduation ceremony.

Later that spring, the university announced that it had taken disciplinary action against two members of the faculty who, the university said, "had shown serious errors in judgment" by approving Shvarts's abortion art project. Pia Lindman was notably absent from the university faculty the next fall. I'm glad the university held certain faculty members responsible for approving a project that could have put a student at serious health risk. But I can't help wondering if they took action only because the university's reputation was on the line once the project became widely publicized.

Shvarts didn't create her project in secret. She would have needed approval from multiple members of the faculty and administration, such as her adviser and the director of undergraduate studies for the Art Department. She presented her project openly at a departmental forum earlier in the year, long before news of the project emerged publicly. If Shvarts's abortion art hadn't created a huge embarrassment for the university, would administrators have raised any objections to it? Somehow, I doubt it.

There are many ethical reasons why treating abortion like a trivial art project is a bad idea. Beyond the ethical concerns, the Shvarts saga shows just how low the bar is set in the Yale Art Department. Why was such a project considered good enough, in the minds of numerous faculty members, to serve as the crowning work of an art major's career at Yale University? The academic standards—if there are any—are set mighty low.

A short time after the Shvarts story broke, Dr. Edmund Funai, a professor of obstetrics at the Yale medical school, was interviewed in relation to the story. The *Yale Daily News* asked Dr. Funai what the odds were that Shvarts had actually conceived during the course of her nine months of supposed self-inseminations. Dr. Funai's response represents the best summary I have ever read of the problem of bad art at Yale. "The most likely scenario," he replied, "is that all Shvarts was seeing every month was her own menstrual blood. Half of the Yale community sees art of similar quality when taking care of their monthly hygiene."[6]

* * *

During my senior year, I took a class in black-and-white photography. We learned the dying art of processing our own film and making our own prints. Yale has a state-of-the-art, fully staffed photo-processing lab, with numerous darkrooms, and a full-time technician who mixes all the chemicals and maintains all the equipment. It's a stunning facility.

It was a great class, and I put a lot into it. For my final project I stayed up all night, walking around the city, taking nighttime photographs, tapping into my inner Ansel Adams, braving the freezing cold, and carrying an expensive camera through the notorious mugger-filled streets of New Haven. I recall another student had been robbed at gunpoint nearby only a few weeks before. As a reward for braving such perils, I was able to display a couple of the final images in a year-end show at the Yale student art gallery.

On a previous visit to the gallery, I had encountered a collection of photographs of a very different kind. It was a special exhibition of work by one of the grad students in the art program. She had, apparently, spent the entire summer having sex with various other women and taking pictures of the whole process.

I'm not sure what kind of camera she had used, but, thankfully, it didn't appear to be a high-resolution model. Also, the lighting was bad. Unfortunately, it wasn't bad enough to obscure the clear image of the wild-eyed artist as she buried her face in the nether regions of another female. I couldn't believe my eyes. Truly, these images were far too ugly to even qualify as pornography. These images simply turned one's stomach.

I had walked into a gallery of outtakes from some student's scuzzy summer scrapbook of sexual exploits. Somehow, I couldn't see the artistic value in it. Furthermore, I have seen children walking through that building. Putting such things in public view, where even the occasional child who passes by may see it, strikes me as reckless.

The debate over the role of nudity in art has been going on for centuries. When I visited the Vatican Museums in Rome, I found ancient sculptures that had been strategically covered with gilded leaves for the sake of public decency by some wary pope or another. I saw others that had been uncovered and restored to their original naked glory by subsequent, more daring popes. In my view, there is nothing like the beauty and grace of the artfully rendered human form. But is there a difference between images that uplift the soul and those that merely uplift the skirt? Personally, I have found that a masterfully crafted Bernini sculpture, for example, contains inspirational power that is beyond the reach of any greasy tongue-wagging snapshot hanging in a Yale gallery.

One of the most stirring experiences I had when I visited Rome came during a trip to the National Museum of Rome near the Stazione Termini. Near the end of my tour through the galleries I came upon the life-size bronze sculpture known as the Boxer of Quirinal. The work was carved in Greece in the first century B.C.; the artistry is stunning, the features so lifelike, and so full of feeling. It was hard to believe that such craft existed at a time in which technology was so primitive by today's standards. Yet could anyone alive today create something to equal it? We don't even know the name of the artist, yet his work lives on, inspiring, moving, and touching people thousands of years later. Yale has within its own extensive collections countless masterpieces by artists such as John Trumbull, Edward Hopper, and Vincent van Gogh, to name a few.

By way of contrast, I doubt anything being made today in the Yale art program will be celebrated a thousand years from now. Instead, I think the art being made there will be looked upon then with the same indifference that so many professors and students seem to harbor toward their own work today.

We should not be surprised that Aliza Shvarts entered such a program, and emerged four years later with a deranged project that seemed, above all, designed to promote herself, stir up controversy, and gain fifteen minutes of fame. Ultimately, it worked. She was invited later that year to present her work at the Tate Modern in London. The ink on her diploma was hardly dry, and already Aliza, the abortion artist, had gone global. How on earth did she score an invitation to present at a prestigious gallery like the Tate? Here's a clue:

A member of Yale's faculty happened to be curating the event. Art history lecturer Seth Kim-Cohen said he decided to include Shvarts's work in the exhibit after observing the tremendous media coverage she garnered with her abortion project.[7]

People were quick to criticize Shvarts. But, ultimately, didn't she do just what her professors trained her to do? Isn't she the logical product of an artistic culture that celebrates mediocrity and meaninglessness? Wasn't she trained by faculty who, much like Pia Lindman, had been hired largely because they were good at creating shock value, good at creating art aimed at the news cycle, art that amounts, too often, to little more than shallow self-promotion?

By these standards, Shvarts may be the greatest artist who ever attended Yale, better than any of her professors, I would say. Perhaps she should have been teaching rather than studying at the university. In our irony-drenched, ante-upped, shock-loving, minute-by-minute, media-whoring culture, Shvarts represents the essence of what the university has shown—through hiring decisions and through countless exhibitions—that it values. When it comes to art at Yale, as far as I'm concerned, Aliza Shvarts is a living "locus of ontology."

5

DIRTY LANGUAGE

C students—you too can be president.
—George W. Bush, B.A., class of 1968, speaking at
Yale's three hundredth commencement

It's always a tough decision when one is trying to decide what language to take in college. On one hand, you can take something like French, which you probably already studied in high school. It's a well-worn path, and if you're a guy, it's a good way to meet women. On the other hand, you can go the route of the intellectual all-star and study something like Chinese. You will work tirelessly for years, and if you're lucky, you'll be able to order kung pao chicken in the mother tongue by senior year. There are also Russian, Hebrew, Hindi, and Sanskrit offered at Yale, not to mention Czech, Hittite, Serbian, Sumerian, Syriac, Yiddish, Yoruba, and Zulu. Once you learn Persian, there's "Old Persian" to add to your repertoire. For your elective pleasure, don't fail to take advantage of the courses in Akkadian, Arabic, Amharic, and Aramaic. There are Old English, Old Norse, and even Old Church Slavic.

What you might do with Old Church Slavic, once you achieve

fluency, is entirely up to you. I hear the local Bulgarian Orthodox congregation in Blagoevgrad is looking for a new choir director. Go for it.

I spent a semester and a half flexing my linguistic muscle in an attempt to learn ancient Greek. What I learned in all that time was basically just one sentence, which, loosely translated, means: The barbarians do not speak well.

Greek class was held in the oldest building on campus, Connecticut Hall, built more than 250 years ago. It is the building that once housed Nathan Hale, the famous Yale graduate and revolutionary patriot, who upon the gallows proved himself to be a much better orator than he was a spy when he uttered the famous line "I only regret that I have but one life to give for my country."

A bronze statue of Hale stands outside the building. On the way to class each day his likeness would stand there erect and defiant. I figured that if Hale could die for his country, then I could hang my GPA upon the gallows of the third declension.

Greek is the language of philosophy, a beautiful, rhythmic language. When spoken aloud it produces an almost musical cadence. Greek is the linguistic instrument of Aristotle and Plato, the epistolary brick and mortar of much of the Bible. From alpha to omega, it would be no exaggeration to say that the very foundations of Western civilization were built upon its every jot and tittle.

Sure, it is challenging and time-consuming to learn. You can lose years of your life in the bowels of its morphological complexity. But in my tiny class of five students, we all strived to learn the language, as if doing so might gain us entrance into a kind of intellectual pantheon, a rarefied realm inhabited by only the most brilliant minds. Despite the language's great difficulty, not one of the devoted students in my class was going to let a couple thousand hours of painstaking study stand between him and the parlance of Zeus. Except possibly me.

Early in my second semester of Greek I scored a low D on my first exam. Prior to that, I had never had a grade of less than B+. Looking back, my attitude was very unlike that of the fearless

Greek heroes I was supposed to able to read about. I suddenly realized that my desire to learn Greek represented a clear and present danger to my GPA. After a couple of hours staring at that bright red D on the test paper, I did what any reasonable performance-obsessed student would do: I registered for Spanish.

I had no idea how dramatic a change I was in for.

I had come from the staid and routinized world of Greek grammar (*polis, poleos, polei, polin, poli*-wake-me-up-when-it's-over). But I was about to enter a classroom environment where language instruction was based on more passionate and exciting pedagogical principles. I was about to learn Spanish from naked women.

It is standard practice these days to include movies in just about any upper-level college course in the modern languages. Films are good for a couple of reasons. First, students actually get to hear native speakers talking in a visual context. You can see what the characters are talking about and doing, and you can pick up new grammatical understanding from that context. The second reason is, of course, that movies aren't boring. They are fun, exciting even. The more exciting the films are, the more students pay attention. And boy did they get our attention in Spanish class. At least, I'm quite sure they got the attention of every male student in the room.

There's nothing like a little girl-on-girl action to get students thinking about Spanish grammar. The first film we watched that semester was called *Flores de otro mundo,* or "Flowers of Another World." It was about a group of bachelors in a rural Spanish village who invite a bus full of love-starved women in from the city to town in the hope that sparks will fly. There is one particular young girl, a vivacious, dark-skinned beauty known as "la Cubana," who gets a great deal of attention from the men of the town. In the end, however, true love eludes most of the men. However, they do find time to take in a little lesbo porn. When this part of the movie came on, I couldn't help turning to look at my professor to see if she was surprised or embarrassed. She didn't look surprised at all.

Later I learned that the head of the Spanish Department coordinates the movie selections at Yale. All Spanish classes at Yale show the same films, regardless of which professor is teaching them. I don't like to see women objectified on film, and I certainly felt odd sitting next to my sixty-year-old Spanish instructor while two naked women writhed and moaned on screen. Some of my classmates probably didn't object to the material, but there was a palpable sense of embarrassment in the room, if for no other reason than the fact that our professor was the one showing it to us. Some of the girls giggled nervously.

There was a tall girl named Tia* who usually sat across from me. We walked out together after class. She was dark-complected, a bit like "la Cubana." I had noticed during class that she didn't appear particularly amused. Wanting to gauge her feelings a little further, I mentioned casually that I thought the material was a little overheated for language study. "I know!" she said with an exasperated tone. She went on to explain that what we had seen was actually pretty mild by Yale standards. "A friend of mine told me she had to watch a movie in Portuguese class. It was basically a porno." Apparently, Yale takes the concept of "the Romance languages" quite literally. Consequently, learning a Romance language at Yale is an erotic experience.

The next film we viewed kept the sex, but also added a religious element. *The Crime of Father Amaro* tells the story of the steamy romance between a lecherous young priest and an innocent parish girl. We witnessed another nude scene in class, but this time there was a clerical collar involved. The priest then gets the girl killed by forcing her to have an illegal back-alley abortion in order to save his own reputation. Very edgy stuff!

I took four semesters of Spanish in college. I observed a few common traits among college Spanish instructors. First, almost all of them are women. Second, many of them grew up in native Spanish-speaking countries where Catholicism was the dominant religion, and where, generally, a bit of patriarchal machismo is the

---

* In this instance, as with several others in this book, the name has been changed to protect the student's privacy.

cultural norm. The curriculum is written and taught by women who, universally, it seemed, felt repressed and victimized by their native culture. Put all this together and you have a recipe for identity politics disguised as a vocabulary lesson. I don't think I ever read a chapter in a Spanish textbook that didn't have some element of criticism of the Catholic church, of racism, of sexism, or of the political hegemony of the white man. I actually think there is validity to some of these points. On the other hand, I sometimes longed for a grammar lesson that would focus on something other than the brutality of the conquistadors, the inequities of migrant agricultural labor, or the history of how America supposedly stole California from Mexico. Maybe I would have found it easier to master that pesky subjunctive if, just every now and then, when reading the textbooks, I hadn't had to simultaneously ponder multiple insights into why Americans' reluctance to celebrate *el día de los muertos* demonstrates the "cultural sickness" of Americans as evidenced by their inability to cope with death. (This latter argument is one I actually read in a Spanish textbook!)

I sent an e-mail to Professor Beatriz Peña, the director of undergraduate studies in the Spanish Department, asking her whether it might be possible to show students films that didn't require them to watch lesbian sex while sitting next to their professor. She responded with a nice and generally apologetic e-mail, half in English, half in Spanish, explaining that choosing movies related to the topics of the textbook "was a difficult task." *Flores de otro mundo* touched on the themes of immigration and racism. Meanwhile, *The Crime of Father Amaro* dealt with the themes of the law and individual liberty—concepts which, in the context of the film, I interpreted as code words for the debate over legalized abortion.

In other words, these films were chosen, not because they would help students learn the language or understand Hispanic culture, but because they advanced a particular political agenda. What I found interesting is that both films could be viewed as critiques of sexism—critiques that I think are well worth making. Nevertheless, both films arguably objectified the female body by showing female nudity that wasn't essential to the story and was probably there to sell movie tickets rather than to make any political statement. In this way, the films reinforced the sexism they were supposedly criticizing.

I appreciated Professor Peña's kind response. In her defense, these films probably didn't offend most students, and they were by no means "porn" films, in the conventional sense of the word. No, no. Leave it to the Film Studies Department to bring the real XXX material into the classroom.

You may already have asked yourself: What on earth is a Film Studies Department? Film studies is one of those wonderful postmodern majors. If you think about it, who's to say that reading books is somehow intellectually superior to two hours at the local multiplex, with popcorn and a jumbo Coke? Once upon a time, dusty, outdated books written by dead white men dominated almost every academic discipline. But times have changed.

Consider the following old-school disciplines: In the Philosophy Department you've got your Aristotle, your Descartes, your Locke, Hume, and Heidegger—all very white and very dead. In the Physics Department you've got Galileo, Copernicus, Newton, Einstein— again, all white and all dead. Einstein even flaunted a gigantic shock of white hair. Hair, as we all know, is also biologically dead.

I forgot to mention that some people at Yale consider it a bad thing, from an enlightened academic standpoint, to be a man. Over in the History Department you've got Napoleon, Hitler, and the Marquis de Sade—all men, and also, I might add, notably evil. In the English Department you do have Jane Austen, who, luckily, was not a man. Still, her ethnicity, her oldness, and her overall lifelessness could possibly be held against her. So you can see there is a problem. To achieve the *right* kind of diversity, we needed ideas that were newer and less white.

About forty years ago, a bunch of forward-thinking intellectuals realized that there was a shortcut to overcoming the fact that dead white men dominated all the academic disciplines, and that was to create brand-new disciplines that definitionally excluded white men. New fields of study were born, including women's studies, gender studies, black studies (later renamed African American studies), Latino studies, Chicano studies. To be fair, Yale also has European studies, and even British studies, two disciplines that buck the nonwhite, non-Eurocentric trend. But the point is that universities, including Yale, have created ever-narrower programs of study, slicing and dicing history and literature, and arranging literary works by the chromosomes and skin color of the authors.

I'm not sure what such narrow academic fields accomplish except, perhaps, encouraging people to be narrow-minded. I have never felt that Shakespeare should be read as a white writer, or as a male writer. Instead, he should be read for what he was—simply a great writer. Shakespeare managed to capture themes about life, death, and love that are universal to all of mankind, regardless of race or sex.

But the intellectuals were eager to make lots of mini academic universes, each with its own set of assumptions and political agendas, each with as many prejudices as the dead white disciplines they sought to supplant. Programs meant to diversify the educational experience had the unintended effect of producing less integration. I've been to a couple of African American studies classes, and they were (surprise!) populated mostly by black students. You find the same trend in other race-specific or gender-specific departments. It never felt right to me. Call me crazy, but I think students of every color would be better off if they attended the same classes and learned from one another, rather than occupying separate academic worlds. I thought "separate but equal" was a policy long ago discredited in this country. Yet I see that it lives on every day at Yale. Blacks and whites attend the same college, but not always the same classes. It's self-selecting segregation. It's Jim Crow incognito.

In the process of creating many mini academic universes, another odd innovation of academic forward thinkers appeared: It was the Department of Film Studies. I could be wrong about this, but it has always made more sense to me to include film studies as part of a broader study of literature. If you think about it, Shakespeare, who wrote plays, was the equivalent of a medieval filmmaker. He made visual spectacles to be enjoyed by common people. And movies are, at some basic level, really nothing more than recorded plays that can be watched on-screen rather than onstage. The two art forms are closely related. But in the academic setting, you won't find much evidence that they are related at all.

Like the ethnic- and gender-based academic disciplines, film studies has always struck me as too narrow to really constitute a meaningful college major for an undergraduate. My classmates who chose it would surely disagree. Nevertheless, there was always a bit of a stigma on campus surrounding the film studies major. You could see those students flinch a little when someone asked: What's your major? They tended to cast their gaze to the ground and answer under their breath. I remember one guy telling me that he had to double major in history just so his parents would keep paying his tuition. Can you imagine how a parent feels to pay nearly a quarter million dollars over four years to send his kid to Yale, only to find that he is spending his days ponderously watching *Citizen Kane* and writing essays with titles like "Rosebud: A Deontological Examination of Moral Memory"?

To be fair, there is plenty of shallow intellectualizing going on in all of the humanities and social science departments at Yale. And I have written my share of overwrought essays. But I have other reasons to doubt the intellectual seriousness of the Film Studies Department. If I had to pin down the exact point at which I lost respect for the program, I think it would be the day the director of undergraduate studies for the department, a professor named Aaron Gerow, posted flyers all around campus, inviting students to attend what one might characterize as soft-core Asian porn.

* * *

There are corkboards hanging in the hallways of just about every building on campus. Professors and student groups use them to post flyers advertising campus events. One day, during my first year at Yale, I was walking past one of these boards when Professor Gerow's flyer caught my eye. It announced a series of hour-long softcore porn films. These films fell into a particular Japanese porn genre known as "pink films." Like most other screenings on campus, they were free and open to all students.

Half of the films were to be shown in Luce Hall, a building where I once attended a lecture by Lord Patten of Barnes, the chancellor of the University of Oxford. Now, in his place, students would be shown films with titles like *Uncle's Paradise* (a movie that was also released under the alternate title *Mighty Extreme Women*). Luce Hall happens to be right across the street from the official residence of Yale's president, Richard Levin. I'm not sure if Levin made it over to see *Mighty Extreme Women* that night or not, but I'm guessing he steered clear.

What isn't clear to me is how to calculate the educational value of *Mighty Extreme Women,* a film one reviewer described as a "surrealistic comedy about the erotic trials and triumphs of a pep-tonic addicted middle-age man and his squid-fishing nephew, climaxing in a descent to a love-hotel hell, with Satan as the desk clerk."[1] Nor is it clear to me how Yale can hope to maintain a respectful environment for women when a professor sits around ogling nude Asian girls in the company of students—when he does so in a Yale classroom, no less. At Yale, this sort of thing does not take place in secret. On the contrary, it is advertised openly around campus. No one in the administration, so far as I know, even pauses to question what message this sends to students. No one in the administration seems to wonder what message this might send to a young freshman girl who hopes to be valued by her peers for reasons other than her body or her sex appeal.

In addition to his position in the Film Studies Department, Professor Gerow, who sponsored the "pink film" screenings, holds a faculty appointment in the Department of East Asian Languages and Literatures. As a director of undergraduate studies, he works closely with young students and is responsible for advising and counseling them academically. He is a person of considerable influence and authority. In most cases, the faculty at Yale is ultrasensitive, almost to the point of paranoia, about racial prejudice or racial stereotyping. One of the stereotypes that feminists often complain about is the hypersexualization of Asian women in film and pop culture. In her book *Pornland: How Porn Has Hijacked Our Sexuality*, the feminist scholar Gail Dines describes the way Asian women are typically portrayed in porn:

> Depicted as perfect sex objects with well-honed sexual skills, Asian women come to porn with a baggage of stereotypes that makes them the idealized women of the porn world. . . . We see a mind-numbing replaying of the image of Asian women as sexually exotic, enticing and submissive in both the text and pictures. Using words such as naïve, obedient, petite, cute, and innocent, the Web sites are full of images of Asian women, who, we are told, will do anything to please a man, since this is what they are bred for. It seems from these sites, however, that Asian women are interested in pleasing only white men because Asian men are almost completely absent as sex partners.[2]

Professor Gerow, who happens to be white, told a reporter for the *Yale Daily News* that he was "excited" to bring Japanese pink films to Yale.[3] In addition to *Mighty Extreme Women*, he screened several others, including one called *The Glamorous Life of Sachiko Hanai*, about a psychic Japanese prostitute fleeing from international spies.

Racism in porn is rampant and problematic, not just when it comes to the way Asians are portrayed, but also in the depiction of Blacks and other racial groups. For some reason, at Yale, where racial sensitivity dials are always turned up to maximum and where the hounds of political correctness can smell the blood of every bleeding-hearted victim of racial slight within a hundred miles, I never heard a single complaint about Gerow's Asian women film fest. Nor did I hear any of the dozens of feminist scholars on campus raising any concerns about the screenings. Racial issues aside, the most problematic issue is how women are portrayed and, frequently, humiliated in porn. Yet, it seems that when it comes to nude girls on film, Yale's usual hypersensitivity to racism and sexism does not apply.

I'm sure Mr. Gerow would claim that his intention was was not to demean Asians, or specifically in this case, the Japanese, but to enrich students' awareness of Japanese culture. I'm sure that he would also say something about the important artistic influence soft-core "pink" films have had on Japanese society. (Seriously, he probably would!) But I don't think you need to show students images that objectify women in order to help them analyze the place of women in Japanese culture any more than you need to expose them to radiation sickness in order to help them analyze the effects of nuclear war in that country. It is a fallacy to think that students must always "experience" something directly in order to understand it. If that were true, studying ancient history would be a pointless enterprise. In this instance, I would say the danger of causing female students to feel demeaned outweighed whatever cultural insight students might gain.

Regardless of his intentions, I find it ironic that Professor Gerow, one of the people chiefly responsible for teaching Yale students about Asian literature and culture, also happens to be the man who screened an entire series of films portraying Asian women as sex objects, and in so doing may single-handedly have done more to reinforce negative stereotypes about Asian women than anyone in the entire university. Nevertheless, if you go along with Gerow's line of thinking, and take it to its logical extreme, you can see he would have a valid point. At a university that so proudly trumpets its racial diversity, its multicultural sensitivity, its ethnic precocity—at such a place—it would be a crime to find that students were in their dorms watching only white porn, full of white bodies. It is therefore, in a sense, the university's duty to introduce smut of every color, to saturate its campus with a veritable rainbow of naked women. No wonder Professor Gerow took no pause as he removed *Mighty Extreme Women* from its case, slipped the disc into the video player, and huddled down in a dark room with a group of students. In his own mind, he was planting a seed of cultural enlightenment in each of them. He was enlarging the international breadth of their education. At Yale, multiculturalism thrives alongside moral relativism. Even the perverse is diverse.

Political correctness and multiculturalism have come to dominate modern academic life, particularly in the humanities and social sciences. For example, literature is now examined almost exclusively, it seems, through the lenses of race, gender, and modern political concerns. While these are certainly legitimate modes of inquiry, they have come to be, quite often, the *only* modes of inquiry. Multiculturalism was supposed to broaden academic inquiry; paradoxically, it only narrowed our intellectual horizons. Checking off boxes on a political laundry list became a substitute for free and genuine academic inquiry. With academic life increasingly broken down into narrow subdisciplines that fail to communicate with one another, the methodological narrowness of modern deconstructionism is compounded by the narrowness of intellectual isolation, as each race- or gender-specific academic department becomes an echo chamber, full of people who think exactly alike.

Looking at great and timeless works of the past exclusively through the narrow lens of today's hot-button political issues reduces our ability to grasp the works in light of the context in which they were actually created. The larger meaning and importance are lost. And truth becomes a political commodity, to be molded and manipulated in service of narrow and ever-changing ideological concerns. To a lesser degree, this is even true of the sciences, which are sometimes thought of as value-free inquiries into the hard facts of the natural world. Because science is relevant to some of the most volatile political issues of our time—take abortion, gay rights, and the environment to name a few—it's not hard to think of positions that would be politically problematic even if they turned out to be scientifically valid. These days, all knowledge is political. Not even something as seemingly innocuous as the learning of grammar and syntax can be considered free of ideology. Thus, at Yale, even teaching a language has become, at its core, an avenue for advancing a political agenda.

6

HOW A LONG SHOT
GOT INTO YALE

There are lots of people saying "I was the president's room-mate." But I only had one roommate—named Barbara Bush.

—George H.W. Bush, B.A., class of 1948

People ask me all the time: "Where did you go to college?" Usually I answer: "In Connecticut."

Many of my classmates have told me that they answer the same way. When you are young and fresh out of school, it's natural for questions about your education to come up in casual conversation. Ordinarily, I feel a tinge of embarrassment when I utter the words, "I went to Yale." It's as if there were something inherently pretentious about that statement. I don't know why. Maybe it's because our culture is so obsessed with elite colleges.

There is a certain segment of our society made up of people who wait with bated breath each year for the release of the new *U.S. News & World Report* college rankings. These people are afflicted with Ivy League fever. It's not just the prep school parents. Many university administrators are completely obsessed with their position in the *U.S. News* rankings. It's laughable how the top ten list changes every year. One year Harvard is supposedly better than Yale. Then a year later Yale is better than Harvard. All of the sudden the next year—surprise!—Princeton is ranked higher than them both. If *U.S. News* used the same basis for ranking these schools each year, there would be very little change from year to year. But *U.S. News* frequently adjusts the algorithm it uses for ranking schools in order to create the illusion of a never-ending Ivy League horse race. It sells a lot of magazines, but that's about all those annual rankings are good for.*

Occasionally, I meet high school kids who want advice about applying to college. But usually it's the parents who start pummeling me with questions. I can tell right away by the panicked expression on the mother's face that she probably has a copy of *U.S. News* rolled up under her pillow. Every parent wants his or her child to do well. I sympathize with what parents are feeling. But I try to tell them to relax a bit.

Most top-ranked schools are wonderful places. But students are all different. And not all colleges are a good fit simply because some magazine says so. You've got small schools, large schools, schools with great science programs, schools with great athletic programs, schools in big cities, schools near beaches. The truth is, a bright and motivated student can do well almost anywhere. And I find that most people end up loving their alma mater, no matter where they attend. Personally, I think the University of Hawaii wouldn't be a bad place to spend four years.

There was a time, however, when I was just as obsessed with the Ivy League as anyone else out there.

I was ten years old when I first caught Yale fever. Around that time, someone had given me a series of children's books—biographies of some of history's great scientists: Newton, Galileo, Kepler. I

---

* On a side note, I do feel strongly that Yale is better than Harvard. (See chapter 9.)

devoured them. Later, I read books about Niels Bohr, Enrico Fermi, and Einstein. Somewhere along the way, I decided that I was going to join their ranks as one of the great theoretical physicists of the modern age.

I was particularly obsessed with Einstein, with his great shock of white hair. He was a rock star intellectual, an icon, a symbol for intelligence itself. I believe it was around this time that I started using lots of hair gel.

I read about how Einstein had spent his final years at Princeton's Institute for Advanced Study. And I decided right then that, in addition to the hair gel, getting into the Ivy League was my ticket to intellectual superstardom and, most likely, a Nobel Prize.

Of course, the irony is, Einstein never really fit well into the university system. As a young student in Germany he skipped class a lot. And much of what he learned, he taught himself. Somehow he managed to do what he did without so much as a day's worth of instruction from a *U.S. News & World Report*–certified, top-ranked university.

Nevertheless, at the age of ten, I was convinced that the Ivy League was my destiny. It would allow me to follow in Einstein's footsteps. Back before the Internet, people had these things called encyclopedias. They were big dusty books, made of actual paper. My parents had bought a set from a traveling door-to-door salesman. I remember carrying the big book outside into the backyard one sunny afternoon. There, under a massive oak tree, I shuffled the pages back and forth until I found the *I* section. Igloos, Iguanas, Illinois, Ireland, Istanbul, ah—there it was: Ivy League, The.

The article mentioned eight schools, most of which I had never heard of before. I saw Yale on the list. I had definitely heard of Yale. In recent decades, it has begun looking more and more like a requirement that in order to become the president of the United States, one must first graduate from Yale. At the age of ten, becoming president of the United States was just another item on my to-do list—right after discovering the great unifying quantum theory and winning the Nobel Prize. As I held that weighty book, I felt the gravity of the moment. The cover of the encyclopedia was deep blue, just like the Yale logo. There was a quantum shift in the space-time continuum. On that day, lightning from heaven struck my ten-year-old heart and, mysteriously, turned it Yale blue.

It took me a quite a few years to figure out that I wasn't cut out for physics. Sure, I was good at math and science—to a point. But I lacked the primal instinct for numbers. Somewhere between calculus, quarks, and quasars, I became aware that I was blind to the "poetry" that supersmart science types were apparently able to perceive while composing ninety-nine-step equations. Consequently, unless I manage to turn myself into Mother Teresa someday, and win it for peace, I guess the Nobel Prize is off the table.

The dream of being a scientist faded, but the little Yale seed that had been planted in my soul would not die. Nay, those Ivy roots grew deeper with each passing year. I wanted it more than ever. Unfortunately, along the way, my educational career took a few . . . detours. To any objective observer, my life would have looked nothing like that of a future Ivy Leaguer. I came from a lower-middle-class home. No prep schools, no private tutors. By the age of seventeen, I was basically a homeschooled dropout with a part-time job loading sacks of cow manure at Walmart.

Back when I was about to enter the fourth grade, my mother had pulled my brother and me out of public school and had decided to homeschool us. I think she had heard one too many stories about kids selling crack on the playground or bringing loaded pistols to school. She also believed she could give us a better education. We lived all over the South: Florida, Georgia, North Carolina, Tennessee. Since I was homeschooled, the constant moving wasn't as disruptive as it might have been.

Looking back on the homeschooling experience, it had its advantages. I was able to move ahead to higher grade levels in subjects where I excelled. I didn't have to wait for thirty classmates to keep pace. I also became an independent learner—something that is very useful in college. My brother and I maintained high scores on state tests, and I think we turned out fine.

Most homeschooled kids I knew were very bright, probably most of all because they had parents who were, by default, deeply involved in their educations. For me there were gaps here and there—especially as I moved into the high school years. I missed a lot of the standard high school English canon.

By way of contrast, when I got to Yale, I was amazed by how much some of my classmates knew before they even got there—and by how much they had read. Many had attended top prep schools. They started out at Yale already knowing more than most American college graduates. Some, who went to places like Exeter and Andover, actually felt that Yale was easier than high school. Students at Yale are bright, creative, and ambitious. That's part of what makes it so fun to go there. As a rule, I'd say if you are bright enough to get into Yale, you won't have any problem with the academics. The hard part is getting in.

After the getting in, there's the question of fitting in. Probably the greatest risk a homeschooled kid faces is becoming a painfully awkward social misfit. You know, the type that live way up in the mountains and spend their days churning butter and making their own clothes out of discarded burlap. Thankfully, I wasn't quite so removed from civilization. And to this day, I have no idea how to make butter. Rather than resenting the fact that I didn't come from a fancy private prep school, I was proud of the fact that I got into Yale despite my humble beginnings.

An admissions officer at Yale once told me the university was very reluctant to admit homeschooled students, for fear they would not be able to integrate socially. After I got to know the social scene at Yale a little better, I was amazed she felt that way. At Yale, being a little bit dorky is essential if one hopes to fit in. For instance, one of the coolest things you can do at Yale is to sing in an a cappella group. Enough said.

At most schools, students get drunk and do keg stands. At Yale, students get drunk and recite Shakespeare—I observed this phenomenon more than once. I may have been homeschooled, but I felt like James Dean next to the guy with the tumbler full of bottom-shelf gin and the phony Elizabethan patois.

The path from homeschool to the Ivy League was not a direct one. For me, high school didn't have a definite ending. It sort of faded out gradually. Over the summer prior to what would have been my senior year, I quit altogether. I took a job loading fertilizer at Walmart. You have no idea what fifty-pound bags full of cow dung smell like in the heat of a Tennessee summer. The sun beats down and cooks the manure inside the plastic bags. Inevitably, some of the bags tear and liquid dung oozes down on your hands and forearms, onto your clothes and shoes. I was getting $6.75 an hour at the time, barely enough to buy all the new clothes I needed in order to keep myself from smelling like the intestinal tract of a Brahman bull.

By the time I turned eighteen, I had had enough of life as a manure loader. I had to make a change.

On my eighteenth birthday I loaded all my belongings into the back of a ten-year-old Ford and drove west to Seattle, which was about as far away from Smyrna, Tennessee, as I could get. I got a job as a baggage handler for United Airlines. Since I was already accomplished at loading manure, loading luggage was a cinch. Plus, I smelled better. And I got to crawl around in the bellies of 747s. Best of all, I never had to handle fecal matter of any kind, although I did load a cage full of monkeys once that smelled just as bad. And there was the occasional corpse, being shipped across the country for burial.

I once unloaded a cargo hold full of about $10 million in freshly printed currency. It was being shipped on behalf of the United States Treasury in dozens of rectangular bundles, wrapped in clear plastic. As I loaded each bundle onto the conveyor belt, I did begin to wonder if the United States Treasury would miss just one of those bundles if I happened to forget to send it down the belt. But when

I saw the man with the assault rifle standing next to the armored car outside, I decided it wasn't worth finding out.

There were a lot of older guys on my crew at United. Most of them had spent their entire careers with the airline. The job entailed a lot of kneeling and crouching in cargo bays, lifting suitcases so big and heavy that they must have been packed by tourists who were planning to vacation for the rest of their lives. It was tough on the body. I had shooting pains running up my back and down my legs. Then I started getting chest pains. I thought I was having a heart attack, but the doctor informed me I simply had an inflamed rib cage due to too much heavy lifting. One day, during a break, I looked across the room and noticed all the older guys had one thing in common—giant scars across their knees left over from reconstructive surgery.

I left the break room and walked out onto the tarmac. I looked up at the cloudy Seattle sky. As usual, it was raining. I believe I hadn't seen the sun in about one hundred days. I thought long and hard about my situation. Then I did what any sensible young man in my position would have done. I went home, packed up the old Ford, and moved to Florida.

Florida is known for three things: beaches, jai alai, and retirees. I was too skinny to be a lifeguard. And my knees were still too stiff from airline work to make it in professional jai alai. So I ended up as a waiter in a country club in what marketing consultants call "an active-lifestyle community." It was basically a giant retirement village, full of former factory managers who couldn't bear to live through another Michigan winter.

As it turned out, I had a knack for serving up tiny cuts of steak and overpriced Pinot Noir. But that was just one side of my job. Before I had finished my second month as a waiter, I had also finagled a side gig as a lounge singer.

I have been a musician my whole life. I started with piano lessons at the age of five. I took up the guitar at twelve. At the age of nineteen, I taught myself how to sing Sinatra-style. I had never done anything like it before. But, somehow, I convinced the club manager to hire me to sing "Fly Me to the Moon" and "Unforgettable" for three hours every Wednesday night for $75 plus tips.

I parlayed my lounge act into a full array of entertainment services for the fifty-five-and-over crowd. In addition to my suit-and-tie Sinatra gig, I had a poolside tiki bar show. Every Sunday, I put on my flip-flops and a tropical shirt straight out of Jimmy Buffett's closet. I'd stand outside with my guitar for hours and sing for the old ladies while they cooked themselves beside the pool. I did corporate parties, social club luncheons, concerts on the town square.

I was beginning to make quite a name for myself. Unfortunately, I was also getting hit on by women who were older than my grandmother. At first I thought they were just being playful. But eventually I started getting letters at home, and suspiciously large tips. It was all very strange.

I had been thinking for some time about where my life was headed, or perhaps, where it wasn't headed. I was twenty years old by that time and still wasn't sure what I was going to do with my life.

Then 9/11 happened.

I remember my best friend called me and I ran over to his house to turn on the news just in time to watch the first tower fall. I can still hear the sound of Tom Brokaw's voice coming over the television, and that feeling of disbelief. It's hard to remember now, when we are used to thinking about terrorism all the time, but 9/11 was such a shock when it happened. It was sobering. Life and liberty couldn't be taken for granted anymore. And all the privilege and opportunity that come from being lucky enough to be born in America—those didn't seem like givens either.

Armed with a new sense of urgency about being purposeful with my life, I joined up with a medical relief charity called Mercy Ships International as a volunteer. Mercy Ships transports doctors and other health workers to impoverished countries where medical care is often otherwise unavailable. It operates ships that are, essentially, floating hospitals. They will pull into port in Africa or Latin America, and the medical staff spend weeks treating the poor, doing fistula surgeries, removing cataracts, repairing cleft palates on children. It's remarkable work. I spent nearly six life-changing months with Mercy Ships, doing menial labor. I was a deckhand, which means I spent most of my time swabbing the deck, painting the mast, and chiseling rust until my skin was as black as the face of a West Virginia coal miner.

It was hard, beautiful work. In the Dominican Republic, we brought food and clean water to Haitian émigrés who lived in an enormous trash dump near a resort town. It is a revelation to watch little kids forage for food through bags of garbage. The stench, and the swarms of flies—it's something I'll never forget. Those kids had so little opportunity. They were doing their best just to survive. I, as an American, on the other hand, was born into a life of comparative ease and privilege.

My family wasn't rich by American standards, not even close. In fact, I know what it feels like for your parents to be unable to pay the rent. I know what it is like to fall below the U.S. Census Bureau's official poverty line. But compared to those kids in the trash dump, I had the life of a prince. I had never gone hungry, not even once in my life.

I remember having such a strong and urgent feeling—*I've got to do something with my life*. I picked up a college guidebook that very day.

How one goes from being a homeschooled dropout lounge singer with a GED to a Yale undergrad is a story in itself. Suffice it to say, I spent six months preparing for the SATs. I took the main test twice, scored well both times, and, thanks to a lot of hard work, managed a perfect verbal score the second time.

Those who have been through the process before know that I

was still a long shot at any elite university. But I was a bit naïve about the whole thing; with good test scores and an interesting backstory to my credit, I believed most any school would welcome me, GED and all, into its ranks.

After my stint with Mercy Ships, I moved to Nashville, near my old hometown, while I prepared for college. Things were going very well. I had applied to a number of colleges, including a little liberal arts college called Sewanee, which sits on a beautiful spot high atop Tennessee's Cumberland Plateau. It was a great school. And they wanted me. They wined me and dined me, and treated me to special one-on-one meetings with the faculty. They awarded me a generous scholarship. At a special dinner for admitted scholarship students, the president of the college got up to speak. "Whether you have already decided to attend here," he said, "or whether you are holding out for a long shot at Yale, we welcome you." He seemed to be speaking directly to me. Later, when I met with one of the professors, she told me that her two daughters had attended Yale and found it to be large and impersonal. "You don't want to go there," she said.

Oh yes I did.

I remember poring over my Yale application, making sure every word was spelled correctly. I even called the admissions office to see if I could charm them just a little over the phone and, perhaps, gain a slight edge. I had the most inspiring conversation with a college admissions officer one could hope to have. The officer on the other end of the line was overflowing with can-do spirit. As I talked with him about my application, I began to feel that my admission to Yale was a matter of destiny: "You know what you need to do," he told me at the end of our conversation. "Now go do it!" I could almost hear the triumphant theme music from the movie *Rocky* playing in the background. When I hung up the phone, I was on an epic high.

Just as I expected, I was called for an interview. I met with an alumna, who worked as a lawyer in a skyscraper downtown. "You're going to love it at Yale," she told me. "And it's going to open so many doors for you." When I got home, I pulled out the shiny Yale brochure I had filed beneath my desk. There was a line on it about how Yale offered one of the finest undergraduate educations in the world. There were images of Gothic stone towers reaching up to the sky. I saw a photo of a group of students smiling and posing with the university president. Something inside me told me I would soon be standing there too.

Finally, April arrived. When I opened the rejection letter it came as quite a shock.

Not only did I fail to get into Yale, I also managed to get rejected from almost every other university I applied to. Even schools that I'd considered "safety" schools seemed to have no interest in a home-schooled dropout with good SAT scores and an electric guitar.

I was still waiting tables to support myself. A few weeks earlier, I happened to serve the former Tennessee governor and presidential candidate Lamar Alexander. He had just been elected to the U.S. Senate. Between courses, he and I got to talking, and he got excited when he heard about my lofty Ivy League ambitions. "Aim high," he told me; "there's a lot of room up there."

I had aimed high. But there wasn't as much room up there as I had believed. Three colleges took a chance on me. In addition to Sewanee, I got in at Columbia, in New York, and a little liberal arts college in California called Claremont McKenna. While Columbia was immediately appealing, the scholarship they offered was quite a bit lower than what I was offered at the other two schools. I weighed the usual factors, including academic reputation, location, cost, and financial aid. In the end I chose Claremont. I tried to resign myself to the path in front of me. I tried to get over Yale. I started preparing myself to move to California.

But then a girl changed my life.

A few months before, I was with a group of friends. Across the room I saw this girl and I decided I had to talk to her. I can see

why the ancient poets came up with the idea of Cupid's bow, because sometimes attraction hits you so suddenly, it can be overwhelming. Amazingly, this girl was not only attractive, she was also
an extraordinary person, a generous soul, and—I shouldn't fail to
mention—an artist. There was no furniture in her living room. Instead, it was covered wall to wall with easels and canvases and paintings in progress. I'm afraid I found the whole thing irresistible.

There's nothing like love to change a man. I soon started doing
things I had never done before. I was talking on the phone for hours
at a time. I was spending money like I was the Sultan of Brunei. I
took her to nice restaurants. We saw shows together. Other times,
we hung around and did nothing. And we were happy. When you
can sit for long periods of time in silence with someone, without
doing anything or saying anything, and it's not the least bit awkward, you know you have something special. Within weeks we were
something like best friends.

Suddenly, we had a bit of relationship drama. Things were moving fast. And we were falling hard for one another. Meanwhile, I
was getting ready to move across the country in order to start college. I tried to break things off. Late one night we were sitting in
her car. I gave her some sort of talk about how I loved her, and she
was beautiful and wonderful, but I was moving to California and I
just didn't think it was going to work out.

That lasted for a few days.

Late one night, I was wrestling with the misery that is unique
to love and I decided I didn't want to live without her. (I mean that
in the nonsuicidal sense.)

There was only one thing to do. I had to take her with me.

Six weeks later, Jennifer and I got married in her parents' backyard.
I believe there were a few people who thought our marriage would
last no longer than our engagement. Now, years later, they all realize it was the best decision I ever made. A perfect fit. It seems so
rash. But that's part of what was so brilliant about it. It was a bright

flash. I saw something marvelous and went after it. I only wish that all others could be so lucky.

Jennifer was that rare mix of the good and the lovely. She was the vegetable and the dessert all mixed into one. Our attraction was unlike anything I'd ever felt. So wild, and almost dangerous. Two weeks with her in Puerto Vallarta served as a prelude to my freshman year.

California, here we come. It seemed like almost as soon as we returned home it was time to move west. As soon as we moved in together, it was time to move out.

We piled all our collective possessions into a U-Haul trailer, which we towed behind our car. The car itself was loaded floor to ceiling. We had our bicycles tied to the roof. We looked like the Clampetts on their way to Beverly Hills.

Jennifer took a full-time job and started working part-time on her master's degree. I took a part-time job and started working full-time on my B.A. I was twenty-two when I started college.

We had a little apartment near campus, in a quiet suburb outside L.A. We rode bikes to school together, ate little meals together, went on jogs together, and struggled to make ends meet together. And we had a hell of a wonderful time. We were that sickening couple that constantly engages in public displays of affection, and always looks so annoyingly happy together. We were enjoying love and going about our life.

It went on this way for a couple of years. I became famous around campus as "the married student"—a true anomaly. As a freshman, I was the same age as most of the seniors on campus. But my added life experience was a real asset. I excelled at Claremont. It is a truly fantastic school. I had pretty much gotten over Yale.

And, then, all of the sudden, the old hope came roaring back to life.

* * *

Many of my classmates were taking semesters abroad, studying in places like the UK, Spain, or Japan. There were also a few exchange programs available at U.S. schools on the East Coast. As a married student, it never seemed feasible for me to participate in these programs. Then Jennifer got a new, better-paying job as a graphic designer, which allowed her to work from anywhere. Around the same time, I heard about a visiting student program at Yale, and I figured it would be great—if only for one term. I could experience a little bit of what might have been. Plus, we were young and adventurous, and it seemed like fun.

Unfortunately, the application deadline had already passed. I was about to toss the paperwork in the trash, but at the last minute, Jennifer stopped me. She told me, basically, what the heck, give it a shot. So I mailed in the application.

Three weeks later we were living in New Haven.

As a visiting student, I was at Yale for only one semester. Being "sort of a Yale student" wasn't as good as the real thing. But it was still pretty awesome. I was captivated by the beauty of the place, by the talent and energy of the other students, by the sense of history that seemed to seep out from every wall and drip from every cornice. I loved the classes. I loved the environment. I loved everything about the place, except for the fact that I wasn't part of it—not completely.

By the end of the term, I had made a decision. I would try to transfer permanently. This time, I had a far more impressive application to present. My transcript showed plenty of challenging coursework and a high GPA. I had enthusiastic references from faculty who knew me well. I even had a letter of recommendation from one of the professors I had studied with at Yale that term. Those were the things that would ultimately make the difference.

But, in the end, those things didn't make any difference. Instead, I got rejected again. This rejection letter looked very much like the one I had received a couple of years before. I should have started a collection. The letter said something about how impressive my credentials were, but, regrettably, there was insufficient space to accommodate the gazillions of qualified applicants who had applied.

After we heard the bad news, Jennifer and I took a walk. We ended up on the campus grounds. It was maybe ten o'clock, and dead quiet. All the buildings were glowing softly under the moon. We sat down in Beinecke Plaza, a kind of marble wonderland of architectural majesty, and just took it all in. We held hands in the moonlight.

"You seem like you belong here," she said.

By this time I had already withdrawn from Claremont McKenna. The thought of going back to California seemed, somehow, like going backward. We didn't really know what to do. So I went back to doing what I had been doing before this whole college thing began. I went back to the guitar.

We moved to Manhattan and got a tiny one-room apartment. Not a one-bedroom apartment, a one-room apartment. It was about as big as a nice walk-in closet. It had a view of the rusty water tower on top of the building next door. And I think it cost us about $400,000 per month.

I started playing clubs and bars again. I recorded and released my own record. By this time I had moved on from Sinatra covers to rock 'n' roll. Of course, I wasn't making any money doing this. Fortunately, I managed to land a research job with a public relations firm. So, by day, I put on a coat and tie and worked a respectable job in midtown. At night, I sat around writing songs. Jennifer still had her same work-from-anywhere gig.

We tried to have fun. But we discovered that having fun in New York takes a lot of money. We did, however, manage to take in a show here and there. We bought the cheap standing-room tickets at the Met. We haunted free nights at the local museums. We ate a lot of $4 hummus dinners. We took a lot of walks in Central Park.

Luckily, we liked each other a lot, so when we couldn't afford to go out, we didn't mind being stuck in the same small room to-gether. We'd stick our heads out the windows and take pictures of each other. Sometimes we'd sit and watch all the people moving around like little ants in the building across the street. Or maybe we'd just make love—that was free. Like I said before, when you're really close to someone, really in love, you can do almost anything, or else nothing, and it's still good.

I had a plan. In spite of my burgeoning rock star career, I wasn't quite ready to give up on school. I decided I'd apply to Columbia. They were right up the road, just a few subway stops from our apartment. They had said yes to me before, so I figured there was a good chance they would again. At the same time, I started think-ing about giving it one more shot at Yale. By this time, I imagined, they had a poster with my face on it stuck up in the admissions of-fice, warning committee members to be on the lookout for the guy who kept applying over and over again. Instead of a most-wanted poster, it was a most-unwanted poster.

Babe Ruth hit more homers in his time than any other player, but he also led the American League in strikeouts five times dur-ing his career. I found out that there is a rule at Yale that if you are rejected from the college a third time, you are forever banned from applying. Three strikes and you're out. So I figured I might as well take my last swing.

I applied to Yale for the third time. When my application ar-rived, they must have sent out an emergency memo. Perhaps it read something like this:

URGENT—Members of the Illustrious Yale Admissions Committee, I regret to inform you, Nathan Harden has applied yet again. The top priority this week for all members of the committee will be determining how to make him go away and leave us alone.

After a couple of months, I received a phone call. Someone from the admissions office wanted to meet with me in person. This had never happened before. I assumed it was a case of morbid curiosity. Or else maybe they wanted the satisfaction of rejecting me in person. Nevertheless, I put on my best suit, which I don't think I had worn more than once since my wedding, and took the train up to New Haven. I met with a nice lady there in a big office.

We sat down. She looked at me. "I tried to make you go away last year," she said, "but you just keep coming back." That's how our conversation began. I was roundly questioned for half an hour and then sent on my way.

Then I waited.

Finally, the news came.

I got in.

The lady I had met with in the admissions office called to congratulate me. Strangely, I felt very little excitement during the call. It all felt very matter-of-fact. It was only after I hung up that it hit me, and Jennifer and I did a little jig around our closet-sized apartment. We were Lords of Manhattan that night. And man, what a sweet feeling after all that trying.

Even for the brightest students, getting into Yale is a long shot. Yale turns away scores of valedictorians every year, thousands with perfect 4.0 grade point averages, and numerous students with perfect SAT scores. Those who do make it in don't always know why. There is a lot of mystery to it. When I look at my own saga, I'd like to think all the things I worked so hard for—the excellent grades, the thoughtful essays, the quality recommendations, the interesting bio, and the high SAT scores—are what got me in. But in the end, I think I just wore them down.

7

FINDING MY CHAKRA AT YALE

Who will deny that true religion consists, in a great mea-
sure, in vigorous and lively actings of the inclination and
will of the soul, or the fervent exercises of the heart?
 —Jonathan Edwards, B.A., class of 1720

In the summer between my junior and senior years, I had the chance to experience what was, without a doubt, the highlight of my Yale education. I had been taking a class on Roman intellectual history over the spring term, and there was an option to go study in Rome for six weeks during the summer. Under normal circumstances, there's no way I could have afforded to go. But, once more, Yale worked its magic. The financial aid office gave me a $10,000 grant to cover the cost of the course, the flight, lodging, and food for the entire trip. The stipend even included an extra amount to cover "lost income" for students who would normally take a summer job. With this amount, I was able to pay for Jennifer's flight as well. These are the kinds of perks that make Yale a truly extraordinary place to study.

We had our own little apartment in the historic Trastevere district, near the river. We shopped in the local markets, picked up fresh bread at the local neighborhood bakery each morning, cooked our own meals with fresh Italian produce, and got to know our neighbors.

Our professor was living la dolce vita. She taught at Yale each spring but lived full-time in Rome the rest of the year. As a result, she was able to share her intimate knowledge of the city with us, and was able to use her connections to access the very best of what the city had to offer. About a dozen of us Yale students were on the trip. We spent our days scouring museums and archaeological sites, getting our hands down in the dirt, and walking through the places we had been learning about all spring.

We sat for outdoor lectures under the ruined aqueducts south of the city, and visited many hidden places tourists seldom discover. We were given private tours of places like the Roman Forum and the Capitoline Hill, with guidance from leading experts in the fields of archaeology and art history. We visited the ruins of the ancient city of Ostia Antica, where Augustine's mother, Monica, was buried. You can walk down the streets and enter the ancient bathhouses, still tiled with the elaborate mosaic floors the ancients walked on two thousand years ago. We ate lunch outside what was once an ancient Roman pub, and you can still see the stone shelf behind the bar where the bartender kept the wine. We were granted special access to the Vatican Observatory at the pope's summer retreat, Castel Gandolfo in Lazio. We saw the strange rainbow-winged angels on the mural at the basilica of Saint Cecilia, and ate lemon jam made by the nuns who live there. We stood speechless before Bernini's *Apollo and Daphne* at the Galleria Borghese. Two of my buddies and I walked five miles one afternoon up the Appian Way from the Mausoleum of Cecilia Metella into Rome. We passed the mighty baths of Caracalla, where Shelley sat composing *Prometheus Unbound* two centuries before. We got lost for hours in Rome's mazelike streets. We ate great food. We drank great wine. Our days were full of wonder after wonder—the catacombs, the Colosseum, the Pantheon at twilight. It was like we were lost in some beautiful, cerebral dream.

Yale made it all possible.

Meanwhile, I wasn't the only one having fun. As an artist and a lover of art, Jennifer was in heaven. After I left with my classmates each morning, she would spend her days taking in the art all over the city, and being admired by hundreds of Italian men. One merchant gave her free cherries as she passed through an outdoor market; another gave her free gelato every day when she passed his shop. An artist working on the street chased her down as she passed through the Piazza Navona in order to give her two paintings he had made. I didn't begrudge the attention they showered upon her. The Romans have, in their city, much of the greatest art ever made, and they know beauty when they see it.

Near the end of the trip, I went back to the Borghese to see Bernini's *David* one more time. I had heard for years about the greatness of Michelangelo's *David*. But his representation of the shepherd king was, in my opinion, nothing compared to Bernini's. Bernini did something impossible. He made stone look like a living material. He captured the softness of skin, the weight of suspended arms and legs, and the subtleties of the face. I'll never forget the fierce determination in the eyes of his David. Maybe it sounds corny, but looking at those eyes reminded me of all the grit and defiance it had taken for me to get to Yale—and now Yale had brought me to the other side of the world to take in experiences unlike any I had ever known. I felt so content in that moment, and so grateful that I hadn't given up. Yale had carried me to places that were so beautiful they were almost transcendent.

I'm living in Rome, I thought to myself. *Isn't that crazy?* Little did I know that as soon as I got back to New Haven, Yale would take me on another kind of quest for transcendence that actually was crazy.

Hoping to get ahead a bit on credits leading up to my senior year, I got it in my mind to take a summer class at the Yale School of Drama. I had always wanted to study acting, and many consider

Yale's drama program to be the foremost in the world. Some of the best actors and actresses of the last fifty years have trained there, including Meryl Streep and Paul Newman to name just two. I figured if it was good enough for them, it was good enough for me. It was an intense program, often running twelve or more hours a day. We had movement class, acting class, improvisation class, dramaturgy study, and rehearsals day and night. I don't think I made it up to Streep's level that summer, but I sure tried.

They make you do a lot of strange things when you study drama. You have to walk around in circles pretending you are moving through air as thick as mud. You have to stand and hold a chair over your head while you shout your lines to the far corners of the room. We also had something called "speech class," which, it turned out, was the strangest class of all. For one thing, it had nothing to do with speech. For another, it had a curriculum that seemed to have been written down in the midst of an acid-tripping, New Age love-in.

The instructor for "speech class" was a woman named Pamela Prather. I love that name—Pamela Prather. It sounds like a character out of a suspense-filled detective novel. But, actually, Pamela wanted nothing to do with suspense. She was hell-bent on relaxation. I don't think I have ever seen someone so relaxed. This woman lived three steps from Nirvana all the time. And she went the extra mile to make sure her students got there too.

In addition to being on the faculty at Yale as a speech instructor, Pamela was also a certified yoga instructor. She was a beautiful woman, lithe and blond, and constantly giving off a fresh herbal aroma.

On a typical day, I come in to "speech class" and find her sitting cross-legged on a mat at the front of the room, in a semimeditative state. She starts us out with a series of breathing exercises and yoga positions. We do the crouching cat, the slinking spider, and one pose that looks like the praying mantis. So far, we've been listening to the soothing sounds of synthesizers and sitars, wafting out from a portable CD player in the corner of the room. But now it's time to jazz things up a bit.

Pamela goes over and changes the CD to a kind of Hindu hip-hop. The room starts to rattle with a powerful downbeat underneath bellows of mystical yodeling straight out of a Bollywood sound track. I'm not sure if hip-hop is standard protocol for yoga. But I think she got her training in Marin County, not Mumbai—so maybe that explains the difference. As the singer groans and squeezes out an endless stream of semitones, the whole class of about twenty students starts moving in step with our leader. We bounce up and down, and jive back and forth with the beat. We are practicing transcendental aerobics. Our arms swing forward as if we are holding imaginary baskets of magic flowers. Now comes the vocalizing. And it's "Haw, haw. Hoh, hoh. Haw, haw. Hoh, hoh." Kind of like we're all training to be Hindi-rapping Santa Clauses.

Pamela's long ponytail swings back and forth as she leads the dance. And that smile—it never leaves her face for a second; it's frozen in place, either by dozens of Botox injections around the mouth, or else by a willful insistence on projecting positive energy into the room. And, I have to admit, all this bobbing and weaving is kind of fun, even if, deep down, I'm laughing at the ridiculousness of the whole scene.

After we've worked the heart rate up into the appropriate realm of positive vibrations, we go back down onto the mats. And, once again, Pamela switches the music to a mellow, meditative drone. She tells us to lie on our backs with our knees up, and to lift our hind ends slowly off the floor. Now we wait for the involuntary tremors to begin.

Thus began my weeks-long quest to find my chakra at Yale. And it proved, in due time, perhaps the greatest of all the challenges I faced in my Yale career. I had once memorized attributions, dates, places of origin, and obscure facts about hundreds of objects for an art history exam—I thought that was hard. I had once written a thirty-page paper on the indispensability of the city in Aristotle's *Politics,* with references in the original Greek—that too seemed like a challenge at the time. But, however difficult such tasks were, I was able to achieve them in a matter of days, perhaps a week or two at most. But the quest to find my chakra went on for six weeks, yet I don't think I was ever really able to get there.

There were some in the class, however, especially a couple of the girls, who seemed to be able to tap into their inner energy stream at will. Almost as soon as the droning music started, their knees were up and starting to shake like bamboo towers on a seismic fault line. Pamela had told us that there were several chakra points throughout the body, but the most powerful of all was—wouldn't you know it?—right in the groin. It seemed like this was the chakra point these girls had tapped into. Pamela had a young assistant, a grad student in the drama program, who was also some kind of part-time yoga instructor. He sat by the girls and held their heads while they raised their midsections into the air, and he looked on while their legs wallowed and twitched and shivered. A few of them were only high school girls, who had come to Yale as special non-credit, visiting students for a few weeks that summer.

Much of yoga is an exercise in holding various positions until you feel you can hold them no longer. After a lengthy session in one of our charka-channeling poses, we all collapse down to our mats in exhaustion. Pamela asks us to close our eyes and continue to breathe slowly and deeply. I can't see what she is doing, but I hear her moving slowly from one student to another. When she gets to me, I begin to smell something strange. I still have my eyes closed. Suddenly, I feel her fingers moving slowly around my temples. I must have twitched, because she reminds me again to relax. While the music drones on, she slowly massages me with scented oil. The fragrance, the music, the sound of her voice, the soft touch of her hands, all melt into a synesthetic haze of sensual delight.

All of this is designed to help me find my chakra. But if this goes on much longer, I believe I'm going to begin to start feeling something else altogether. I suddenly remember that this woman is my professor, and whatever feeling she is about to tap into may be pushing the edge of what is appropriate within a healthy student-teacher relationship.

This is basically how "speech class" went, day after day, week after week. Despite Pamela's best efforts, I never did achieve the right kind of leg tremors. I wasn't the only one who struggled to find my "Kundalini energy." Others in the class went tremorless for weeks on end. I felt sorry for them. All of the chanting, hip-hop how-hawing, and scented oil in the world wasn't enough to push them over the edge into the realm of the transcendental.

There was an intellectual side to the class as well. On one occasion, I arrive to find Pamela distributing a handout featuring the wisdom of an Indian guru. It consists of photocopied pages from a book called *Light on Life: The Yoga Journey to Wholeness, Inner Peace, and Ultimate Freedom.*[1] The handout is full of mystical nuggets: "The word tapas," it reads, "contains the meaning of inner intellectual heat, which burns out our impurities"—whatever that means. Other gems of advice include: "Do not be attached to your body" and "Create within yourself the feeling of beauty, liberation, and infinity." Pamela tells us that yoga is compatible with Judaism, Buddhism, Hinduism, Islam, and Wicca—just about any religion. Notably, however, she leaves Christianity off her list.

In "speech class" I strive for bodily detachment and the feeling of infinity. It's a brave New Age world at Yale. I soon realize I have entered an alternate academic universe. I'm on my way to becoming Maharishi Mahesh Yalie.

As we neared the end of the term, I got the feeling that Pamela had grown a bit frustrated with me. Her admonishments to relax became a bit sterner. Despite all of her creative methods, and despite my apparent willingness to follow her instructions perfectly, something just wasn't clicking inside, and she knew it. She asked me to pay her a visit in her office. When I arrived, she asked me if I was practicing the yoga exercises on my own, outside of class. And if so, why wasn't I tapping into the chakra energy? I believe she became suspicious that, while I was performing the exercises without flaw on the outside, perhaps my heart wasn't really into it.

Pamela handed out our grades at the beginning of the final week, before the course was actually over. She gave me a B−, which turned out to be the lowest semester grade I ever received in college. I was always a bit of a freak about my GPA, and I wasn't happy about the grade. So I visited her again in her office, and asked what I could have done to improve my performance in her class. She told me that I was at Yale University, where standards are very high.

Pamela told me she didn't believe in giving out As to everyone in the class. She told me that some students have an innate gift for yoga, just like others have an innate gift for calculus. I guess she was implying that I didn't have the yoga gift. The difference between calculus and yoga, of course, is that one skill can be tested and graded on the basis of objective standards, while the other requires the professor to exercise a kind of mysterious spiritual perception when doing the grading. I'm not sure that grading students on the basis of a mysterious innate gift is a practice the university would wish to publicize.

There is a lot of talk these days about grade inflation—universities giving out As to everyone, passing students through with no real care about the quality of the work. B is the new D; C is the new F. I think there is something to these concerns. But I also think that when a school is gleaning nearly all of its students from the top 1 percent in the country, there is a good reason why most of those students are doing A-level work. So some of the concern about grade inflation is overblown.

The next day we had our final class of the term. Seeing how the grade for the course was already in, I had nothing left to lose. I decided I would go all out. I was going to show my teacher just what a yoga prodigy looked like. I decided I was going to tremble and moan with an intensity never before seen. I have long hair, and people often mistake me for a yogurt-sucking hippie anyway. It wasn't hard for me to slip into the part. It was, I reminded myself, supposed to be a drama course.

Pamela had something special planned for us on the final day. As we entered the room, the atmosphere was decidedly more solemn and spiritual than usual. Instead of her usual wide smile, the look on her face conveyed a sense of gravity. The lights were dimmed. Exotic smells filled the air. She asked all of us to take off our shoes and gather in the center of the room. One by one, she blindfolded us. My classmates and I stood there, huddled together in the dark, waiting.

Then the music began. What was about to transpire fell somewhere between a hallucinogenic séance and a pagan funeral rite. She ordered us to move. And we began to circulate around the room in a blind huddled mass, holding out our arms to keep from knocking into one another. Gradually, the volume and the intensity of the music began to increase. An earnest feeling began to take hold. I started to hear some of the girls moaning, first one, then another. Pamela turned up the music and told us to move faster, and to let our limbs fly freely. The pulsing beat of the music began to stir the class into a trancelike frenzy.

"Faster!" Pamela shouted. "Release your Kundalini energy!"

The room had transformed into a New Age mosh pit. Blindfolded students were bashing into one another, and dissolving into violent convulsions. The music was swelling to greater and greater levels of intensity. My classmates and I had given ourselves up to the mania. We were dancing like jungle heathens. I heard girls screaming all over the room.

I followed Pamela's voice and found my way over to the side of the room where she was standing. There, at her feet, I dropped to my knees, reared back my blindfolded face, and let out a howl that could have terrified a pack of rabid wolves.

I shuddered and shook and pounded my fists. I did everything short of foaming at the mouth. And I did it all right there where she could see me. It was an Oscar-worthy performance.

After perhaps a half hour or more of the mania, Pamela told us all to be still. The music fell silent for a moment and there was no sound except heaving breath. Then the sound of soft, droning music filled the room.

We had reached the climax of the ceremony. She led us all, still blindfolded, into a circle in the center of the room. She passed in front of us, holding a soft, velvety bag. It was full of magic stones. She told each of us to reach in and pull out whatever stone our hand was drawn to. As we held the stones, a powerful feeling fell over the room. One by one, we placed our stones in a pile in the middle of the circle, and we were told to release our negative energy into the stones. One of the young men in the class was so overcome that he began to weep openly as he placed his stone in the pile.

Once we had released the negative energy, Pamela told us we could undo our blindfolds. I saw that several of the girls in the class had also been weeping. As a group, they stood, embracing our professor in the center of the room.

After it was all over, Pamela came up to me, her eyes as wide as saucers. She told me she had been astonished at my level of spiritual energy during the final class, and she only wished that she could have seen that intensity in me sooner. I was somewhat amused by her change of heart. Perhaps she was wondering if she had misjudged me. Perhaps she now wondered if I had that special yoga gift after all.

It was the only time in college I can ever remember not taking a class seriously. I had acted my part in the whole charade, and I felt a little bad about it because I realized that day that many of my weeping classmates were desperately hungry to connect with some kind of spiritual reality, which they obviously hadn't found elsewhere.

Professor Prather's class was supposed to be a course in speech training. But there was precious little speech involved. Instead, it seemed designed to indoctrinate students into a certain kind of

Westernized yoga religion. Ironically, I think her course did help make me a better actor, in a backward sort of way. When it came to all the dancing and wailing, I had been good enough to convince her.

The lack of legitimate academic standards in "speech class" left me dissatisfied. I had wanted only to study drama, but Yale asked me to find my chakra instead. A few weeks later I filed a complaint with the director of the drama program and got my grade changed to a B+.

My experiences with the Yale yoga master made it clear to me just how much Yale's academic standards have declined. Whether students are viewing porn in the classroom, being advised on abortion art, or graded on the basis of their mystical connection to the chakra—these are all symptoms of the same problem. Yale seems to no longer know what is or isn't worth teaching in its classrooms. The pursuit of truth—if Yale's leaders would even admit that there is such a thing—is no longer important. Yale seems to have lost its sense of intellectual purpose.

In the course of one summer I had experienced the best and the worst of what Yale has to offer. I had followed Alice down the rabbit hole into a warped academic wonderland. I fell from the glorious vistas atop Rome's Palatine Hill, down a long intellectual chasm, past secularism, historical relativism, and postmodernism. I landed in a windowless room in New Haven, surrounded by confused students mumbling incantations over magic stones.

At Yale, the decline of academic standards and the decline of moral standards are two manifestations of a single problem. That problem is Yale's loss of academic purpose. The university's mission is no longer defined by the pursuit of empirical knowledge. Instead, the academic culture is animated by an all-out commitment to accommodating the whims and dictates of political correctness. Ideas are appraised according to their multicultural value, and are sometimes integrated into the educational experience on that basis alone, without regard to educational merit. Thus, finding the chakra—remember, in a speech class—becomes a basis for handing out academic grades. Other ideas are approved solely for their political value. Thus, abortion art is approved by the faculty—at least until it becomes a public relations liability for the university.

In the modern academic world, political considerations reign supreme. Facts are not permitted to stand in the way of political agendas. Eventually, people begin to act as if reality itself is governed by politics. In other words, if my politics are different from yours, then my reality is different from yours. It's all relative. For this reason extreme multiculturalism is a form of intellectual relativism. It entails an implicit denial that there is any such thing as absolute truth.

Our perception of the facts forms the basis of our moral conclusions. Consequently, if truth is relative, morals are also relative. For this reason, the abandonment of the pursuit of empirical knowledge as a guiding principle has brought about both intellectual *and* moral decline.

PART THREE

Yale's War on Women: *How Yale*

sends the message to students that

women should be valued for their bodies

rather than their minds

8

PORN 'N' CHICKEN

I loved all the pizza places and Basil's, a great Greek restau-
rant that closed when I was president. By happy coincidence
I was in New Haven and was able to eat there one last time
just before it closed.
                    —William Jefferson Clinton, J.D., class of 1973

The year is 1973, and Yale students are gathering in a large lecture
hall in the law school building for one of the regular movie nights
sponsored by the Yale Law School Film Society. The screening is
open to anyone in the Yale community, not just the law students.
Many undergraduates are in attendance. Students pay a small admission fee. On the bill tonight: *Deep Throat.*

Produced by a New York hairdresser on a budget of $25,000,
Deep Throat was the first movie to bring hard-core porn into the
mainstream. It generated tremendous political controversy and public calls for censorship. Police raided a number of theaters where it
was being shown in cities across the country. All the news headlines related to the controversy generated enormous publicity for
the film, and it went on to gross more than half a billion dollars
worldwide, making it possibly the most profitable film ever made.

Porn films had been around since at least the early sixties. But

films of that era were what is now called "soft-core." A little vocabulary lesson may be helpful here on the difference between
hard-core and soft-core porn. "Soft-core" films, while they feature
plenty of nudity, depict only simulated sexual intercourse. The actors are not actually having sex on-screen. In this way, soft-core
films are only a bit more graphic than what you might find in some
of the more sexually explicit R-rated films. This is the kind of thing
shown on HBO in the middle of the night. "Hard-core" porn, on
the other hand, features actual sex and may include depictions of
genitalia, male ejaculation, sexual violence, and sadomasochism.

Now a word on letter ratings for movies: The language about
hardcore and softcore should not be confused with the letter ratings granted by the Motion Picture Association of America (MPAA).
In the sixties the MPAA started rating movies with explicit adult
content with the X rating. Later, when home videos became common and the audience for porn began to grow, hard-core pornographers adopted the XXX rating as a kind of marketing gimmick, in
an attempt to suggest that their films were even more extreme. In
fact, however, most porn films are not rated by the MPAA at all.
And the MPAA stopped using the X rating in the early nineties,
replacing it with the equally misunderstood NC-17 rating. To be
clear, films rated X or NC-17 are actually much milder than the
majority of porn produced today.

At Yale, the Law School Film Society continued to screen porn
throughout the seventies. Eventually, the screenings ceased and the
society itself went defunct. These days, all students have to do to
access porn is turn on their computers. But for many years, slipping
in for a public porn screening after a hard day of hitting the books
was a normal part of the Yale experience. Aviam Soifer graduated
from Yale College in 1969, and then from the law school in '72
(just ahead of future president Bill Clinton, '73, and future Supreme
Court justices Clarence Thomas, '74, and Samuel Alito, '75). Soifer went on to enjoy a stellar legal career, which saw him rising to
become the dean of the University of Hawaii Law School. He was
also a film society member during his law school days, and he once

spoke to a reporter about the lassiez-faire environment at Yale in those days: "It's hard to recreate that era," he explained. "There was a general 'breaking out' in the late '60s; it was about defiance of authority. . . . Yale Law School would have been among the last places to crack down on a student group."[1]

In the seventies, porn was a public experience, often consumed in seedy dollar theaters on deserted avenues. Men slipped in and out with their collars pulled up high and their hats down low. Today, porn is much more a private affair, consumed mostly over the Internet. Because of the anonymity and relative convenience of the Internet, porn has become a far more pervasive part of American culture than it was in the seventies.

I came of age in the era of the Internet and of pay-per-view television. Therefore, it is hard for me to relate to a time when public porn screenings were the norm. In addition, I find it hard to reconcile the sleaze of low-budget porn with the power and prestige of Yale Law School, chock-full—as it was—of future presidents and Supreme Court justices.

Nothing goes together like porn and fried chicken. At least, that was the opinion held by a group of students who, a few years ago, started a group on campus called, well, "Porn 'n' Chicken." It began quite by accident. A group of guys began gathering on occasion to watch porn (nothing unusual on a college campus). But the innovation—the particular genius that seemed to set this particular group of young men apart—was that, prior to each gathering, they would make a run to the local Popeyes Chicken and Biscuits restaurant.

Popeyes stands on Whalley Avenue, just outside the perimeter of campus. It marks the border between Yale and a poor, largely black neighborhood to the north. In case you need a clue as to this demographic transition, Miriam's Hair and Braiding Salon sits right next door.

Like many poor urban neighborhoods, this area has a lot of

problems with drug-related crime. Newspapers report muggings and shootings fairly regularly. For this reason, Yalies tend to avoid walking around at night in the area north of campus. And I imagine it must have taken some boldness, a certain daring determination, on the part of the Porn 'n' Chicken club, to make the trip to Popeyes prior to each meeting.

I'm not sure what the connection is between porn and chicken; maybe it has something to do with all those breasts and thighs. But whatever the connection, it seems to have struck a chord with the student body. Within a short time, the small group had grown to more than one hundred in number. Even a number of girls began attending.

One thing I admire about Yale students is their relentless ambition. After a while, it wasn't enough for this growing flesh and fowl club to simply watch porn. Emboldened by the growth and success of the movement, the students of P 'n' C announced they were going to produce their very own porn film, entitled *StaXXX*. The title alludes to the voluminous central library building, which includes a large multifloored complex known as "the stacks." The stacks, which are something like fifteen stories high, are full of countless rows of dimly lit books, and endless nooks and crannies. It has long been a rendezvous point for students seeking a romantic liaison. Roommates can make privacy hard to come by in the dorms, I suppose. But it sounds a bit geeky, doesn't it? Leave it to Yalies to turn the library into the most erotically charged location on campus.

The announcement that Yale students were planning to make a porn film stimulated something of a media frenzy. The story was picked up by the *New Yorker* and *Time* magazine. Initially the Porn 'n' Chicken club tried to avoid the media. But a reporter for *Time* convinced the group to grant him access in exchange for his bringing a porn star to a P 'n' C meeting. He persuaded Sydnee Steele, star of more than one hundred porn films, to accompany him to Yale. According to his report, he, Steele, and all the students gathered to watch a film together:

More than 100 people squeezed into a dorm suite, even though the group had sent only 20 invitations. Sydnee was concerned because she had packed only 30 goody bags with T shirts, key chains and thermoses. Fortunately, everyone was understanding. The audience was half male, half female, including eight couples holding hands, one woman bearing an Erotic Poetics textbook and one who had a pint of Ben & Jerry's Chubby Hubby. The students were very supportive during the showing of Hell on Heels, cheering when Sydnee's name appeared onscreen. During a three-woman sex scene, Sydnee offered commentary. . . . As the film continued, students raised their hands to ask questions such as "What do you think of feminism?" and "Do you like to have sex with your shoes on or off?"[2]

At least on this occasion the porn wasn't being shown in an actual classroom, although it sounds like there was some attempt to intellectualize the evening's entertainment. Then again, maybe intellectualizing wasn't the main point.

The originators of P 'n' C had begun sending out e-mail invitations to the student body under pseudonyms. And they continued to use these noms de porn when talking to the media. According to the reporter from *Time,* there was one who went by Baby Gristle, and another fellow known as Fruit on the Bottom. The ringleader called himself Sweet Jimmy the Benevolent Pimp.

Sweet Jimmy was, in fact, James Ponsoldt, the student body president.

Ponsoldt never got to make *StaXXX,* and his porn-producing career ended before it ever began. But he did go on to become a successful writer and director of several feature films. Fresh out of college, he sold his story to Comedy Central, which eventually produced a made-for-TV movie based on his college adventures. The movie even featured a cameo from our old friend Ron Jeremy. I'm not sure if *Porn 'n' Chicken*—the movie—is available for sale or rental anymore. But if you ever get a chance to see it, don't judge too harshly. Instead, be grateful that it got made, rather than *StaXXX.*

Ponsoldt, aka Sweet Jimmy, grew up and married an Episcopalian minister. Truly! I saw the wedding announcement in the *New York Times*. And judging from the couple's engagement picture, I'd say she may well be the most attractive minister of the gospel I have ever seen.

Having discussed in an earlier chapter how the porn business exploits performers, it is worth discussing some of the ways it can negatively affect consumers. I think most students at Yale would disagree with my criticism of porn. Many argue that porn is, at its core, just a bit of fantasy and fun. If some people find porn offensive, they can choose to avoid it, right? Others should be able to enjoy it so long as it does no harm. There is a line of thinking out there that anyone who questions porn is either sexually repressed or a deeply conflicted religious hypocrite.

Porn advocates often cite the fact that Utah, one of the most religious and most politically conservative states in the United States, also has the highest rate of porn subscribers in the nation.[3] Pakistan, a largely Muslim nation with extreme cultural restrictions on sex and public indecency, also ranks number one in the world in Internet searches for pornographic content per person. A nation where women are commonly compelled to wear head coverings and head-to-toe robes in order to safeguard their "modesty" is the same nation that leads the world in Google searches for the terms "rape sex," "donkey sex," and, "child sex."[4] Wherever there are severe cultural restrictions on pornography, people are all the more compelled to access it privately—without risk of cultural stigma—via the Internet. It begins to look like there is a pattern of hypocrisy: Those who condemn porn publicly often consume it privately.

But a closer look at the porn industry reveals that it isn't always harmless. And, while many critics may be hypocrites, there are valid reasons to criticize the industry. Turn on your television and you see Hugh Hefner prancing around in his silk pajamas with an entourage of bottle blondes on his own reality television series. Hefner represents the flashy, lighthearted public face of the sex industry. But the reality is much darker. If you are like many people, when you think of porn, you may think of a blushing *Playboy* centerfold, or some thinly plotted film with a pizza delivery boy, a lonely housewife, and a lots of goofy sex. In fact, if you grew up prior to the existence of the Internet, there is a good chance that you have no idea what I mean when I say "porn."

These days, most of the porn you can find on the Internet is what is known as "gonzo" porn. In the gonzo genre, all the flimsy plots are done away with and the emphasis is on "real" rather than scripted scenes. Since the arrival of the Internet, porn producers have been coming up with material that is more and more extreme. If the girl is vomiting, crying, or even bleeding, that's gonzo gold. In her book *Pornland,* author Gail Dines explains how mainstream pornography has grown more brutal, more vicious, and more violent than most of us could imagine.[5] Dines relates what she has seen in the course of two decades of research, and her description of what goes on in hard-core porn is truly shocking, and tough to read. She describes one nightmarish scene after another, full of men punishing and humiliating women sexually on camera. It is commonplace to encounter every kind of bodily waste and fluid in today's porn, and to see a woman's body being punished in every conceivable way, often at the hands of two or three men at a time. I physically gagged more than once while reading Dines's book.

According to Dines, it is not uncommon for gonzo pornographers to film close-ups of the injuries that have occurred to the girl's body, as a kind of twisted climax to a scene. Mainstream porn today is about punishing a woman, not pleasuring her.

While porn is more extreme than ever, it is also more pervasive than ever. Here are a few current and eye-opening statistics on Internet porn use:

- Every day, there are 68 million search engine requests for porn.

- One out of every four times that someone types a search engine request on Google, it is a search for porn.
- The porn industry generates $57 billion worldwide; $3 billion is from child porn.
- Twelve percent of all Web sites on the Internet are porn sites.
- There are 100,000 Web sites offering illegal child porn.
- The average age of first exposure to Internet pornography is eleven.[6]

The Internet has made it a lot easier to access porn. And, increasingly, children are the ones consuming it.

Whether we like it or not, porn affects all of us, including the people we love. Like most young people today, I encountered porn first as a child. My first experience came at the age of five, at the hands of an older cousin. Later on, a friend would occasionally find a girlie mag, or I would stumble onto something online. (Putting a teenage boy in a room with a computer and an Internet connection and expecting him not to look at porn is like putting him in a room with a stack of *Playboy* magazines and expecting them not to take a peek. It ain't gonna happen.) My parents believed strongly that porn would negatively affect the way I thought about and related to women. They taught me to avoid it, and generally, I did. Nevertheless, I have certainly seen my share.

Personally, I find images of naked women to be the neurological equivalent of crack cocaine. I am the first to admit that porn can be really exciting and fun. If it weren't fun, it wouldn't be so addictive. I understand why many people (both men and women) have no problem with porn and see it as a healthy outlet for sexual fantasy. But like crack, porn has an inevitable downside.

I see no way to avoid the fact that porn, these days, is full of violent sexism. It is not simply about men looking at naked women or watching sex acts. Rather, the aim of much of it seems to be to depict the maximum amount of humiliation for the girl on-screen. I think many people who have a favorable view of porn really don't realize how brutal much of it has become over the last couple of decades.

Consider the following: "Among the 50 top-rented porn films, 88% of scenes include physical aggression against a woman, including spanking, slapping, and gagging; 48% include verbal aggression, including calling the actress 'bitch' or 'slut.'"[7] In *Pornland,* Dines describes one Web site that proudly offers its customers the opportunity to "access total degradation" of young women.

Porn teaches young boys that girls are inferior. Many young men now grow up thinking that porn sex, with all its brutality, is normal sex. To take one graphic example, the climactic scene in hardcore porn frequently includes what is known as the "cum shot," which consists of one or more men ejaculating onto the face of the female. Is this really the kind of sex education that young boys should be receiving? If you take porn at face value, you would have to come away believing that the willingness to be humiliated sexually is what makes a woman good in bed. And you would have to believe that it is only when a girl has fake boobs and becomes a passive receptacle of male sexual aggression that she becomes truly desirable.

Young people today are part of the first generation to be raised with free and open access to pornography. This generation has grown up experiencing and learning about sex in a way that is profoundly different from what our parents experienced. We are the porn generation. Our ways of relating have been shaped, inevitably, by our immersion in a kind of sexuality that distorts gender roles and constantly confuses sexiness with sexism. Porn isn't just fantasy, it is a powerful force shaping our sexual culture.

And porn is not just a male pastime. Increasingly, women are consuming it as well. Nevertheless, I am convinced that porn, perhaps more than any other force in our culture, is working against women, reinforcing negative ideas about them, what they want, and what they are capable of being and doing. Porn dehumanizes women and, in this way, demeans all of us, both male and female.

Our parents' generation came of age in the sixties and seventies, just as porn was going mainstream. As members of that generation, they embraced new ideas, including the sexual revolution and women's liberation. But they did not realize that the permissive ideas about sex they embraced would, within a few decades, usher in a pornified sexual culture that would completely undermine the idea of women's equality.

Linda Lovelace, whose real name was Linda Boreman, was the star of perhaps the most well-known porn film in history, *Deep Throat*—the same film screened at the Yale Law School back in 1973. She was always remembered most for her appearance in that movie. However, she left the business shortly after becoming famous. For a while she kept a low profile, had children, and tried to live a fairly normal life. Eventually she became an outspoken antiporn activist. Lovelace died in a traffic accident at the age of fifty-three. Her performance in *Deep Throat* represents both a watershed moment in the mainstreaming of porn, and a crucial moment in the history of the sexual revolution. But when Lovelace published her autobiography, a darker story emerged surrounding her appearance in the film. In it she told of her violent and abusive ex-husband, who she claimed had forced her to act in the movie under threats of violence. Accordingly, she came to think of the film itself as an ongoing glorification and commercialization of what was, for her, a deeply traumatic experience. She was once quoted as saying, "Each time someone watches that movie, they're seeing me being raped."[8]

Richard C. Levin received his Ph.D. from Yale in 1974, just a year after Linda Lovelace's movie was first screened at Yale. Twenty years later, he became president of the university. Levin was already married by 1973, and I doubt he attended the *Deep Throat* screening. But he did come of age as part of a post-sixties generation of academic leaders who take a broadly permissive view when it comes to porn. Perhaps in keeping with the general sentiments of his generation, he has felt reluctant, as Yale president, to place restrictions on the kind of sexual material that can be shown in Yale classrooms.

Unfortunately, however, that sexual material turns out too often to be violently sexist.

Earlier, when I wrote about my experiences at Sex Week 2008, I left out the most controversial event of the week. I mention it now because I think it illustrates so well how Yale's permissiveness has boiled over into an environment that is functionally antiwoman.

On Friday morning that week I received an e-mail, breathlessly announcing that night's main event, which harkened back to the law school porn screenings thirty-five years before:

7:30 p.m., Law School Auditorium
SCREENING followed by panel discussion and Q&A with Vivid Girls Monique Alexander & Savanna Samson, and acclaimed director Paul Thomas
FREE Vivid DVDs. Porn screening. In the Law School. Enough said.

No, I didn't go.

However, I did hear all about what happened that night. The big porn screening had been billed as one of the highlights of Sex Week at Yale. But it turned out to be a real bust. According to a report in the *Yale Daily News*, organizers had to shut down the movie midreel. The film's director, Paul Thomas, was on hand to talk about the film, which was described as "a graphic porn film that featured violent sado-masochism."

According to the article, the coordinators of the event said they were "appalled" by the film, which they hadn't bothered to watch prior to airing it in front of a crowd of more than two hundred students. Meanwhile, the reporter wrote that "members of the gender-balanced crowd did not appear upset by the movie" and that the whole room "reacted with disappointment" when coordinators shut down the film early. Among some of the film's highlights that evening were depictions of "fantasy rape, bondage and piercing"—practices the event coordinators emphasized that they didn't support. "We really dropped the ball on this one," Colin, one of the coordinators, said afterward. He added that while he felt the images were "sexually unhealthy and disrespectful to women" there was "a sense of revelry" among members of the audience, which he found disturbing.

Joe, the director of the event, considered violent porn from a more pedagogical perspective. He said that while he had problems with the material, he still felt the event "was positive overall." He felt the event gave students the opportunity to speak out against violent pornography and to consider how it affects the public's view of women. "I questioned Paul as to whether these graphic, violent images are OK," he added, "knowing that there is someone on the other end who is enjoying it."[9]

Apparently, some Yalies discovered that night that porn can actually be demeaning to women. (Who knew?) But they still seemed to think it was worth viewing so that students could "challenge" it and "speak out against" it. As for me, I find it difficult to see how students can "speak out against" something while simultaneously displaying "a sense of revelry" over it.

I felt sympathy for Joe and Colin while I read their attempts to explain to a reporter the difference between "good" and "bad" porn. They obviously didn't know what they were getting into when they fired up the film. While they thought this particular film was over the line, the reporter makes it clear that many others in the room had no problem with it at all. Rather, they seemed to be enjoying it.

If Yale students were reveling in "violent sado-masochism" and "fantasy rape," I would say it is because they had probably seen it all before. Yale students aren't abnormally cruel, or sexist, or depraved. On the contrary, my classmates at Yale are some of the most conscientious people I've ever met—good-natured, imaginative, intelligent. Most of them worked relentlessly to improve themselves in high school just to have the chance to study at Yale in the first place—showing incredible drive and determination along the way. I never met anyone at Yale who wouldn't publicly advocate respect and dignity for women. Yale students are inspiring people. They are the kind of young people who would make any parent extraordinarily proud.

What does it mean that many of these extraordinary young people could revel, as a group, in the pain of others? I think the answer is quite simple. As part of a generation that has grown up on a steady diet of hard-core gonzo porn, they are profoundly desensitized to sexual violence.

If I had to make one single argument as to why porn is a problem in our culture, it would be this: It really isn't possible, in today's porn industry, to separate pornography and sexual violence. They have become virtually one and the same.

Yale students may be overachievers, but in every meaningful sense they are normal, everyday kids, who grew up in a porn-saturated culture so extreme and so pervasive that they could not help being shaped by it. What is different about Yale students is they will grow up to have an outsized influence on our culture once they enter the working world. They will be legislators, authors, artists, producers, screenwriters, and media executives. That's why I think it's such a shame that Yale allowed the public screening of violent porn. Yale's permissive approach to all matters sexual seems, in this case, to have reinforced the worst ideas about women, sex, and power. If Yale is willing to host violent pornography, in the same lecture hall where students study law, history, and literature, it gives a stamp of legitimacy to images that dehumanize women. Ultimately, we are all diminished.

Ironically, by advancing a morally unbounded notion of free speech, Yale may actually be silencing women. No student wants to come across as a prude or a killjoy. If women are publicly demeaned, some will be less likely to feel empowered to speak up for themselves in the public arena. For this reason, Yale has taken a position that is utterly incompatible with the notion of women's equality.

One can trace a downward trajectory, starting around the Law School Film Society's presentation of *Deep Throat* in 1973, and ending somewhere around Sex Week's sadomasochist peep show in 2008. It is striking that while Linda Lovelace claimed that she was coerced or "raped" in a way that is not apparent to the viewer, now, thirty-five years later, rape or "fantasy rape" is openly accepted.

If I try to argue that all porn is harmful, I realize I am in the minority. There are many I will never convince. But I hope that even those who defend porn will realize that much of what is produced today—especially that which features violence and the flagrant degradation of women—has a potentially harmful effect on how we all relate as sexual beings. It is not enough to say that those who don't like porn may simply ignore it. We are all affected, those who consume porn directly, and those who simply live in a porn-saturated culture.

While most Yale students would probably say there is nothing wrong with porn, it's a safe bet that not one would want his or her sister or mother to appear in a hard-core porn film. If porn is harmless, why wouldn't we want our sisters, sons, or daughters to perform in it? For many, there is a disconnect between what they view as entertainment or fantasy, on the one hand, and real life, on the other. But fantasy isn't wholly separate from reality. Beliefs affect behavior. Negative images can spawn negative actions. If support for women's equality is unanimous, at least publicly, among students at Yale, how then do we explain students' sadomasochistic revelry back in the law school auditorium? It is hard to reconcile a culture that professes women's liberation by day, and then sits back to enjoy a bit of "fantasy rape" at night.

At Yale there is a growing intellectual rift between facts and values. Likewise, when it comes to women's rights, there is a rift between actions and professed beliefs. This may be one reason why otherwise conscientious students occasionally say and do things that clash with the sensitive modern values they profess. Here, as you will read in the following chapter, a student can call a woman a "slut" one moment, and then talk about how much he respects women the next.

9

FEMINISM AND FOOTBALL

I don't want to go to Harvard.
> —Rory Gilmore (*The Gilmore Girls*)

Some things in life are inscrutably and cosmically bound together. So it is with feminism and football. And if the connection isn't obvious to you, then you only have to ask a Yale student to explain. I will start by recounting a particularly infamous event in Yale history, one that brought upon the school no small measure of humiliation. The day was November 17, 2007. I was in New York that morning after an overnight visit to the city. It was a Saturday, but, sadly, I had no time to sleep in. Instead, I made my way to Grand Central and boarded an early train back to New Haven.

Normally, an early weekend train such as that one would have been nearly empty. But on that occasion the train was bursting at full capacity. People were left standing in the aisles for lack of seats. It was an odd sight to behold. Hundreds of loud passengers huddled together, all wearing one of two colors—either Harvard crimson or Yale blue. We were all on that train for one reason: "THE

GAME"—that is, the annual Harvard versus Yale gridiron melee. Manhattan, that great repository of tireless investment-banking and management-consulting machines, had given up its Ivy-educated keep. There were many young, fresh-faced alumni as well as the occasional briny old banker among us, all hoping to relive the bright college years.

Every year the Harvard versus Yale football game provides an occasion for students and alumni alike to revel in their deep-seated, never-ending rivalry. The premise is a bit absurd. (My fantastically elite institution is better than yours! Just look at our football team! Ha, ha!) And the awesome and exclusive name given to the event (THE GAME) greatly outweighs the athletic prowess of the two schools involved. It would be much more fitting if the rivalry were battled out as a *Jeopardy*-style geek tournament hosted by Alex Trebek. But Trebek, who went to the University of Ottawa, is smarter than most Harvard and Yale graduates. If this fact were to become known to the general public, it wouldn't reflect very well on the two mighty Ivies. Plus it's hard to drink beer and answer trivia at the same time. So THE GAME remains a football contest. And, in spite of the modest athleticism involved, it is a huge event every year.

On the train, I ended up surrounded by a bunch of Harvard kids. They were fairly recent graduates, close to me in age. In addition to their crimson shirts and hats, they carried bottles of "cranberry juice," which I would guess, judging from the jocularity of the group, contained copious amounts of 80-proof vodka. One of them was a bit less discreet than the rest. All throughout our journey, he guzzled from a twenty-four-ounce Budweiser tall boy, which he clumsily concealed in a brown paper bag. I might add that it was only about eight o'clock in the morning. It was all very classy. But that's Harvard for you.

That day, the Ivy League championship was on the line, and Yale was bidding to finish the season with a perfect record for the first time in nearly fifty years. It wasn't the Rose Bowl, admittedly, but it was as close to that sort of experience as Yale will ever get.

Our team was ranked first in the league and had dominated all season. Many were predicting a twenty- or thirty-point victory. As my train pulled into New Haven, I had reason to feel confident that those Harvard kids would soon be drinking in sorrow rather than joy.

There were fifty-seven thousand people packed into the Yale Bowl when I arrived. I reached my seat just in time for the kickoff. To my dismay, it took Harvard only about a minute to score its first touchdown. And things just got worse from there. Over the course of the game, Harvard's quarterback threw for 316 yards and four touchdowns. Ours, on the other hand, went 2 for 18 for a grand total of 29 yards, with two interceptions. It looked like the rough-and-tumble Yale football team had been replaced by the New Haven ballet. By halftime the score was 27–0. By late in the fourth quarter it was 37–0. It was more than a defeat. It was a total embarrassment.

For those who aren't football fans, it may be hard to understand why tens of thousands of Ivy League alumni, most living charmed lives of wealth, privilege, ease, and comfort, would get so distraught about losing a football game. But I can tell you that I, along with about forty thousand other Yale fans, sat there that day in total shock and disillusionment. Meanwhile about twenty thousand Harvard fans gloated and jeered at us from the other side of the stadium. They were beating us on our home field. And they were really enjoying it. It was going to be a shutout.

With only four minutes left in the game, many Yale fans had already hit the exits. The mood in the stands had hit an absolute low. But at that moment a little magic happened. Harvard lined up to punt. A young Yale freshman named Gio Christodoulou stood for the return. Christodoulou fielded the ball and found a crease up the middle, then exploded into open field on the left side. There was no catching him. Eighty-seven yards later, as he sprinted into the end zone, ecstatic cheers erupted from the Yale side. Our enemies sat in silent disbelief. In our hour of despair, Christodoulou had served us a juicy morsel of schadenfreude. He had silenced the Harvard rabble.

Somehow Yale's dignity was restored with that single touchdown. The frustration of the previous three hours gave way to a sense of relief. Sure, the championship was lost. But at least there would be no shutout. On the Yale side, we held our heads just a little higher. You can bet Christodoulou was a hero on campus that day.

As it turned out, however, his dazzling reputation wouldn't last for long.

Fast-forward to mid January—less than two months later. Around midnight a female student is walking alone toward the Yale Women's Center—an on-campus facility that serves as a home base for feminist political activity and also provides women's health services (contraception, pregnancy tests, rape counseling, etc.). As the young woman approaches the building, she finds the entrance blocked by a rowdy gang of frat boys, who, in unison, are drunkenly shouting "Dick! Dick! Dick!" into the cold night air. (Whoops! Didn't I just make a snide remark about those unclassy Harvard kids?) The girl, feeling intimidated, decides to avoid the frat boys and goes around to the rear of the building in order to enter by the back door.

The whole incident might have passed without much notice if only one of the frat boys hadn't felt compelled to broadcast his fraternity's drunken exploits by posting a photo on Facebook, which depicted what had taken place. The photo quickly spread around campus via e-mail. Visible were a dozen male students in pathetic "gangsta" guise, complete with do-rags, "West Side" gang hand signals, and smoldering clove cigarettes. I had to roll my eyes when I first saw it, knowing that those Yale boys undoubtedly grew up about as far away from the ghetto as one could get. Yet there they were in the photograph, posing like the Bloods and the Crips. Behind them, I could read the signpost over the door of the Yale Women's Center. Right smack in the middle of the hooligan posse, one guy was holding up a single sheet of paper that read "WE LOVE YALE SLUTS" in all caps. That guy was none other than our football hero of two months before, Mr. Christodoulou.

* * *

The day after the photo came to light, I found in my inbox an angry e-mail, which included a copy of the guilty photo. It had been sent as a mass message to the student body. The e-mail read as follows:

> **From:** Yale Women's Center
> **Date:** Jan 21, 2008 10:50 AM
> **Subject:** This Time We Sue
>
> Dear Yale,
>
> The photograph below was taken during a recent Yale fraternity initiation. This is sexual harassment. Lawyers have been consulted, and we are taking legal action.
>
> If you are unwilling to be enrolled in a school where woman-hating is a subject of pride, email yalewomenscenter@gmail.com now. We will keep you informed.
>
> "WE LOVE YALE SLUTS" uploaded to facebook.com January 16, 2008.
>
> Sincerely,
> The Yale Women's Center Board

Apparently, the stunt in front of the Women's Center was part of the initiation activities for new recruits of the Zeta Psi fraternity. No female student appeared to be directly targeted by the frat boys. Even so, as a group, they had certainly shown themselves to be crass and obnoxious. The national Zeta Psi organization, according to its own Web site, aims to "turn out into the world self-respecting, original-thinking, self-controlled, purposeful gentlemen."[1] Yale's Zeta Psi pledges struck out on all four counts.

Yet the idea that the Zeta boys actually hated women, as the e-mail indicated, seemed a bit over the top. And it wasn't clear to me what sort of "legal action" the board of the Women's Center hoped to take. Zeta Psi deserved a big institutional jack-slap. But the notion that the Women's Center had grounds to sue for damages or press criminal charges seemed several steps beyond reality. Since when is it a crime to be a jerk? However, college is a different world. Little problems can become big ones—especially when issues of race or gender are involved. The "WE LOVE YALE SLUTS" saga was about to take on a life of its own.

After the photo leaked out, Zeta Psi entered public relations panic mode. The fraternity promptly issued a public apology in the *Yale Daily News*, calling the incident "a lapse in judgment" and declaring that it was "deeply sorry" and hoped for the forgiveness of its peers.[2]

In a local news television interview, Christodoulou claimed ignorance (rather implausibly): "I never even read the sign," he told a reporter. "They gave me the sign, and I held it up. . . . I never disrespect women—that was very uncharacteristic of myself," he added. "We're all terribly sorry, and we learned our lesson."[3]

The Zetas also claimed that they had been yelling "DKE! DKE! DKE!" rather than "Dick! Dick! Dick!" that night, as the girl who heard them had claimed. (DKE is the abbreviation for a rival fraternity.) Regardless, there was no getting around that incriminating photograph. Lame explanations notwithstanding, Zeta Psi's response was thoroughly apologetic. The president of the fraternity even offered to meet with student leaders of the Women's Center in order to discuss the issue further. Most students considered censure of some sort from the Yale administration to be sufficient punishment. But not the Yale Women's Center. It had bigger plans.

The Women's Center published a saber-rattling opinion essay in the *Yale Daily News* that week. It compared the "WE LOVE YALE SLUTS" photograph to a hypothetical case in which a group of all-white students stands in front of an African American building with a sign reading "WE LOVE YALE N-GGERS." I had to cringe when I read it. The center's leaders were out to dramatize their sense of victimization. And they didn't mind using a tasteless analogy in order to bring home their point.

Newspapers and blogs all over the country picked up on the story. In an official statement, the Women's Center governing board admitted that its real grievances were beyond the scope of any single incident. The statement reflects the kind of dramatic grandiosity to which college-aged political activists are prone. "The bigotry of Zeta Psi is unexceptional. It is pervasive, at Yale and around the world. This sort of behavior has to change, everywhere, here, and right now." In other words, the prank of some drunken frat boys had become, for them, a symbol for the oppression of women "around the world."

There are plenty of students at Yale, both male and female, who call themselves feminists. But the students who run the Women's Center have the reputation of being somewhat extreme in their devotion to the cause. Zeta Psi's "WE LOVE YALE SLUTS" sign was intended, no doubt, to cast some irony on the quorum of radical lesbians and bitter man haters who supposedly haunt the Women's Center. This conception of their membership is caricature rather than pure fact. As it so happens, I have an acquaintance who served on the board of the center at the time. She is, for the record, neither a lesbian nor a man hater. As for the rest, well, the caricature is not completely without basis. What all these women have in common is a fervent devotion to feminist political activism. As activists, attention is what they crave.

Once the Women's Center got some attention, the activists didn't want to let go of it. The Zeta Psi photograph became a tool to leverage the news media and the Yale administration. The incident sparked a series of administrative hearings. The university created two new committees to deal with women's issues, and (this one amused me) promised to renovate the Women's Center facility.[4] The students of the Women's Center treated the Zeta Psi incident like some kind of lucky break. They used it as a platform from which they could demand, among other things, a bunch of shiny new furniture. No apology, however sincere, was going to get in the way of their quest for a double plush sofa set. It was, of course, a matter of global injustice.

The public airing of grievances has become a staple publicity tool in the age of identity politics. And the litigious students of the Yale Women's Center know how to play the game. That, dear reader, is what Yale's brand of feminism has in common with football. All too often, it is nothing more than a game.

There is, in fact, plenty of genuine oppression of women "around the world." Consider the real-life story of a Pakistani woman named Zafran Bibi who was raped in 2001, became pregnant by her attacker, and then was sentenced to death as an "adulterer" in accordance with fundamentalist Islamic law.[5] Now that kind of injustice should get a person angry. And what about millions of girls who suffer genital mutilation in Africa? These are examples of damnable oppression and genuine bigotry.

Persecution of the kind suffered by Zafran Bibi is something deeply and uniquely evil. I don't associate it with the pranks of Ivy League frat boys. Neither, I suspect, would the student leaders of the Yale Women's Center, if they hadn't been too busy constructing an overdramatized publicity campaign, to think about what they were actually saying. Yes, the Women's Center had every right to speak out against Zeta Psi. A statement like "WE LOVE YALE SLUTS" is deplorable, especially in front of a place that some female students consider a "safe place" on campus. At issue is the scale of their response. The fact that the pranks of fraternity pledges loom larger in the day-to-day political activism of some Yale feminists than the stoning or mutilating of women on the other side of the world is indicative of the self-centeredness of identity politics in general, and the short-sightedness of the Yale Women's Center in particular.

Of course, the Yale Women's Center, despite its all-encompassing name, does not by any means speak for all Yale women. And not surprisingly, many Yale women were unhappy with the way the Women's Center handled the "WE LOVE YALE SLUTS" incident. A spokesperson later said that even several members of its own managing board were upset by the center's "drastic" response at the time of the incident.[6] The Women's Center may have scored some attention and new décor in the bargain, but those benefits came at a cost to its status as a serious organization.

Some offenses (like name-calling or being a jerk, for instance) really don't merit a lawsuit. When a group like the Yale Women's Center manufactures a hyped-up sense of its own victimhood, it loses credibility. And it gives feminism a bad name. This is undoubtedly one reason why nearly 70 percent of American women refuse to call themselves feminists, even though most women have a favorable opinion of the women's movement in general.[7] Women want equal treatment; but they don't want a gender war. Yale's feminist leaders don't seem to understand this.

On April 5, 2008, Yale's Executive Committee handed down a verdict of not guilty to the Zeta Psi pledges on the charge of intimidation and harassment.

"Some of the actions the Center took were polarizing," admitted Isabel Polon, a student who was the group's political action coordinator at the time of the incident. "But they gave the Women's Center leverage and brought issues to public discourse that otherwise were not talked about."[8] Hmmm, did you get that? At the Yale Women's Center, overhyping one's sense of offense for the sake of political leverage is viewed as a good thing. What Isabel does not realize, however, is that—far from enhancing public discourse—such phoniness causes most people to tune out altogether.

By holding up the word "slut" in front of a facility known for radical feminism, the Zeta Psi boys became unwitting cultural commentators. Is it possible to be both a slut and a feminist at the same time? The women's movement was supposed to offer women sexual liberation. At the same time, it was supposed to free them from being defined as mere objects of male desire.

My friend Emily, who sat on the board of the Women's Center

at the time of the Zeta Psi affair, once complained to me about the double standard applied to women in romantic relationships. "If I go up to a guy and offer to buy him a drink," she told me, "he won't want to have anything to do with me." As a feminist, Emily hates being relegated to a passive role. But she's right; in our romantic culture an aggressive woman can easily appear desperate. As a result, the woman is usually left waiting for the man to make the first move, or else she risks repelling the very man she desires.

But before we all start gloomily reciting the maxims of Betty Freidan, we should remember that women hold one big advantage in the battle of the sexes, and that is the fact that most men will do almost anything for sex. If a woman is given a choice between an extravagant shopping spree, a box of chocolates, or a roll in the hay, chances are good that she'll choose one of the former. On the other hand, if a guy has to ride thirty miles uphill on a tricycle for sex, he will probably do it. If he has to crawl over broken glass, or stand on his head naked in some public place barking like a wild hyena, he will probably do it. There is no pain or disgrace that outweighs the male's urge to merge. So who really holds the power? I don't know.

When it comes to sex, a major source of a woman's power is the control she exercises over her own body. It is only if she gives this up and conforms to a typical college existence, consisting of endless hookups with men she barely knows, that a woman really loses power in relationships. At Yale, a guy doesn't have to ride thirty miles or stand on his head. He only has to show up at a random party and talk to some girl for a few minutes—and make sure she has a few drinks. It's so easy. This is why sexual liberation never really empowered women in the way it was supposed to. A woman is truly objectified when men don't even have to get to know her in order to get her into bed. Without any commitment to modesty or sexual restraint, the worthy cause of deobjectifying women loses much of its gusto. I know it sounds very 1950s, but playing hard to get might not have been a bad idea for feminists, if power is what they were after.

Feminists at the Yale Women's Center talk about birth control as a form of empowerment. And they dole it out freely to all comers. But they never talk about keeping one's zipper up as a potential form of empowerment. Ultimately, sending women out the door with fists full of condoms doesn't do much to prevent them from being seen as sex objects.

When sex comes casually and with no relational strings attached, as it often does at Yale and on other college campuses, women are essentially commodified and objectified in the eyes of men. Here's why: When no real relationship is involved, there is no need to treat one's sexual partner like anything more than a functional object—a sex doll that breathes. On any given Friday night, one girl will do just about as well as another. This is exactly what Yale guys are thinking when they show up a party on the weekend, hoping to find a willing one-night stand. Under this arrangement women lose the respect they want and deserve. It's hard to be a randy sexpot and a deobjectified feminist at the same time. Even the strongest woman who ever lived couldn't pull it off. And she was a superhero.

In July 1972 the inaugural edition of *Ms.* magazine hit newsstands across the United States. Charging across the cover was the figure of Wonder Woman, rendered in Godzilla scale, halting a war plane in midair with her left hand while, with the other, carrying to safety an entire block of American suburbia, sacheted neatly within the bonds of her magic lasso. She towered over the chaotic scene of bombs and flames below, her earnest face bearing the look of a woman on a mission. As she forged ahead, her lengthy gait stretched from beyond the horizon, seeming to echo the momentum of an American feminist movement that was just hitting the peak of its stride.

The radiant Amazonian beauty was clad in skintight star-spangled panties, high boots, and a curvaceous red bustier fronted by the emblem of a golden eagle—wings outstretched across an ample bosom. Above her read the headline "Wonder Woman for President," augmented by the captions "Money for Housework" and, with no apparent irony directed toward the voluptuous cover illustration, "Body Hair: The Last Frontier." The contrast between this idealized (and well-shaved) representation of feminine beauty, surrounded by such captions, on the cover of a magazine dedicated, in part, to the deobjectification of women, captures vividly the tensions present among competing conceptions of women's liberation.

The voluptuous vigilante who graced the inaugural cover of *Ms.* magazine has a fascinating backstory, which sheds light on the paradox of her sexed-up feminism. Created by the Harvard-trained psychologist William Moulton Marston (famous for inventing the polygraph), Wonder Woman has been among the most popular comic-book superheroes since her inception in 1941. Marston always envisioned Wonder Woman as a character of social significance, and he hoped to present young girls with progressive models of female behavior through his comic books.

He professed a strange brand of feminism, believing America to be headed for matriarchal domination "politically and economically," meanwhile living with, and having children by, two different women at the same time. Other females rotated in and out of his life. The strangeness of his personal life presents us with evidence that Marston saw, more clearly than many who followed, that movement toward economic and vocational equality would liberalize sexual and domestic relationships between men and women. By appropriating some of those "liberties" for himself, he demonstrated that new lifestyles for women would correspond to new lifestyles for men as well. The flow of money and sex was about to undergo a revolution.

If you were to search the frat house of Yale's Zeta Psi brothers, you could find plenty of magazines full of women even more scantily clad than Wonder Woman: *Playboy, Maxim, Stuff, FHM,* etc. The ideal woman in these magazines comes over for a quick tryst (with birth control please!) and then goes home. She does not live off the man. She is, economically speaking, a feminist woman—a *Ms.* magazine kind of woman. By the time *Ms.* magazine began publication, *Playboy* had been selling the theme of female economic independence for twenty years. Reliable birth control (heralded also by the playboys) was the final pillar of women's liberation, uniting lifelong economic independence with the possibility of childless sexuality.

Here we discover the big secret behind Wonder Woman. Her blatant sexual appeal, seemingly out of sync with the feminist message she is supposed to embody, is not, as it turns out, out of sync with the proposition of female independence. Ever resisting the wooings of her desperate suitors, this "liberated" woman, adopted by feminists, rewritten and recast over the decades to inspire a young female audience, has always been read and loved predominantly by males.

I have met a lot of women in college who try to play the role of the super sexed-up Wonder Woman. They seem caught between two personas: part pin-striped professional, and part pasty-wearing pinup. (You should see what Yale girls wear on Halloween, or, rather, what they don't wear. I wish I had a dollar for every prostitute outfit I came across on October 31.) These are not airheaded bimbos I'm talking about. These are seriously talented women, many of whom will go on to enjoy high-powered careers in the corporate world. Nevertheless, as Yale students, they are part of a culture in which both feminism and laissez-faire sexuality are simultaneously embraced. But the two ideas don't really work together.[9]

Men, of course, should be held to the same standards as women when it comes to sex. But my point for now isn't to argue about the virtues of virginity so much as it is to point out that Yale's loose sexual culture has certain consequences that are not at all beneficial to women. Early feminists embraced sexual liberation, but I think if they saw the actual results on today's college campuses, they would say it wasn't what they had in mind. Ultimately, it probably isn't possible to be both a "slut" and a true feminist at the same time. And making one's body easily available *to* men probably isn't the best way to fight oppression *by* men.

This is the problem embodied by the bustier-wearing superhero: For all her impressive strength and notable achievements, she never quite got the deobjectified thing down. In this sense, she is a fitting emblem for far too many Yale women: strong, wonderfully capable, but hypersexualized and, consequently, hopelessly objectified. When I see the emblem of the golden eagle on Wonder Woman's chest, I think it looks a lot like the Yale Y. I don't blame Yale women. I blame the culture they are a part of. Think about it. When porn films are shown in the classroom, what message are female students supposed to take away from that experience?

It's one thing to find porn in a frat house, and another thing altogether to find it in the classroom under official university sanction. Sometimes I wonder what the feminists at the Women's Center think about all the porn that is on display around campus. Doesn't porn objectify women? Why don't they sue someone over that?

As for Wonder Woman, she has enough sex appeal to be a *Playboy* centerfold if she wants to be one. But it's an open question whether she, as a feminist, would actually do it. On the issue of pornography, feminists are deeply divided. Some see it as inherently demeaning, while others see porn as an expression of a woman's right to choose what she wants to do with her own body. Among those who oppose porn, it is one of the few issues where feminists find themselves politically aligned with social conservatives.

Chyng Sun, a feminist academic who has argued extensively on behalf of the antiporn faction, wrote about a typical example she found in the course of her research. In this case the porn producer had come up with a concept called the "BangBus," in which men would drive around in a large van, persuading what appear to be random women on the street to have sex with them. After the sex scenes, the men would then degrade the women in some way by hurling insults at them, dropping them off in some desolate location, or throwing their belongings out into the dirt.[10]

While feminists may be divided about pornography, it is clear that women as a whole take a mostly negative view of it. In a 2005 Harris poll, women agreed with the statement "Pornography is demeaning towards women" by a margin of 58 percent to 37 percent.[11] It is remarkable, therefore, that Yale—a university so well known for its political liberalism, and so adamant about its commitment to women's rights—should demonstrate such ambivalence about the pornography that is displayed year after year in its own classrooms. To my knowledge, no feminist has ever directly challenged Yale's president, Richard Levin, on his apparent willingness to turn a blind eye on past occasions when professors or student groups have used university resources to create a humiliating environment for women.

Feminists have a great deal of power in academic circles. They pushed Larry Summers, the former president of Harvard, out of his job after he suggested that inherent aptitude might partly account for the gender disparity in the sciences. Since they have such power, why don't feminists put pressure on Yale to end the screening of porn at officially sanctioned events? Sadly, their commitment to sixties-era sexual liberation has left them deeply divided on the issue of pornography, and hesitant to render moral judgment on any sexual issue. It's unfortunate because the Women's Center is probably the one group on campus with enough political clout to get Yale to clean up its act, if only it would speak out. All too often, feminist leaders at Yale fail to address the issues that actually affect female students' day-to-day lives.

Because of their ideological conflictions, feminists at Yale are unwilling or unable to take action on what should be a straightforward women's rights issue. Even if some women have no problem with porn, it should be enough that many women find it demeaning. The latter should not be subjected to it as part of their Yale education. Again, we aren't talking here about what some guy watches while alone in his dorm room. We are talking about public presentations, which have official approval from Yale leadership. Each time Yale puts its stamp of approval on porn, it sends a message to women that they exist to serve men's sexual desires, even when those desires entail "BangBus"-style humiliation.

If you think about it, the sign those frat boys held up in front of the Women's Center is a fairly accurate description of the sexual culture at Yale. It's a culture nurtured by the faculty and administration, which have failed to provide moral guidance where it is needed. Yale's leaders subjected the Zeta Psi pledges to an ethics review. Good for them. But they should have subjected themselves to an ethics review while they were at it.

Ultimately, screening porn isn't a very good way to show respect for women. From a moral standpoint, I would suggest that doing so is at least as misogynistic as the pledge night exploits of Zeta Psi. Therefore, if Yale's president, Richard Levin, fails to respond whenever porn is shown in Yale classrooms, he could do no worse if he were to simply stand in front of the Women's Center with a sign of his own that says WE LOVE YALE SLUTS.

While he stands there with the sign, fellow administrators should take his picture. Then they should put the photo on the glossy brochures they send out to prospective students, and put it up on the home page at Yale.edu. That way everyone would know what the university stands for, and female students would know what to expect even before they arrive.

Best of all, such a photo might finally generate a Women's Center controversy worth its while.

10

HOOKING UP

Today's first base is kissing. . . . Second base is oral sex. Third base is going all the way. Home plate is learning each other's names.

—Tom Wolfe, Ph.D., class of 1957

On my way back from Rome during the summer before my senior year, I scheduled a three-day layover in London. I had always wanted to see London, and I wasn't sure when I would ever have the chance to return to Europe. So while I was traveling on the university's dime, I figured, I would take advantage of the opportunity to visit the motherland.

I didn't really have any money for lodging. But, through a mutual friend back in the United States, I managed to contact the proprietors of a boardinghouse about a half hour south of the city. It was an enormous old Tudor-style manor, surrounded by green fields. Thanks to my friend's connections, I was charged the equivalent of a charity rate. I think I paid something like £10 for the night.

That evening, after dark, I decided to take a walk out in the surrounding fields. It happened to be the Fourth of July. And there I was in England, a patriot among the redcoats. I figured I was in for a low-key evening, less celebratory than usual.

Not long after my walk began, however, and to my great surprise, I discerned a burst of light cutting through the darkness above the trees. A split second later I heard a familiar screaming whiz and pop—the unmistakable sound of fireworks.

How in the world? I thought to myself.

Instinctively, I rushed across the road and through a stand of trees. On the other side, I met a group of perhaps a half dozen young people who, by now, were setting off one explosive after another, to a chorus of whoops and hollers. It was, as I soon learned, a group of American students—staying at the same boardinghouse. Somehow, they had laid their hands on a mountainous pile of fireworks at a local market. As a fellow American, I easily fell in with their number. We were all, I suppose, a bit homesick. As a result, we took extra joy in our little countryside fireworks show. Before long we were standing in a row, spontaneously singing the national anthem while one bottle rocket after another shrieked up over our heads, past the stone wall at the edge of the property, and out into the fields beyond.

Nearby, a group of British students stood rather stiffly, arms folded, looking on, grinning and shaking their heads at the spectacle. I suppose we looked like delirious pyromaniac cowboys to them. So be it. To this day I maintain that that little $50 pile of pyrotechnics was the best fireworks show I've ever seen.

My real business was to see London. I headed up on the train early the next morning and set about seeing the sights. Madeline, a friend of mine from Yale, was doing an internship in the British Parliament that summer. She, along with several other Yale girls—also doing internships of various kinds—had a flat on the north side of the city. They were kind enough to let me crash on their living room couch during my last night in the UK.

Luckily, Madeline had the day off. She dutifully showed me around the city—a kindness for which I was very grateful. She was a lot of fun. We had had a couple of classes together, but this was the first time we had hung out one-on-one. Over a lunch of fish and chips, she made casual mention of her boyfriend back in the States—I had a feeling it was a subtle way of clearing the air and making sure that neither of us had anything other than platonic intentions for the evening ahead. Once we got that out of the way, we were able to have a good time without the kind of tension and ambiguity that so often accompanies even the most casual interactions between twenty-something guys and girls. *Is he or isn't he into me? Are we just friends or something more, or what?* We saw Big Ben, took in a hilariously over-the-top show on the West End—the stage production of *Lord of the Rings*—and drank some English tea. And that was it.

The next morning I awoke to find myself sprawled out on one of the couches in the living room. Several of the other girls who lived in the flat were sitting around talking on the other side of the room. They had been out partying the night before and their conversation, naturally, turned to talk about boys. It was a kind of fly-on-the-wall experience. I heard a bit of girl talk—the kind girls usually indulge in only when there are no guys around. For whatever reason, they didn't seem to mind that I was in the room. They started talking about the hookup scene back at Yale. The conversation went something like this:

—Oh my gosh. Have you ever been with a football player?
—Yeah, they can be pretty awesome. They work out a lot.
—Yeah, and you know what's best about them? They're not that smart. If you go up to them at a party and just get them drinking, and start dancing with them and kissing them, they will totally end up sleeping with you. They don't even know they're being played. They have no clue.
—Ha-ha! Totally.

I was amazed. Could it be possible, I thought to myself, that these girls don't understand a fundamental fact about the human male? You normally don't have to trick a man into having sex. Most men are willing, eager, happy to oblige. I was baffled by these girls' apparent lack of understanding of this basic fact about men. Don't they realize that's why most guys show up at college parties in the first place?

However, in these girls' defense, there is a great deal of confusion today among college students when it comes to negotiating sex and love. As far as the college years go, sex often has precious little to do with love, or with any real emotional connection. These days, as you might have heard if you've been paying attention, sex in college is all about the hookup.

For most college students, hooking up is the only way to carry on any kind of romantic relationship at all. Dating, in case you haven't heard, is dead. You know dinner and a movie? Holding hands? That kind of stuff? It's exceedingly rare at Yale.

In college, very casual relationships can turn into sex almost instantly. So you can see why it becomes very confusing for students who are trying to figure out which relationships are or are not romantic in nature. After a few beers, almost anyone you meet around campus could be a potential sexual partner. Actually taking a girl to dinner is tantamount to a college marriage.

The funny thing is (well, maybe it isn't that funny), I realized later that my day of casual sightseeing with Madeline was more of a "date" than many Yale students ever have in college, even with people they are having sex with. No wonder Madeline seemed to feel the need to be sure we both understood that we were hanging out that day in London as mere friends. Young people today don't have the old dinner-and-a-movie script to go by. The line between a friend and a "friend with benefits" is thin and hazy. Everyone is confused.

This book is ultimately about the academic culture at Yale, not about the details of students' sex lives. But this book would not be complete without a brief description of "hooking up," what it means, and how it affects students.

"Hooking up" is a broad term that can refer to almost any kind of physical interaction between a guy and a girl. It can be a single kiss, it can be making out for two hours, it can be oral sex, hand jobs, anal sex, intercourse, spending the night together, spending three minutes together—anything, everything, and nothing.[1] Even though no one can say precisely what hooking up is, or what it isn't, there is one aspect of hooking up that everyone agrees on: It involves no expectation of commitment, no expectation of exclusivity, and no emotional attachment.

It used to be that dating led to sex. At Yale, and many other colleges, sex is most often seen as the first step toward a possible romantic relationship. Things are backward.

The hookup culture couldn't survive without the inhibition-lowering power of alcohol. Alcohol is the oil of Yale's sexual machine. If you talk to any guy at Yale, he'll tell you that the first and most important step to a random hookup is to get a girl drinking. Problem is, when a student's judgment is impaired, so is her ability to give or deny consent. It's sad but true: The line between drunk sex and rape is, all too often, painfully thin. It is my own observation that alcohol is involved in the vast majority of on-campus cases of sexual assault. In any case, drunk sex often leads to serious regrets on the morning after.

Here is a staggering fact: About 25 percent of college women report having had at least one nonconsensual sexual encounter. The hookup culture has exacerbated the problem. When students hook up, it can mean anything from simply making out, to sexual stimulation with the hands, to oral sex. Many girls draw the line at intercourse. But what often happens is this: A girl leaves a party with a guy, and she starts making out with him in her room. Soon she ends up naked on the bed with the intention of kissing and engaging in some kind of heavy sexual touching; but she has no intention of engaging in intercourse. It's a very common scenario. All of the sudden, the guy decides kissing and touching are not enough and he forces himself on her. At that point she may try to say no, but she's already lying on the bed with him and has very little chance of escape. I've heard stories like this so many times. Talk to any girl at Yale, and she will tell you she knows someone who has been assaulted in this way. This sort of thing is often referred to as "acquaintance rape."

Call it what you want: Rape is rape. It's the hideous, hidden reality behind the hookup culture—far too often, students get intoxicated, then move on to dorm room liaisons that begin consensually and end in sexual assault. These kinds of crimes almost always go unreported to law enforcement because girls often blame themselves for letting things get too far; or they blame alcohol. And their rapists often go unpunished. Hooking up can be very risky for females. The inherent risk of sexual violence is built into the hookup culture because it is fueled by alcohol and involves intimate encounters with others whom one may not know well enough to fully trust. Yale actively endorses this culture with its juiced-up sex-ed programs.

Since Yale sets the tone for the hookup culture on campus, it is no surprise, then, that students carry it off campus as well. A local bar and nightclub in New Haven called Toad's is ground zero for Yale's hookup scene. It's a huge club with several different bars, stages, and dance floors. On any weekend night, you can find many hundreds of Yale students there, all gettin' down to a heavy hip-hop beat in their mildly geeky ways.

The last time I was at Toad's it was a Friday night. Downstairs an Indian DJ in a turban was pumping out dance music with a Far Eastern flair. It was all subwoofers and sitars—a real booty-shaking combination. It was early and there weren't many people out on the dance floor. I sat back and nursed a beer while the first tentative students made their way out onto the massive dance floor. At first, there was only one girl out there. Three hip-thrusting dudes quickly surrounded her, and they started dancing awkwardly—like a troupe of excited robots at a middle school prom. Eventually a pair of girls got out and started dancing with each other and giggling in that hilarious way girls sometimes do when neither has a guy to dance with (yet).

There wasn't much going on downstairs. So, after I while, I decided to check out the bar upstairs. Toad's has a kind of VIP room on the second floor, with a smaller dance floor and a different DJ. Upstairs they were playing a mix of hip-hop and teenybop. There were two bikini-topped go-go dancers in the room, each perched atop a raised platform, dancing with remarkable energy. Down on the floor itself, the barmaids were working the room in thong bikinis—covered head to toe in rainbow-colored body paint. Oh yeah, there was also a basketball game on the television by the bar. Liquor, girls, sports. It was a room catering to a male audience, and not a very polite one. I left before long, but not before I observed one of the barmaids getting groped by a scuzzy guy in a trucker's hat.

By the time I got back downstairs the room had undergone a magic transformation. There was a new DJ at the turntable, playing more traditional American bump-and-grind music, rather than the Hindi variety I had heard before. And the floor was packed with what seemed like a thousand guys and girls, crammed in pelvis to pelvis, a drink in seemingly every hand. Judging by how sticky the floor had become, I'd say a lot of the booze had been spilled by that time.

I had seen a couple of friends and chatted for a while, and I was about to leave. Before I headed for the exit, I turned for a moment to take in the scene. Sure, most of the students couldn't dance very well, but still, I was overwhelmed by the intensity of the crowd. Hundreds and hundreds of young people with so much life and passion, moving around in a great throng, trying to connect with one another. It was almost beautiful. Except I knew that most of them, especially the girls out there, weren't going to find the kind of connection they were looking for that night. And that made me sad.

I know we're not supposed to say there is any difference between guys and girls. But science tells us that even our brains are wired differently. On average, women have more connections between the left and right hemispheres and a larger deep limbic system for processing emotions—to name just two differences. I think the hookup culture negatively affects both men and women. I've heard guys say that they too wish for more meaningful relationships than hookups provide. But, let's face it—a lot of guys are thrilled to have sex with no strings attached. Some girls feel that way too. But a disproportionate number of college women say they are dissatisfied with "no-strings-attached" sexual relationships.[2] There's a reason for that. It's because men and women are different. They value things differently.

Some girls may be happy with the hookup culture. But, in general, the girls I know tend to be more interested in forming meaningful, longer-term relationships. I've heard many of them say that they often hope that sex will lead to "something more," but instead they find themselves continually disappointed with their options. They either play the hookup game, or spend Friday night alone.

The post–Monica Lewinsky generation marks a shift in the cultural expectations placed on women, particularly with regard to oral sex in casual relationships. In 2001, a female student wrote an article in the *Yale Daily News* that, last I checked, was the most read article in the history of the newspaper's Web site. The title of the famous article? "Spit or Swallow."[3]

It's hard to understand how we got to a place where girls are expected to serve guys sexually on the mere basis of some slim hope that the encounter will develop into a more meaningful relationship down the road. If this is where sexual liberation has led us, then we took a wrong turn somewhere along the way.

A lot of girls dive headlong into the hookup culture during their freshman year. By the time they are sophomores or juniors, they are fed up with it. They are fed up because they feel like they are giving a lot more than they are getting out of their relationships. When students reach their junior or senior years, you start to see more committed or semicommitted relationships. Relationships among upperclassmen tend to last longer, and are more likely to be exclusive. But even then, the hookup rules the day.

— 144 —

During my senior year, a religious couple on campus got engaged a few months prior to graduation. They planned to get married that summer. This turn of events was shocking to many on campus. The *Yale Daily News* did a story on the engagement because the idea of two Yale students getting married so young was such a novelty. It wasn't always that way. One famous alumnus, George H. W. Bush, was married and a veteran of World War II when he entered Yale in the midnineteen forties. By the time he graduated, he was already a father. In the hallway on the first floor of the Yale gym, there is an old photograph on the wall showing the future president Bush, standing with his young wife, Barbara, and holding another, pint-sized future president, George W.

To take a more recent example, Richard Levin, Yale's current president, got married right out of college during the sixties. These days, for a host of economic and cultural reasons, very few Yale students, male or female, picture themselves getting married before thirty. Students may not be eager to go back to the custom of marrying early, but many, especially young women, aren't happy with the total emotional detachment of the hookup scene either.

If so many students are dissatisfied, why do they continue to hook up? I believe that the ambitiousness of Yale students is a big part of the answer. Most Yale students expect to have high-powered, prestigious careers. For Yale women who want to become mothers and have families, it is sometimes hard to imagine how they can become doctors, lawyers, or professors and still have families too. Many imagine spending their late twenties and early thirties attending graduate school and building their careers. They plan on getting married perhaps in their early thirties, and, hopefully becoming mothers in their mid to late thirties.

Sadly, female biology doesn't always cooperate. I attended a presentation at Yale once by a group of fertility experts. They said that for many women, it can be next to impossible to get pregnant once they reach their mid to late thirties. Many of the girls in the classroom were shocked. You could hear their collective gasp. We see a lot of Hollywood types having babies in their late thirties or early forties these days. What most people don't realize is that these celebrities have often used egg donors, and sometimes surrogate mothers. They may have spent hundreds of thousands of dollars to have those children—something that isn't feasible for most women.

Many of the Yale women I know feel conflicted about how to balance a desire for a future family and a successful career. They feel constant pressure to delay love, out of the fear that it might interrupt the educational and career achievements they have worked so hard for. Thus, hooking up, even though it leaves many girls unsatisfied, looks like a safe bet for girls who want to guard themselves against heartbreak in their early and mid twenties. After all, if they don't get emotionally involved, then maybe they won't feel as much pain when they have to leave a boyfriend for law school, or to take a job in a different city. Part of the problem is that workers are now expected to have graduate degrees for positions that, a few years ago, would have required only bachelor's degrees or high school diplomas. Women and men spend more years in school as a result. And they delay getting involved in serious relationships. Many parents too, because they are hoping for great things for their daughters, encourage them not to get too serious about love until their careers are well in hand. Nevertheless, I don't think years of random hookups would be what most parents have in mind either.

There is no easy solution. Several years ago, the *New York Times* published a story about how more girls at Yale were altering their career expectations, planning to spend at least some part of their careers away from full-time work in order to start a family. The article set off a firestorm of protest from a number of sixties- and seventies-era feminists, who viewed the article as evidence that the current generation of young women were throwing away hard-won gains in workplace equality.

Ultimately, I think we need to expand our ideas of what a woman's career can look like. Take former Supreme Court justice Sandra Day O'Conner for a model. She married at twenty-two, and had children in her twenties, and then put more effort into her career later in her thirties. Ultimately, she enjoyed a long and—by any measure—successful career. She became one of the most powerful women in the world. Love didn't hold her back.

Women today are outperforming men in the educational arena and, increasingly, in the workplace. Today they are earning more bachelor's degrees and more advanced degrees than men. They are taking more managerial and professional positions in the workforce. But there is no doubt that some of this success has come at the cost of delaying starting families and putting off developing meaningful relationships. If a woman chooses to concentrate on motherhood in her twenties or thirties, that shouldn't mean that she can't have a high-powered, full-time career in her forties, fifties, and sixties, and beyond. I think women should have those options if they want them.

The conflict many young women feel between their hearts and their careers is at the heart of the sexual dysfunction on college campuses today. This leads us to a surprising conclusion: While the hookup, with its commitment-free sex and zero emotional attachment, seems to be skewed toward the desires of men, the hookup culture, is, arguably, largely controlled by women.* The hookup culture endures, largely, because ambitious young women face a tremendous amount of social pressure to delay love. If real love is not an option, a hookup might seem better than nothing at all.

Casual sex has been around forever. But the sexual culture at our colleges has changed in dramatic ways over the last few decades. Men used to have to work much harder to get sex. There used to be lots of dating and wooing and pleading going on. Now, it's just so easy.

---

* This is the conclusion the feminist and Pulitzer Prize–winning journalist Laura Sessions Stepp reached in her groundbreaking book, *Unhooked: How Young Women Pursue Sex, Delay Love, and Lose at Both* (New York: Riverhead, 2007), in which she follows the lives of real college students for an entire year, interviewing them and detailing their experiences in the hookup culture. Stepp's book is insightful, and should be considered essential reading for college students, parents of college students, or anyone who wants to gain a thorough understanding, through students' own words, of how the hookup culture works.

The problem is made worse by the fact that women now outnumber men 57 to 43 percent in our universities. All too often, college guys reject young women who press for emotional commitment, because easy, commitment-free hookups can easily be found down the hall. The "cost" of sex, in terms of emotional commitment, is exceedingly low. If that's not the way a girl wants it, then too bad for her. The link between women's professional ambition and the incentive to delay love means that the more elite a university is, the more extreme the hookup culture tends to be.[4] The situation at a place like Yale is, for this reason, likely to be more extreme than the situation at a typical state university in middle America.

I don't want to overstate the gender dichotomy. Meaningful relationships are important to both men and women. And men can be hurt emotionally by random hookups, just as some women can engage in hookups without any apparent emotional toll. But women, more often than men, are unhappy with their sexual experiences in college. That's not mere speculation; that's a statistical fact.[5]

All too often, hooking up ends up being a one-way street: Guys get what they want, but girls don't. Consequently, young women tend to grow less satisfied with the hookup culture over time. In one study, 30 percent of ninth-grade girls said they would be willing to have sex after a great first date, but only 5 percent of college seniors said the same.[6] A 2005 study found that the majority of women who engaged in hooking up, or casual sex, said they felt "disrespected" afterward, while only one-fourth of men said they felt that way.[7]

Overall, women don't seem to be thriving in the hookup culture. There are many different explanations for this. Evolutionary psychologists suggest that differing emotional responses are the result of differing biological incentives between the sexes. Social conservatives and people of faith view it as a consequence of declining societal morals. Feminists often say that the problem arises when girls internalize the repressions of a patriarchal culture. Regardless of which ideological stamp you want to put on it, the fact remains that by the time women finish college, many of them are fed up.

As extreme as things are at Yale, I think many students believe that others around campus are even more sexually active than they really are. Students, consequently, often feel pressure to live up to whatever sort of lifestyle they think is normal. If you read some of the student publications around campus, you can see why students get an exaggerated idea of what constitutes a "normal" sex life.

In one student magazine I picked up, a female student wrote of her study-abroad adventures in Israel, telling in graphic detail all about "power bottoming," and how she discovered she "enjoyed being punished." In another article, a student describes a United Nations–like sexual history, having sex with students from four different continents and at least two different sexual orientations, while another details a week's worth of constant booty calls. This is the Facebook generation, and the distinction between private and public life is fading fast. The fact that these students feel compelled to publish their sex diaries for everyone to read in campuswide publications is a symptom of how trivial and banal sex has become at Yale.

Sex can be casual, but it is never really trivial. It isn't possible to completely remove the emotional realities of sex from the equation. Scientists now tell us that the act of having sex actually alters our neurological makeup through the release of hormones that strengthen the emotional bond between two people, whether they want such a bond or not. Sex is like the Cupid's arrow. It produces a sense of emotional attachment by way of a chemical reaction in the brain. This bond can remain even after you sober up the next morning. Sex with no strings attached often produces confusion, especially for girls, who tend to be more tuned in to the emotional side of life. There is a very good biological reason for this. It's because sex, literally, messes with your mind. It's a drug. In spite of your best efforts, it imposes a bond between you and your partner. It makes you think, Hey, maybe I love this person.

When I was a teenager, my parents warned me that if I had sex with someone, I would carry that relationship around with me for the rest of my life. At the time, I thought they were talking about memory, or merely referring to some kind of ethereal connection of the soul. Turns out, however, there was a bit of scientific truth behind their words. And sex really does impress a lasting neurological bond.

Sex is the occasion for a miraculous meeting of the carnal and the divine, a profound link between the purely physical act of getting it on, and the deepest bonds of human love—love being the force behind the noblest human acts of self-giving and self-sacrifice, and the source from which spring the highest sensations of contentment and spiritual peace. Love gives life meaning.

In some ways, I'm an unlikely person to write about the hookup culture because I never took part in it. By the time I got to Yale I was married, and happily so. Yet, my position outside today's mainstream sexual culture helped me to see it for what it was. While I didn't hook up, I was, by virtue of being married, perhaps the most sexually experienced undergrad on campus. Unlike many of my classmates, I was having sex with someone I loved, cherished, and knew intimately, both good and bad, with someone I was committed to—for better or worse. In short, I was in an actual relationship. I was in love. A lot of students at Yale are having sex, but they remain lonely. Some of them, I fear, may go through their twenties, thirties, and beyond never figuring out how to tie sex and love together.

Occasionally, Yale's senior administration seems to take a prurient interest in students' sex lives. In October 2010, on the eve of the anticipated Halloween-night debaucheries that were to come, dean of students Marichal Gentry sent an e-mail that was supposed to warn students about the connection between drunkenness and sexual assault. He got awkwardly enthusiastic about students' sexual prospects for the evening, writing wistfully about how "having the sex you want" is something that "makes you smile the next day."[8] A year earlier, Dr. Carole Goldberg, the head of the sexual assault resource center on campus, wrote a similar e-mail to the student body in which she expressed her wish that students would find "just the right words that would lead to glorious, consensual sex."[9]

"Glorious consensual" sex?

You can't make this stuff up. This strange suggestion caused more than a few grimaces among students who felt it was a little weird for Yale's leaders to be taking such a colorful interest in the quality of students' sex lives. Yet, this is what passes for responsible administration at what is arguably the most influential university in the nation.

Several months later, Yale took the weirdness to another level by announcing that it was launching a Web site where students would be encouraged to publish essays about their sexual experiences. These essays would be made available for other students and the general public to read. Once again, the Yale College dean's office was at the forefront. Professor Melanie Boyd, professor and director of undergraduate studies for the Department of Women's, Gender, and Sexuality Studies and special adviser to the dean of Yale College on gender issues (I wonder how she fits all of that on her business card) led the effort. With a link from the dean's official Web site, the new "Sex@Yale" site would allow students "to think about what happens to them and what they want to have happen," Boyd said after the announcement.

And once again, students winced at the idea that the Yale administration was taking such eager interest in the sex lives of undergraduates. When the *Yale Daily News* published an online report about the new initiative, comments on the article ranged from "Are you kidding me?" to "Oh my God!! What is happening to this school?"

Rather than simply educating students about STD prevention and health risks related to sexual activity—like most other universities—Yale's leaders seem determined to take things a step further. They seem to almost want to manage students' sex lives, creating scripts and narratives that make it seem as if having sex as often as possible, with as many people as possible, in as many unusual ways as possible, is the key to health and well-being. What continually surprises me is the way the university seems determined to shift student views about "normal" sexuality to ever greater extremes—whether by posting details of students' sex lives online, or by hosting yet another porn star lecture.

Yale's leaders have moved beyond simply being permissive. Instead, they seem to be pushing a specific sexual agenda. At Yale, if you're not having "glorious consensual sex," and having it all the time with all the battery-powered objects and all the different partners you can muster, there is probably something wrong with you.

Yale may be a liberal university, but that doesn't mean it has to be perverse. Yale's leaders are desperate to avoid appearing moralistic. They would never advise students that participating in lots of hookups might possibly make them unhappy, even if studies have shown that hooking up doesn't work well for some people. Addressing issues related to students and sexuality is difficult and, at times, politically controversial. Yale's leaders don't have to join the religious right in order to do right by students. They need only exercise common sense and a bit of restraint.

The problems this generation faces are considerable. The difficulty starts well before students even arrive at college. There was a particularly disturbing episode at prestigious Milton Academy a few years ago—some sort of ménage à six in a locker room—in which five boys received oral sex from one girl. When I read about it, I realized just how extreme things can be, even at the high school level.

College girls are the special target of today's radical sexual culture. It is a culture that asks of them everything and offers them nothing. It is presided over by a legion of academics who have been enamored of the sexual revolution ever since the Summer of Love.

These academics enjoy calling themselves feminists, but they fail to see that the sexual revolution left many young women feeling powerless.

What's a girl to do if she wants—you know—real love? Some girls (and guys) are searching for better ways to love and relate. Have you ever noticed how girl-oriented pop culture is loaded with chick lit (think of the bestselling Twilight series of novels with its cast of virgin vampires) and music (think of the PG-rated love songs of Taylor Swift) that offer a narrative of emotionally deep, committed, and largely chaste love. Young girls are spending their cash as fast as they can to get a dose of romance and emotionally meaningful love. It's what many crave. But they have to get it in books or music because cheap casual sex is all they see around them in the real world. By the time they get to college, I think, many of them realize that the kinds of emotionally meaningful relationships they dreamed about as younger girls just aren't on the menu.

Yale didn't create the hookup culture. But, in the name of "free expression," Yale seems to be doing all it can to reinforce negative sexual behaviors and prejudices. Today, young men are being taught that it's normal to use women and toss them aside. Young women are being taught to accept this kind of treatment as a necessary stage on the path to one day, hopefully, maybe, having an actual "boyfriend." When these students arrive at Yale, the lewd material in the classroom only reinforces such negative assumptions about women. How are women supposed to be viewed as valuable when porn stars end up being the ones instructing students on human sexuality?

I can remember walking through the dorms and seeing little packets of personal lubricant, provided by the university, littering the hallway. It sends a message to students: If you're not putting out, there's something wrong with you.

We often forget, in the course of all our fierce debates over sexual politics, religion, and morality, that real people are behind all the issues that fuel our culture wars. Ultimately, maintaining a respectful sexual culture is not a liberal or conservative issue; it's a human issue. Many students see nothing wrong with hooking up. Others, while they may not see it as wrong, are not especially happy with it. And finally, there are those who feel trapped in a sexual climate that they feel doesn't offer them any options other than to put out or shut up. It is this latter group that Yale wrongs the most by pushing a one-sided sexual agenda.

In the college hookup culture women often feel pressured to make themselves sexually available to men more quickly and more frequently than they might want to under normal circumstances. I observed evidence of this firsthand on a number of occasions. One time, while working in the photography lab, a female classmate, Clara, made a point of showing me negatives from pictures she had taken of herself while topless. Clara was a really nice girl. And I hoped, at the time, that she was just goofing around, and that she didn't really feel that she had to expose herself in that way to get noticed. But, I think, in a culture where sex flows so freely and easily, girls can feel pressured to get sexual right away. Remember, sex is thought to be the starting place for romantic relationships at Yale, not the climax.

During my very first term at Yale, I was in a couple of classes with a young freshman, whom I'll call Rachel. As the weeks wore on, I noticed that she was casting more than the occasional glance my way, and making a point to sit down near me. Still, I didn't make much of it. I never really saw Rachel or spoke with her except when we were in class.

Imagine my surprise when, one day, toward the middle of the semester, she caught up to me on the sidewalk and invited me to accompany her on a weekend getaway. Rachel was a very attractive girl, not someone who would have any trouble attracting male attention. Her proposal both shocked and enticed me all at once. If I had been a man of different circumstances or lesser morals, I would certainly have accepted her offer. I stumbled over my words for a moment, eventually declining by awkwardly muttering something or other. I can't even remember what I said. I hoped I hadn't embarrassed her by turning her down. She hadn't known, after all, that I was married. That's just the point—we didn't really know each other at all. We barely knew each other's names. As I walked away, I remember feeling flummoxed, and kind of sad that she had offered herself to me so easily. Sad that she might take my refusal as evidence that she wasn't desirable, when she definitely was. She was a beautiful, intelligent, and talented girl, but she didn't seem to know what she was worth.

Rachel, I now realize, was simply following the normal relational script at Yale. You start by having sex with someone, and if it seems to be working, you hope it turns into something more. That's what the hookup culture is all about.

PART FOUR

The Return of Sex Week: *How I*

ended up in a Yale classroom

being lectured by a naked porn star

11

DEFIANT DESIRES

Once on a hot summer night, I had spent an hour kissing a hairy, ape-shaped law student from Yale because I felt sorry for him, he was so ugly. When I had finished, he said, "I have you typed, baby. You'll be a prude at forty."

—Esther Greenwood
(from Sylvia Plath's *The Bell Jar*)

In the spring of 2010, I wrote a magazine story about Sex Week at Yale. I flew back into New Haven just as the first events were getting under way. I figured it would be easy, since I had seen it all two years before. What I didn't realize was that this time around, Yale was about to take sex "education" to as yet unimagined extremes. Within minutes of arriving on campus I would be wishing that, somehow, I could return to my airplane and retrieve the barf bag I had most regrettably left behind.

I sat near the back of the room and waited for the first presentation, which was entitled variously (depending on which version of the schedule you believed) either "Deviant Desires" or the more combative "Defiant Desires." Personally, I prefer the latter title, even though I suspect it was a misprint. "Defiant Desires" conveys a certain sense of anthropomorphic drama and political urgency.

A student I knew stood up to introduce Katharine Gates, saying, "Her book is *the* book, when you start talking about these topics." And what were these topics? Fetish and kink. The first slide on the PowerPoint summed it all up well by announcing the following maxim: *When correctly viewed, everything is lewd.*

Gates had a smooth, smoky voice. "There is nothing in the world that someone isn't getting pleasure out of," she told us. She made a pretty good case for this claim over the subsequent hour. She lectured us on the "Four Levels of Fetishism" and the "Core Kinks," including leather, feet, fat, and goo.

We learned about sneeze fetishes, slug-killing fetishes, and black power giant fantasies, about gay sneaker fetishes, gay mud fetishes, and gay fur erotica. "I'm probably showing you a disproportionately large amount of gay material because I'm tired of seeing the female," explained Gates.

Gates utilized photos and videos to illustrate each topic. There were pictures of men dressing up as Japanese schoolgirls, and a video of a man having his diaper changed by a grown woman.

Toward the end of her talk she decided to open up a bit about herself. "I'm going to reveal my total geekiness by revealing what I think is hot." Given what I had seen over the previous hour, I really wasn't sure what to expect. What followed was a strange YouTube-style mashup, consisting of numerous pieced-together clips from *Star Trek*. Students watched Spock and Captain Kirk exchange many intense looks over the ensuing minutes, accompanied by the heavy industrial-rock stylings of the band Nine Inch Nails' hit song "I Want to Fuck You Like an Animal."

During Q&A, students criticized the lack of diversity in the presentation. One girl complained that, other than the *Star Trek* montage, there didn't seem to be much fetish material in the presentation that was made specifically for women. Another student suggested that the material was a little too Eurocentric, and wondered if there weren't more non-Western kink materials out there. At Yale, the political correctness police are ever vigilant.

As I looked around the lecture hall, I noticed the ornate stained-glass window on my left, which included a dramatic visual representation of the union of art, science, and religion—once considered the three pillars of higher education. Around the perimeter of the room, we were surrounded by decorative wall carvings, showing the names and artistic likenesses of many of the leading figures of intellectual history: Dante, Shakespeare, Goethe, Kant, Newton, Franklin, Virgil, Aristotle—all gazing down at us under the weight of a high arched ceiling. These were the leading lights of Western civilization, the shining examples to which all Yale students are forever challenged to aspire.

What greater example could we have than Aristotle, whose deep insights into the nature of mankind still inform us after thousands of years? My thoughts were suddenly interrupted when Gates mentioned the great philosopher by name. "There were engravings in the Middle Ages of Aristotle in a bridle," she claimed. "It was said by Aristotle's contemporaries that he enjoyed being ridden by his wife."

I looked back up at the face of the old fellow, gazing down mutely from his molded plaster perch. I really don't think that when Aristotle made his most famous observation: "Man is by nature a political animal," it was fetish role-playing he had in mind.

Using the topic of animals as a stepping-off point, Gates began to talk about "cannibal play." She showed a video of a woman who was being basted with savory marinade by a group of men. "This is Meg. This is her kink. She wants to be turned into a stuck pig, and pretend to be eaten." It was about this time that I began to pine for that barf bag.

Gates mentioned one story that had been in the news a few years before about a pair of German men who found each other on the Internet. One agreed to literally be eaten by the other. The grisly details of their apparently consensual encounter were documented on videotape, although authorities later called the victim's state of mind into question by pointing out something manifestly obvious— that the victim had a severe psychiatric disorder. The cannibal remained unapologetic. "I always had the fantasy and in the end I fulfilled it," he told the court on the first day of his murder trial.[1]

Fantasy can be harmful. Isn't this why people complain when negative racial or sexual stereotypes are reinforced on television? If entertainment and fantasy have no relation to how we act in the real world, then what is wrong with a black minstrel show? If, on the other hand, the images we consume, and the fantasies we indulge, can actually affect the way we behave, then there must be at least some sexual fantasies out there that are potentially harmful as well.

"Anything goes in fantasy," Gates told the class, "but if you're going to act in reality, it needs to be safe, sane, and consensual" (not including cases of consensual cannibalism, presumably). In the lingo of my generation: Hey, whatever turns you on.

Gates's message seemed to discount the connection between fantasy and real life. Yale administrators, it seems to me, have erected a similar barrier between ideas and actions. They have done so in the name of academic freedom. Supposedly, this means that no expression, no matter how odious, is off-limits in the university. Even if one accepts that no idea should be off-limits, that doesn't mean that all ideas are morally equal, and that doesn't mean that every idea deserves to be given a special platform.

Standing there behind a Yale lectern, atop the platform she had been given that evening, Gates said something that I can guarantee no other teacher has ever said in a Yale classroom. I heard a faint, collective gasp in the room afterward. In that moment, she made clear the totality of her belief in the acceptability of any and all desire. She said, "As far as I'm concerned, you can fantasize about beheading babies and fucking them in the neck."

I stepped out into the winter night and braced for the walk to Ezra Stiles, one of the undergraduate residences on campus. The next event on the program was something called the Y-Couture Fetish Fashion Show, featuring Yale students as models. I guess the idea was to allow students to experience firsthand the kinds of things they had learned about in Gates's lecture.

When I arrived, the foyer was crammed full of students waiting for the doors to open. The dining hall at Ezra Stiles had been converted into a catwalk, complete with strobe lights, spotlights, and a high-powered sound system, thumping out the lower registers of the audio spectrum via a couple of oversized subwoofers.

Tickets were $5 and the money went to a charity called AIDS Walk New Haven. I have seen a lot of charity work in my time, but this was the first time I had heard of students baring themselves publicly for the good of mankind.

Seats filled rapidly once the doors opened, and there was tremendous excitement in the room. The music fired up with a singer belting out rapper 50 Cent's "Candy Shop." Next was "Sexy Back," from Justin Timberlake, followed by Shakira's "She Wolf." The DJ also played the very catchy tune "That's Not My Name" by the Ting Tings—which, in this sexually-charged atmosphere, took on new meaning and started to sound like an anthem for the proverbial hungover morning after.

The room filled up, but students kept on coming. Two girls crammed into a single seat on my right, and the nearest one was, consequently, sharing half my own seat as well. I soon overheard them gossiping about how many people various friends of theirs had slept with. Given the atmosphere in the room, I guess discussing the weather would have been a bit beside the point.

No cameras were allowed, we were told. I wasn't sure what we were about to see. But I figured the students might not want it posted all over the Internet the next morning, where future employers or political rivals might easily find it someday. To my left, I noticed a burly middle-aged fellow who was manning the spotlight. He wore black fingerless gloves, cut-off sleeves (revealing arms covered with tattoos), spiked hair, and a braided silver necklace. I wondered if he was getting paid for his work, or if he had volunteered to shine the spotlight on a retinue of skimpily clad girls simply out of benevolent concern for the charitable cause associated with the event.

The subwoofers began to rumble. Then the Yale students–turned–underwear models began to emerge, stomping down the catwalk. They modeled several dozen examples of student-designed lingerie and negligee in the course of a half hour. Often they came out in pairs, a guy and a girl, each ensemble capturing some role-playing theme. There were Secretary and Boss, Housewife and Sugar Daddy, Angel and Devil, and another called "Virgin and Defiler." Several girls came down the walk alone. Among the brave solo girls the themes included a Flight Attendant and a Pinup Girl. One outfit consisted of little more than strategically placed fabric and duct tape.

I watched a girl reach the end of the runway, the part where models always pause, with hand on hip, swivel, and cast a fierce stare. That's what this girl more or less did. I guess she had seen enough of the *America's Next Top Model* television show to have the routine down. When she paused and swiveled, I could see the ogle-eyed expression of a curly blond-haired guy in the row beyond her. He was sitting within two feet of her breasts, which were separated from him now by no more than a single thin piece of satin fabric, which, having been stitched together by an amateur student designer, might plausibly fall off at any second. At least, that's what it looked like that guy was thinking.

The first thing that crossed my mind was: What would that girl's parents think if they knew they had sent her off to Yale only for her to end up half naked in front of a bunch of horny college guys?

How did we get here? I wondered.

It was a surreal feeling. Decades ago when women were first admitted to the all-male college, it was considered a major achievement for the women's movement. And the earliest women admitted to Yale were seen as the best examples of what strong, intelligent women could accomplish if only the barrier of sexism was taken out of their way. The idea that Yale women, in those early years, would have submitted to being ogled under a spotlight by their male classmates seems impossible. When women first entered Yale, there was a political implication to their very presence on campus. Women had fought so hard to achieve respect and equality. I couldn't help wondering what those first Yale women would think had they been sitting there with me, watching some of the brightest female minds in the world march along like a shirtless flight attendant, a pinup girl, or some man's half-dressed secretary.

These servile gender roles may have been assumed in a playful spirit. But is that really all that's going on here? Is there a deeper sociological meaning behind what I was witnessing? Does the fact that Yale women today playfully embrace gender stereotypes that their mothers eschewed tell us something about the state of feminism in the midst of a radical sexual culture? Today, female students at Yale refer to themselves as "girls," not "women," like their mothers' generation did. Maybe that signifies something negative about how Yale women view themselves today. Then again, perhaps today's young women simply aren't as caught up in terminology. Either way, this much is clear: Many young women seem to have internalized the subservient sexual identities that are celebrated in today's porn culture.

I couldn't help noticing how politically incorrect the themes were. In particular, the male/female themes reinforced the kinds of clichéd submissive female stereotypes that are constantly painted as sexist and evil in Yale's gender studies classes. I guess I had gotten so used to certain standards of militant feminist orthodoxy in the classroom that it was a bit of a shock to see those standards so blatantly transgressed outside the classroom. The last pair to come down the catwalk paired two girls in a Dominatrix/Submissive getup that I can only describe as Girls in Leather with Chains.

By the time I left the Fetish Fashion Show, the cold night had grown even more bitter. As I hurried over the great marble courtyard outside Woolsey Hall, I was struck by a wave of beautiful music, cutting through the chill. As I came closer, the sound grew clearer. I neared the western wing, which contains a great cathedral-like assembly hall. I pressed myself against the stained-glass window and felt the soft warmth coming from within. Some lone figure inside was playing the pipe organ. Long, brassy tones echoed out over the stillness.

I am not the kind of person who starts tearing up every time I hear a violin. But at that moment, I was deeply moved by the music: the complexity and perfect beauty of the melody, the emotive swell of the sound, the shattering echo of the notes as they spilled over one another and reverberated through the hall and out into the darkness. The melody felt free and unfettered, even though the notes were actually bound by rigid chord structures and scales. There was freedom in all that order. And the beauty of the notes I heard, I knew, could not be beautiful without that order. If the player had simply stomped his feet across the keys, the same tones that sounded so beautiful would have produced a cacophony, mere noise.

Maybe there was something similar about the Fetish Fashion Show spectacle I had just seen—all those intelligent, amazing young women on parade before a crowd of rowdy oglers. It felt like something valuable had been thrown around with no thought or care. It felt like something was out of order, like the notes had wandered off the scale.

Over the next few days I attended a number of enlightening events. The highlights included a lecture on the benefits of non-monogamous relationships by a self-described "polyamory activist." The lecture was entitled "Getting What You Really Want." What many of us really want, the speaker suggested, is to have ongoing sexual relationships with several different people at a time. Problem is, pesky things like jealousy and insecurity and societal mores keep us from exploring the kinds of relationships that can make us happy. "I think marriage is actually not the model that you want to be adding more people into," she told us. She went on to describe her life as the part-time lover of an older married man, whose wife, she said, approved of the long-term affair. "Having situations where there are multiple partners requires a heightened level of communication," she said.

As an alternative family attorney, she said, she often drew up complicated domestic contracts involving three or four people. I couldn't help wondering how children fit into all these arrangements. How does one go about practicing heightened communication with them? Do you sit the kids down in order to have a talk about Daddy's other special lady? And does the special lady draw a visual diagram in order to teach her daughter about Daddy's "full-time" family? Do the special lady and her daughter come over for Christmas dinner with the full-time family? Oddly, though, kids never came up during the lecture. Instead, it seemed to be all about what might make adults happy.

Normally, the Yale administration kept itself at a distance from Sex Week events. But the polyamory event was unique because it actually boasted an official sponsorship from the dean's office. Dean's office representative Melanie Boyd was there to interject her own comments about Yale's sexual culture during the polyamorist's talk.

Boyd kept saying how it is so important to communicate. "There is a presumption that everybody wants the same thing," she said. Then she brought up Yale's tradition of holding naked parties. (More on that later.) The naked parties, she said, are "a great indicator of how easy it is to define your own sexual space. Many people outside of Yale find the naked parties completely incomprehensible. They say, 'How could this happen?' But Yalies see it all the time. . . . It takes organization."

I was glad she brought up the issue of organization because the organization of this particular talk was baffling me. In total, there were nearly thirty different lectures and presentations during Sex Week 2010. As far as I know, the "Getting What You Really Want" polyamory talk was the only event sponsored directly by a member of the university's senior administration. I didn't know what to make of such high-level, official involvement. Exactly why the dean's office thought the message of polyamory was so important is a mystery to me.

Later that week, I attended yet another pep talk advocating non-monogamous lifestyles. (I guess Yale hosted a second non-monogamy event that week in case students didn't get the message the first time.) The second time around students didn't hear from "an alternative family attorney." Instead, the speaker was a porn producer who offered porno DVDs for sale from the trunk of a car after the lecture ended. This time around, I didn't see Melanie Boyd there; nor was there any sponsorship from the office of the dean.

Perhaps it was inevitable; I eventually found myself at an instructional seminar on masturbation. It was one part theology, two parts physiology, and four parts Oprah-ology: "Our bodies have the power to make us feel good. . . . It doesn't mean your partner doesn't fulfill you," and with a touch of self-evident reasoning that would have made Gertrude Stein proud, "Whatever works for you, works for you."

It's not every day someone reads the Bible in the classroom at Yale. Leave it to masturbation class to provide such an occasion. We heard the cautionary tale of Onan. He was the fellow in the Bible who incurred God's wrath after he developed the habit of having sex with his dead brother's wife, all the while utilizing a devious innovation of timing and technique in order to "spill his seed" and avoid getting her pregnant because, under the law of the land, any resulting children would legally have been considered his dead brother's offspring, not his own. Sheew. It's all very complicated, but I think, in the end, it probably had something to do with who was going to inherit the dead brother's flocks.

After the Sunday school lesson, we moved on to a slide show depicting all sorts of medieval and Victorian contraptions designed to ensnare the genitals, ranging from the chastity belt to the spiked urethral ring and the spermatic truss.

Next came a bit of food trivia. Did you know graham crackers were created for the purpose of suppressing lustful urges? The Reverend Sylvester Graham of Suffield, Connecticut, invented the original libido-quenching wafer in 1829. (As a great lover of s'mores, I've found that the addition of rich, dark chocolate and gooey roasted marshmallows completely ruins the suppressive effect.)

Finally, we got down to the actual mechanics of the process—how one should stroke this or caress that, and whether to use this battery-operated contraption or that one. The speaker was particularly concerned with the architecture of the female genitalia. If you were to attempt to give a respectable title to this subject, you might call it something like "The Autoerotic Ambiguities of Gender 101." And it would almost sound like a topic worthy of serious academic study. But when you get right down to it, it was nothing more than a lesson on how to touch yourself—an act that any ultrasound technician can tell you most babies figure out in utero. I'm pretty sure all of the students in the room had a handle on it already.

Before we left, we were presented with a brief thematic musical survey, piped in over the classroom's sound system. It included the song "She Bop" by Cyndi Lauper and, of course, the greatest ode to self love in pop history, the Divinyls' 1991 hit single "I Touch Myself."

12

ORAL EXAMINATIONS

I was studying in the library, and Bill was standing out in the hall. . . . I noticed he kept looking over at me. He had been doing a lot of that. So I stood up from the desk, walked over to him, and said, "If you're going to keep looking at me, and I'm going to keep looking back, we might as well be introduced."

—Hillary Rodham Clinton, J.D., class of 1973,
on meeting her future husband for the first time

In general, Yale students are full of energy and ambition. On top of a challenging academic workload, they tend to stay heavily involved in extracurricular activities. It wouldn't be unusual for a Yalie to participate in a debate in the Yale Political Union, write an article for the *Yale Daily News*, perform in an a cappella group, compete in a club rugby tournament, and cram for two midterms in the course of a single week. On top of all this, there are dozens of artistic performances, presentations, and special guest lectures happening every week. Sometimes it is overwhelming just to realize how many great things you have missed on any given day, simply because you can't be in two places at the same time.

I've had quite a few conversations with myself that went something like this: *Hmmm, should I go to a special prerelease film screening by a Hollywood director at the Humanities Center, or should I attend a reading by the current poet laureate of the United States at the master's house? Oh yeah, there's the presentation by the Nobel Prize–winning astrophysicist over on Science Hill, maybe I should go there. Nah, I probably won't understand anything he's talking about. Okay, I'll go to the poetry reading; they'll have food there. On second thought, maybe I should just go to the library and do the readings for class tomorrow.*

I could sum up my entire Yale education as an exercise in deciding what not to do—how much of my five or six hundred pages of reading I could afford to skip that week without letting my grades suffer, which once-in-a-lifetime event or experience I could bear to pass up without impoverishing my soul. It's a tough life when you have the intellectual riches of Western civilization right at your fingertips. I was never shrewd enough to take advantage of all I should have, but I was wise enough to know that these were beautiful dilemmas to have. And I savored them.

Nevertheless, as you can see, it was hard to make time for unplanned events. Consequently, guest lectures, even by relatively well-known speakers, were sometimes sparsely attended. On one occasion, I took it upon myself to organize a special guest lecture. It was during the height of the presidential primary season in 2008. Hillary Clinton and Barack Obama were fighting tooth and nail for the Democratic presidential nomination. Among the overwhelmingly liberal students at Yale, there was quite a bit of contention and debate going on between supporters of the two candidates. There were Obama and Hillary posters in dorm windows all over campus, as well as the occasional lonely McCain sign.

During my junior year, I worked part-time for a public relations firm. It was a great gig that allowed me to work remotely from New Haven, with only the occasional trip back to New York. I had a connection, through my boss, to a pollster and pundit of some renown. He was working as a political commentator for Fox News at the time, and had been a senior adviser to President Clinton in the nineties. I figured that with all the intense interest around campus over the Democratic primary, it would be a great time to invite this particular expert on elections and public opinion to speak on campus. So I invited him.

With a little help from the administration, I booked a big lecture hall that seated two or three hundred. I printed flyers and posted them around campus. I took out an ad in the school paper, and had a promotional e-mail sent to the entire Political Science Department. The guest of honor arrived in a black limousine, which had carried him from his Park Avenue apartment in Manhattan to Yale's front gate—a trip of about two hours.

I have paid as much as $15 for a ten-minute ride in a New York yellow taxi. I wonder: What does a seven-hour, 150-mile round-trip cost in a Manhattan limousine? I have a feeling I never want to find out.

As I escorted the speaker and his assistant across the quad to the lecture hall where he was scheduled to speak, I could barely manage to make small talk because I was so busy trying to calculate the limousine fare this fellow had paid out of his own pocket in order to get to Yale. Imagine my feelings when we opened the heavy oak doors and found that there were about five people in the audience, including one elderly couple that seemed to have wandered in off the street.

I stepped up to the podium in order to offer up a witty little introduction, which I had prepared beforehand on a piece of scrap paper. It's very hard to be witty in front of an empty room. I had planned an intimate post-talk dinner at Mory's, a private dining club with old-school roots going back to the days when Yale was little more than a finishing school for all the WASPy young squires of New England. The dinner was supposed to be a chance for Yale students to meet and chat with the distinguished guest in an informal setting. The table seated six, which means there were more people at that dinner than there had been in the audience at the lecture itself. The guest of honor was gracious and polite. He didn't say anything to indicate how he felt about the fact that I had wasted an entire day of his life, or about how he had spent a small fortune in limousine fares just for the chance of giving a talk to an empty room. However, I took note of the fact that he left dinner early.

Sometime later, I attended a guest lecture that drew far better attendance from the student body. In contrast to my measly audience of five, I estimate that nearly two thousand students showed up for this one—somewhere near a third of the undergraduate student body. What the lecture was about, exactly, will require some detailed explaining. But, as a clue, let me start by saying it was billed as "Babeland's Lip Tricks." On that occasion, I observed a burlesque performer named Darlinda demonstrate fellatio and cunnilingus before the rapt student audience for an hour and a half.

I was running late for Babeland's Lip Tricks, and I had to shuffle through the dark over icy sidewalks on my way across campus. Did I mention the wind? I would have worn a pink polka-dotted Gore-Tex jumpsuit if someone had offered one. New Haven sits right on the coast of Long Island Sound, and the winter sea breezes always add an extra bite to the chill. More than once, I encountered winds so stiff that they would turn my spindly six-foot three-inch frame into the equivalent of a human sail, and I would almost fall over.

The wind can be brutal. On the other hand, if you are on the sailing team, those stiff breezes are a wonderful thing. Yale has its own private multimillion-dollar boathouse. If students want to practice for a future part in a Ralph Lauren commercial, they can shuttle over to the coast most any afternoon for a bit of sailing. I once spent an afternoon cruising around the sound on a two-man dinghy. It was heavenly. Then again, it was also a sunny day in early September. Those warm memories were hard to muster as I made my way through the February winter to the majestic Sheffield-Sterling-Strathcona lecture hall, known as "SSS" around campus. If you changed the Ss to Xs you would have it just about right.

When I arrived at the lecture hall, students were crowded around the entrance, pressing, herdlike, up the steps toward the heavy arched wooden doors. The foyer was packed, and I realized it was going to be standing room only. Students were already jockeying for position around the doors leading into the main auditorium, poised to spend the entire lecture standing and peeking in, since there were no seats left. I pushed my way past them.

The main hall in SSS is like a cathedral, with stained-glass windows and a high peaked ceiling. The seats look like traditional church pews. There was seldom a liturgy so well attended in all of Yale's history. Not only was every last seat taken, but students were also sitting shoulder to shoulder on the ground, covering the floor, filling both aisles. I had to step over and around dozens of them as I made my way down toward the platform. At the foot of the stage, the seated hordes were even more tightly pressed together. When I reached the front, I found one of the last remaining pieces of visible surface area anywhere in the room, at the foot of the stairs leading up to the stage. I crouched there and did my best to avoid the harsh stares of all the people I had walked over in order to reach my tiny perch. I looked up and saw that the balcony was also packed to overflowing. I began to imagine that the crushing force of students pressing forward might push the students standing up front, lemminglike, over the edge of the balcony.

By this time, we were beginning to test the limits of certain laws of physics, like the one that says no two objects can occupy the same space at the same time. I think we were also risking the ire of our local fire marshal by violating an array of maximum-occupancy laws and emergency-exit codes. Perhaps in the eyes of Yale authorities, the intellectual magnitude of this particular event justified extreme measures to accommodate student interest. I must say, in the midst of such chaos, I did begin to wonder if there was anyone in charge at all. By the time I settled in my place, students had begun to climb up onto the stage itself, and so several dozen students ended up sitting at the very feet of our instructor, Darlinda.

I watch as Darlinda approaches the podium. She is a dark-haired woman, somewhere in her midthirties, I estimate. The roar and rustle of the crowd come to an abrupt halt, echoing momentarily and melting at last into attentive silence across the vast hall. She begins to speak.

"Today I want to start with a little bit of an icebreaker. Although, I can tell that you guys are a little bit broken in already." There is a brief delay of collective incomprehension. Then the first of the evening's numerous middle-school-grade-level-humor-induced laughs erupts across the room.

She starts by pitching a book entitled *Moregasm*, billed as a "guide to mind-blowing sex."

She says she wants us all to be comfortable with any kind of language, anatomical or otherwise. "Let's start with some words that we like to use for vagina, like 'cunt.' That's a really fun word to use. (Laughs erupt.) So, um, we'll start by saying 'cunt' all together." This time the laughs are accompanied by whoops and cheers and applause. I feel like I have arrived on the set of the Jerry Springer talk show.

"Okay, so let's all do it. Are you ready? One, two, three, CUNT!" The room shouts in unison.

"Okay, one more time, CUNT!"

"One more time, CUNT!" We really get it going on the last try. And the repetitive nature of these collective recitations begins to take on a kind of Zen quality. I feel that I am being transported away into an alternate plane of existence where Yale University has melded into the plane of consciousness formerly accessible only to those who are passionate about MTV reality shows. Without pause, Darlinda takes us on to the next anatomical mantra. "Okay, let's say 'cock' together." And on it goes.

"Pleasure is a very important thing. As you know, you have a whole Sex Week dedicated to pleasure.

"And I hope you're all out there having sex," she adds. "I know when I was in college, I started exploring and learning things about sex. And so, it's all about pleasure. It's really all about pleasure.

"We have a Bill of Rights, based on pleasure." Darlinda begins showing, up on the projector screen, images from the book she's selling. Hers is, apparently, an illustrated Bill of Rights. "So, basically, you're sexy already. You can learn a lot of good things about sex, but, guess what? You're sexy already. Every part of your body is sexy. And you can use your whole body to have sex: your mouth, your feet, your toes, your ears, your nose, everything." She never gets any deeper into the thing about sex with ears, but it sounds difficult.

She moves on to the second principle of her Bill of Rights: Love yourself. "Loving yourself; it's a big, big, big, important thing. Anything we teach you today—well, not the oral sex—you can try out all these things on your own. I really encourage masturbation, it's so important."

Once again, I am baffled by the great urgency applied to the subject of masturbation: the expert instruction, the how-tos, the earnest cheerleading. In general, the speakers of Sex Week seem to consider it a profoundly challenging exercise. And there seems to be a great deal of doubt as to whether the average Yale student can pull it off without proper coaching.

Darlinda continues expounding on the items in her pleasure seeker's Bill of Rights:

3. Enjoy the Journey. ("It's not all about having that orgasm.")
4. Own Your Own Orgasm. ("Masturbate, masturbate, masturbate.")
5. Ask for What You Want. ("Don't be afraid to say, 'I'm ready to fuck you in the butt' or 'I'd really like to sit on your face now.'")
6. Take Charge of Safe Sex. ("It's 2010. Guess what? We should all be having safe sex. You know, there are diseases out there." The room breaks out in applause, presumably for the safe sex, not the diseases. "Where can you get condoms on campus?" "Everywhere," comes the collective response from the room. "If you need to use dental dams you can use Saran Wrap. You can get Saran Wrap anywhere. Okay?")

7. Use Lubrication.
8. Laugh.
9. Don't Be Afraid to Make a Mess. ("If you get real juicy, if you pee, whatever . . . If you aren't messy with the sex, you aren't really free.")
10. Keep Growing. ("Every day I learn new things. I learn them from you. And you can learn them from me. And we can all learn together.")

The spirit of Oprah is haunting yet another session of Sex Week. Once again, a basically tawdry event has come packaged in all kinds of marshmallowy language about self-understanding and self-acceptance.

"Any questions about the Bill of Rights?" she asks.

I can't help it when my mind drifts away from Darlinda's talk into a strange fantasy where a buttoned and whigged James Madison is introducing his Bill of Rights on the floor of the first United States Congress.

"*Numbah nine,*" he says in a highborn Virginia accent. "*The enumeraaation in the Constitution, of certain riiiights, shall not be construuuued to deny or disparage othahs retained by the people, including the riiiiight to make a mess during sex.*" Gentlemen in white wigs stir uncomfortably on their benches across the house floor.

"*And furthamore, numbah ten,*" Madison continues, undeterred by murmurs and fits of coughing all over the room. "*The powahs to keep growing, not delegated to the United States by the Constitution, nor prohibited by it to the states, are reserved toooo the states respectively. I learn from you. You learn from me. And we can aaaaall learn togethah.*"

Suddenly I'm startled back to reality. "Are you ready to learn about sex!" Darlinda continues. Immediately, the room erupts in cheers.

"I don't really teach anatomy on the molecular level," she explains. Nevertheless, she is an expert at the macro level. The next slide on the projector is labeled "V-Town." She clicks through about a dozen pictures of vaginas. One after the other, Darlinda shows us the many faces of the feminine.

Then she moves on to the anus, which she calls "an equal opportunity orifice." Darlinda talks about the anus as though it has feelings and a mind of its own. It "loves to be kissed and touched," she observes. Next, she breaks into rhyme, emphasizing "relaxation, lubrication, and communication," and, for a moment, her advice in this area aspires to the realm of the poetic.

Clearly, Darlinda's presentation, like so many others during Sex Week, is intended to be edgy. In the category of things that break taboos at Yale, teaching anal sex techniques would seem to qualify. At least, it would have qualified in any prior era. But all the edgy stuff strikes me as oddly passé in the Internet age. My generation has grown up with the most extreme and brutal kinds of pornography only a few mouse clicks away. Therefore, I can't help feeling that the relevance of what I'm hearing and seeing is rather imaginary. If the intention is to teach young people sexual behaviors they can't easily discover and learn about online, then there is nothing left to teach. They've seen it all already.

That's when I have to remind myself that education isn't really what this is all about. The Babeland® sex toy company isn't really interested in educating students, or walking hand in hand with them through a long, emotional journey of sexual self-discovery. They want to sell, sell, sell; and that's all this presentation is about. Yale was happy to give Babeland® and other companies like it a free platform to market their products, under the pretext of "education."

It is a bit surreal, sitting through these kinds of marketing presentations. I can't stop being amazed by what I'm seeing and hearing in the classroom. Still, I have to admit that plenty of others around me seem untroubled by the conflicts of interest inherent in this kind of sex industry event. It's all so absurd. I can't imagine the Yale administration inviting McDonald's to come in and give a lecture about healthy food choices, using its own menu as a step-by-step guide. That would be ridiculous. Turning the classroom into a venue for marketing any product is frowned upon at Yale. And there are university rules that supposedly forbid it. Yet Yale seems happy to host sex education lectures from just about any company that sells porn or sex-related products.

Why the double standard?

Did I mention that Babeland® has an entire line of eco-friendly merchandise? "Rechargeable vibrators, body-friendly materials, sustainably harvested woods . . . Be kind to the planet and to your body with these eco-friendly products, and you'll feel good in more ways than one!"[1] I didn't know there were sex toys out there designed to satisfy environmentalist urges. I do recycle. But, personally, I've never been able to get quite that excited about it.

Many lectures during Sex Week seem to be taking cues from *Cosmo* magazine, and they inevitably include earnest advice about finding your "G-spot." Darlinda carries on with her talk, exploring the mysterious wonder zone before moving on to even more rarefied sexual territory.

"If you go to the bathroom before you have sex and you have G-spot exploration, then you know you won't have to pee. And what might come out of the urethra is female ejaculation.

"Has anyone ejaculated before?" There is a brief pause, and then the laughs start rolling.

"Beside the boys?" she adds.

A few girls raise their hands. "That is so wonderful. . . . It's a really exciting thing," Darlinda says. The room breaks out into cheers and excited applause. The girl sitting next to me lets out an earnest "Yay!" in response to the small showing of hands.

Oddly, the applause goes on and on, getting louder and louder. To me, the sudden outpouring of cheers has the unmistakable feeling of catharsis. I get the feeling that there is some kind of sexual glass ceiling being broken here. This unusual and elusive female bodily function has now taken on political relevance, perhaps signifying a new plateau of female sexual liberation. It is as if the possibility that female ejaculation has actually occurred to some woman, somewhere, represents, to many in this room, a kind of victory for women's equality. There is a suggestion behind all those cheers that if other girls in the room could experience such a thing, it would mean that they would have reached nearer to their highest sexual potential.

You need to understand something about Yale students: As a rule, they are highly performance-oriented. They are used to measuring themselves constantly against their peers in an effort to come out on top. In high school they had to have the best SAT scores, the best grades. Being the best, or at least among the best, is a matter of basic self-esteem for many of them. Since grade school they have been overachieving and outperforming their peers. That's how they ended up at Yale. When it comes to sex, this competitive drive makes Yale students a perfect audience for Darlinda's tips on maximizing sexual performance.

"Let's all do some exercises! Are you ready?

"Do you have your game clothes on?"

All of a sudden Darlinda turns into the Richard Simmons of sex. She's got the whole room doing her version of below-the-belt aerobics. "Hold it. . . . Take a breath in, then squeeze." Next, after a minute of slow breathing, we move on to a turbocharged exercise called "the Breath of Fire," which she says is great for women to do while they are masturbating.

"Five, six, seven, eight . . . ho, ho, ho, ho, ho, ho, ho, ho . . . heh, heh, heh, heh, heh, heh, heh, heh . . ." She has two thousand students panting like thirsty dogs.

Having given us a thorough rundown on female anatomy, our speaker now turns her attention to all matters male. Once again, I'm starting to feel like I'm living inside a cover story in *Cosmo* magazine, probably titled something like "38 Ways to Blow Your Man's Mind." I can almost see the blond, photo-enhanced models and smell the scratch-and-sniff perfume. Darlinda shares secrets on how to stimulate the foreskin, the testicles, the prostate.

Darlinda is not a fan of the unsheathed saber, and she congratulates all the uncircumcised young men in the room, telling them they have a part of their body that is "supposed to be there" and promising them that they will have "more pleasure." Too bad for the rest, I guess.

She rounds out her phallic soliloquy by admonishing students not to neglect one often-overlooked part of the male member, calling out, "Let's hear it for the balls!" And the room bursts into yet another round of applause. I feel like I am sitting through the anatomical Academy Awards.

When Darlinda finishes her three-part lesson on how to help a man achieve a "prostate orgasm," her talk seems to have reached a point where its bluntness can get no blunter. At that very moment she turns her attention to the main topic of the evening. "Let's move on to the nitty-gritty.

"We're gonna talk about hand jobs!

"We're gonna talk about blow jobs!

"We're gonna talk about pussy eating, pussy licking!

"Are you ready?"

In response to these questions, I see two female students near the front stand up and head for the exits. Darlinda carries on. "I'm going to need all of you to make a pussy with your hands."

"I'm afraid to see how this is possible," the girl sitting next to me says, giving voice to precisely my own thoughts.

Darlinda leads us by example. "I'm going to actually teach you how to do this," she says. "So here's my hand. Okay?" She puts her hands together to make the intended shape. "Here's the clitoris, right here. Okay?" She interlocks her fingers and wiggles them a bit. "Say hello to my vagina!" she says.

She asks students to mimic her hand motions. "Let's start with some hand job techniques for women. So, first of all, you want to get some lube." She lathers up with silicon lubricant and shows students four different rubbing techniques, including the "pulling technique," the "whole hand" method, and the "popping" method, which consists of slapping the female genitals. "It's very popular in the porns these days," she tells us. Slapping the genitals really gets the blood flowing to the right areas, she adds. "It's like exercise.

"Now I need a couple of volunteers." Two young students answer the call, one guy and one girl. They start shuffling up to the stage, accompanied by riotous applause. People are shouting out the guy's name in a show of support as he makes his way up front. It takes both of them a while because they have to walk over scores of students who are seated on the floor in the aisles and in front of the stage. When they finally get there, Darlinda is waiting for them with a giant tube of lubricant.

She lathers them up with a cocktail of silicone and flavored gels, and then has them practice cunnilingus on their hands in front of the assembly. "What we're going to do is start with some long, slow licks. Okay? And all of you out there, you've got to help these folks out."

Before I know it, the entire hall is full of students holding their hands together in front of their faces as if they were in a somber moment of silent prayer. But, instead of whispering pleas to the divine, they are licking their fingers up and down. And the licking spoils the pious feeling the scene might otherwise have evoked.

"Put your tongue out flat like this. Ahhhhhhhhhhhhhh."

A chorus of "ahhhhhhhhhhhhhhs" echoes back from the crowd.

"And you just sort of take your mouth and slowly lick the vulva."

An older male professor is sitting near me on the floor. "You guys do it," he says, addressing a couple of female students to my right. The girls respond with nervous laughter. To me, it's amazing that a faculty member would even allow himself to be seen at an event like this one, much less actively engage in sexual banter with students. The creepiness factor is very high. But this particular professor is a special case. And I'm not sure if he is even aware of why those girls are laughing nervously. Of the many tactless academic types I've encountered, he seems particularly blind to propriety. He is one of several male professors I have come across who teach sex-related classes of questionable academic usefulness, and who, in my opinion, appear entirely too comfortable experiencing sexual situations alongside young guys and girls forty years their junior.

"Okay, so you're licking, right?" Darlinda continues to coach the two volunteer students up onstage through each lick. Next she leans down and puts her mouth under the live video projector in order to demonstrate various positions of the tongue. For several unrelenting minutes, we are treated to the sight of her monstrous three-foot-wide purple tongue, flicking and dribbling all over the big screen. She shows us all of the most important tongue techniques: the push and hold, the rapid repeat, and the figure eight.

"You want to use your own choreography as well. Take all of these things and make your own choreography. I am teaching you some moves, and then you can dance however the hell you want." She continues miming the motions. If we were playing charades, I would guess she was pretending to be a thirsty puppy at a desert watering hole.

Her next directive conjures another bit of animal imagery. "So, you know how cats clean themselves? Try that. But you do it faster." The two students onstage continue to act out their roles in the production. "I've experienced that a lot," she adds, in reference to this particular technique. In the abbreviated text-speak of my generation, this is what is known as TMI—or, too much information.

"It's all about communication, all about communication."

The professor seated on the floor next to me can't help voicing his assent to this nice notion about communication. "Um hmm. Um hmm," he says. Again I feel the creepy factor rise, and I want to ask him: *Why are you here, exactly?*

Just then Darlinda draws my attention back again. "All right. Moving on, we're going to do the pucker. Okay? It's all about sucking on that clit. Okay? That feels amazing. There's nothing like some great pressure on the clitoris. Okay?" She sucks her cheeks in and pokes out her lips, then begins bobbing her head like a woodpecker with its beak stuck in a log.

All this is making my professor friend very talkative. And he seems to be carrying on a hushed conversation with one of the students behind me. It's probably for the best that I can't make out what he's saying.

Darlinda describes the next move, which I think she borrowed from a contortionist. To me, it sounds like there is a risk of suffocation. Finally, she releases her first two volunteers, who, up until now, have been dutifully mimicking all her motions into their own hand-vaginas for the instructional benefit of all the other students present. To show her gratitude, she sends them away with an armful of free merchandise from Babeland®.

"Okay! Are you ready to move on to the cock?" Students respond with a smattering of whoops and applause.

"We're going to learn how to put a condom on with our mouth." She calls up two new volunteers, a guy and a girl. They start by rolling condoms on with their lips. "Is that one too wide for you?" Darlinda asks the girl. The girl gets a new, smaller piece of fruit.

"Is it really small?" I hear the professor next to me asking.

"All right. We are ready to learn how to give a blow job. Are you ready?" Darlinda teaches several moves, including the testicle squeeze, the over-the-hill method, and the fabled doorknob technique. Next thing I know, both students onstage are fellating bananas.

Darlinda is doing something else with the imaginary testicles. The professor leans over to me and says, "Not something you usually teach in a sex-ed class."

Darlinda goes on to detail the importance of "full coverage" when performing the oral doorknob. Periodically, the professor emits a pensive "Hmm" in response to her instruction. At least, I think his moans are merely pensive. But I'm afraid to turn around and make sure.

Taking a wooden penis in her mouth, she shows us something called "the master stroke." This evokes yet another round of whoops from the audience. "I need more lube. Don't be afraid to add more lube," she says. She moves over to encourage her two volunteers, who continue to perform on their bananas. "Use your whole head and really get into it. Okay?"

Next she tells students to rub the penis all over their bodies. "Just get your whole face into it. Your whole body is aroused. Use your whole body. You can also use your breasts too. Use your butt, not the inner part of your butt but just your butt cheeks. That feels really good too—or the labia just rubbing on it.

"There's so many different things you can do with penises, and your mouth, and your labia, and your anus. It just goes on and on and on. We could really talk for hours."

The professor next to me speaks up again, addressing those of us within earshot: "These things are so important," he says, in all apparent seriousness.

Darlinda interrupts his train of thought. "Okay, we've got someone to do the deep throat for you!"

Before I even realize what is happening, one of the student volunteers onstage is deep-throating a poor, innocent banana. This move provokes general amazement throughout the audience. Students respond with an eardrum-bursting round of laughing, clapping, hollering, stomping, and whistling, the likes of which have not been heard in perhaps any Yale lecture hall in the university's long, storied history.

It doesn't get a whole lot classier during Q&A. In the closing minutes we hear additional advice on how to get at that prostate. Then we receive tips on anal/oral stimulation. "Anything you do with your mouth anywhere else, you can do on the anus as well." That makes it simple, I guess.

We also learn some critical hygienic protocol, specifically, how to avoid pooping during sex. "Before you have anal sex, or any anal stimulation, give yourself a couple of hours—depending on your digestive cycle—give yourself a couple of hours and poop, you know, before you have sex. There might be some fecal matter happening but . . ." She trails off into something about metabolism, but basically assures us there is no need to worry, before admitting that, unfortunately, "some people are poop machines." I look around to see if anyone is taking notes.

"You can always use gloves," she concedes.

This must be, I think to myself, the natural progression of the culture of clinical safe sex, taken to its banal extreme. It started with sex educators' near-religious devotion to the condom—that miraculous wonder-sock that was supposed to cure AIDS, liberate women from the curse of motherhood, eliminate unwanted pregnancy, make abortion obsolete, and, above all, free mankind from so many lingering Victorian vestiges of fearful prudery.

The all-powerful rubber gave us sex with no strings attached. But that wasn't enough. Now our hands are also supposed to be covered with latex. Slowly but surely, our anonymous sex culture is becoming as devoid of physical contact as it is of emotional contact. Touchless, heartless, passionless sex is the inheritance of this porned-out, hooked-up generation.

Pretty soon they will come up with a big latex bag we can put over our heads—a kissing condom. We won't even need to look each other in the eyes. After that, a full-body-length model will emerge, completely eliminating the need for any skin-to-skin contact. This will have the added advantage of suffocating us while we shag, and thus it will put an end to our collective sexual dysfunction once and for all.

"You never want to go from anus to vagina. Never ever, ever, ever. There's bacteria in the anus that belongs in the anus, but not in the vagina."

"Hmm," says the professor.

A male student up in the balcony speaks up: "So if you would like to receive, like, a deep throat during your blow job?"

"Sure."

"And your partner is too, uh, say, frightened to experience that. What advice would you give to a girl or a guy who is too scared to perform that?"

"Sure! Deep-throating takes a lot of practice. You know, it's all about training your gag reflex."

Actually, I've been training mine ever since she brought up the subject of anal bacteria.

"It is really just all about taking your time with it, practicing with a dildo at home, just kind of putting it back to the end of your throat."

Being a sexual high achiever requires serious dedication, I remind myself.

"If you're on the edge of a bed with your head sort of hanging, you can kind of lean into it that way. . . . Again, it's about the dirty you."

The dirty me?

Darlinda winds things down with a bit of advice against engaging in oral sex while driving. Probably the soundest advice I have heard all evening.

Finally, in response to a girl near the front who asks for tips on how to spice up oral sex if it starts to get boring: "If you have long hair, you can actually have your partner hold on to your hair and actually pull your hair. If you like that sensation, hair pulling can be really fun . . . Another thing, which is really great, is just to put your finger in someone's butt while you're giving them a blow job. You can also sit on someone's face. You can do sixty-nine. There are so many things you can do. . . . You can integrate spanking. You can integrate rope bondage."

But Darlinda was getting ahead of herself. Yale's bondage class wasn't scheduled until that coming Friday.

13

LOVE JUNKIES
AND A PORN STAR PRUDE

A whale-ship was my Yale College.

—Ishmael (*Moby-Dick*)

There were far too many events during Sex Week 2010 to detail them all. Altogether there were more than thirty items on the schedule. Even in describing some of the most outrageous moments, I have passed over countless episodes that, in any other academic context, would be shocking. Only at Yale can ordinary porn in the classroom come to seem trivial in the face of the most extreme sexual images and agendas.

Throughout the week, students heard and saw just about everything. At one event, the Reverend Debra W. Haffner introduced herself as a "minister and a sexologist." As a university chaplain, she was scheduled to speak on sexuality, faith, and morality. I've heard of ministers who refuse to marry a couple if they are having premarital sex. But Hafner put a twist on this rule. She said she actually refuses to marry two people unless they *are* having premarital sex. You've heard of homophobia. I think Hafner has what you would call virginophobia—fear of the chaste.

During a panel called "Love Junkies," clinical sexologist Michael Rothenberg had students laughing when he told them how he once gave group therapy to a kindly grandmother and grandfather—and their sex slave. You see, Grandpa was a sadist. The slave girl was a masochist. Rothenberg described the pair's desires matter-of-factly: "He had a need to beat; and she had a need to be beaten." "Grandma," on the other hand, "was just going along for the ride."

It sounds like the makings of another happy polyamory story. But, surprisingly, Grandma developed problems in the relationship. When the couple hired Rothenberg to work on mending their marriage, Rothenberg decided to bring Grandma, Grandpa, and the sex slave in as a group for "family therapy." Maybe Grandma wasn't being sensitive enough to the needs of her husband and his slave girl.

After a presentation all about the female condom, I made the mistake of using the men's room right outside the classroom. When I entered the stall, I found a used condom of the male variety floating in the toilet, along with the discarded foil wrapper. I guess some student(s) couldn't wait to get back to the dorm to try out some of the things we had all been learning about that week.

On another occasion we heard about "The Do's and Don'ts of Dating in College" from a man called "Flyness," aka "Your Royal Flyness." He had written a book called *From MySpace to My Place: The Men's Guide to Snagging Women Online,* all about scoring chicks on the Internet. He claimed to have met more than five hundred women online, and to have gotten one of them into his apartment in "less than thirty minutes."

The main point of the talk seemed to be how to manipulate women into having sex. "Game," explained Flyness, "it's not about cheating. . . . Being a player isn't a bad thing if you're honest." He then cited pimps as an example of being honest. "Pimps, real pimps, not Hollywood pimps . . . they call it being 'true to the game.'"

Finally, His Royal Flyness moved on to give a little advice to the ladies on how to score a good man. But it turned out to be a tough order to fill. When he asked what guys are like at Yale, all the girls shouted back in unison, "Gay!"

I attended a presentation on the current global epidemic of child sex trafficking by a nonprofit group called LOVE146, which builds aftercare facilities for rescued victims. Students received information about how they could get involved in the struggle to prevent children from becoming victims of the multi-billion-dollar global sex trade. Unfortunately, there were only a few students in attendance.

The LOVE146 event was followed immediately by a much better attended event called "Red Light Rights," which featured a panel of pro-sex-work activists arguing on behalf of the sex trade. There was a lady named: Simone Valentino who explained how she got into such work. She described it as a natural progression: She started out working as an escort, but really didn't like it. She then tried Starbucks and the Home Depot, but the money wasn't good enough. Next she got into stripping, and then finally found her calling in the field of professional domination. "I've had clients who want to be beaten and tied up, one who was really into giantess worship. He would be on the floor and I would try to pretend I was stepping on him."

I was astonished during Q&A when one young girl in the audience said that she too wanted to work in the sex trade. I had never before met anyone at Yale who aspired to this particular line of work. You meet students who want to become doctors, lawyers, bankers—sure. But never this. The girl asked Simone for advice: "My biggest issue is like how to bring it up with family," she said. "My family is like Jewish mafia."

From her position at the front of the classroom Simone advised her: "For every family it's very different. You need to be very confident in the choices you make. . . . Hopefully it will be something that empowers you." Another panelist, named Will, jumped in, telling us how he had left a conservative home at the age of fifteen to become a gay prostitute. It wasn't always easy. The clients weren't always good, but the money was. "It was the best year of my life," he said.

As a musician, I spend a lot of time around creative people. Many of them dress in edgy clothes and some have piercings of various kinds. From time to time, I used to think that it might be cool to get a piercing of my own. But that was before I met a buzz-cut body-piercing artist named Elayne Angel, who gave a lecture at Yale on "Erotic Piercings." Elayne is the author of *The Piercing Bible.* We sat for an hour watching a slide show of Elayne's work. It's amazing what some people will do to their genitalia. When it comes to areas below the belt, most guys are instinctively protective of themselves. There's a reason guys wear protective cups on the football field. Yet there are apparently many people who set out deliberately to impale themselves with row upon row of rings and studs and chains. I never imagined there were so many ways to poke painful-looking holes in the most sensitive areas of one's body.

Some might say that mutilation is too strong a word for what Elayne does. But I'd say that when a guy has to use his finger to plug a hole in his penis so that the urine doesn't shoot out the wrong way, there is something wrong.

"Piercing is primal," explains Elayne, "a metaphor for sex itself." The idea of allowing my body to take on a literary form sounds lofty and transcendent. But if it takes a three-inch steel stud in the nether regions in order to get there, I just don't think I'm ready for transcendence.

"Virtually any piercing has the potential to arouse," Elayne tells us. But the only thing being aroused in me is fear, agony, and the instinctive urge to cover myself. In fact, I may never again be able to walk past a piercing parlor without breaking into a nervous fit.

Elayne tells us it ordinarily takes six to nine months for a nipple piercing to heal, "longer for women." She then showed us a series of images of botched genital piercings—a long lineup of labia rings gone bad and failed scrotum impalings. Elayne moves on to a close-up of some poor, foolish woman's mangled vagina piercing. "This woman was feeling shooting pains down her arms and legs."

Not all cases turn out so bad. A report published in the *American Journal of Obstetrics & Gynecology* found a positive correlation between vertical hood piercings and frequency and enjoyment of sexual contact—that is, if you manage to avoid losing sensation altogether, which Elayne said happens occasionally when things go bad. Elayne brings up a slide showing a vagina with no fewer than six piercings in it.

Elayne finishes by reviewing images of some of the most popular piercing techniques. Each one has its own cute name. You've got your Prince Albert piercing for the guys, and it is "the biggest bleeder of all." It involves going right through the urethra. You've got your garden-variety Triangle piercing, the Frenum piercing, and one called Jacob's Ladder. She shows a penis stuck through with a dozen or more bars.

You've got your Scrotum and Lorum piercings, your Pubic piercings. At this point, she shows us a scrotum with at least twenty piercings. Next she shows us a pair of big ugly testicles with barbells through them. There's a guy in the corner videotaping the entire presentation. But, personally, there are many things I will be glad never to see again.

You've got your more exotic European-sounding piercings, including the Guiche ("invented by men in the leather community") and a dainty little number called the Fourchette ("you may be asked to get on your hands and knees for this one"). Rounding out her list of popular male piercings, you've got your run-of-the-mill foreskin techniques, and then the more daring Ampallang and Apadravya. These names sound like they were borrowed from a pair of hideous monsters in Norse mythology. That's probably because the Ampallang and Apadravya really are monstrous, and involve piercing straight through the head of the penis.

Rounding out options for the ladies, Elayne mentions the ultra-rare Clitoral piercing. She figures she has done fewer than twenty of these in her career, explaining how "it can ruin a woman's sexual pleasure." She closes things out with a piercing named in honor of Princess Diana, her own invention, which involves piercing right through both sides of the clitoral hood.

One concerned student asks if all these metal protrusions might tear a condom—a very good question, it seems to me. "If you're using lubricant, there's no reason to think the condom would break," comes the answer.

"Piercings can improve your love life, improve your confidence," Elayne says. "But be careful, a male piercing can cause tooth chipping." If I have learned anything this week about sex, it's that maximum performance in bed requires extraordinary commitment, and a total willingness to practice and pierce and push oneself into new dimensions of sexual exercise. Darlinda told us how we could lean against a bed and force a dildo down our throats in order to overcome the gag reflex. Elayne helped us understand that we should also be sure to take out a hefty dental insurance policy.

Finally, Elayne issues the ultimate challenge, something called "play piercing," where lovers actually pierce one another during sex. In the privacy of your bedroom, you are free to explore this brave new perforated world. "It's your own erotic adventure." Elayne explains the concept further: "It's to some extent more about a power play between partners." I think I understand what she means. After all, who wouldn't enjoy the rush of power that comes from stabbing someone in the genitals? Sure, amateur genital piercing might sound dangerous, but that is all part of the thrill. "You want to definitely get training first."

On that note, Elayne Angel finished her presentation, and went off to sign copies of her book at the Yale bookstore. Nice to know the Yale bookstore has copies of *The Piercing Bible* on hand for convenient reference for students who want to spice things up with amateur genital piercing.

* * *

Sometimes wisdom comes from the most unexpected places—in this case it came from a gay porn star. I attended a panel discussion on the porn business, consisting of five or six porn performers and directors, among them Sasha Grey—perhaps the best-known female porn performer in the country at the time. Also on the panel was a performer called Joanna Angel and another named Buck Angel. For some reason a lot of people in the sex industry like the stage name "Angel."

Buck, I discovered, is actually married to Elayne Angel, the genital-piercing lady. And Buck used to be a lady too, before he wasn't—but now it's getting confusing. Let me back up for a moment.

The porn-biz panel took place in the same cathedral-like lecture hall where Darlinda had given us her Lip Tricks lecture a few days before. Buck arrived wearing a ski cap and a hoodie. Later he stripped down to a muscle shirt, revealing a pair of hefty shoulders beneath.

Despite his broad shoulders, Buck isn't your typical porn star stud. Having begun life female, Buck underwent gender-reassignment surgery in the nineties. But he left one key area unmodified. Ultimately, he decided to parlay his hybrid anatomy into a career in porn. Today, Buck bills himself as the world's only female-to-male transsexual porn star. He performs with both men and women, but his work is generally marketed as gay porn.

As you can imagine, it's not often that Buck Angel comes off as the biggest prude in the room. He is, after all, a porn performer. But during this event, the issue of the lack of condom use in mainstream (heterosexual) porn came up. Buck, as a member of the gay porn industry, took the opportunity to confront the other porn stars on hand about the importance of using condoms during on-screen performances.

In gay porn—the world Buck inhabits—the ghost of the eighties AIDS crisis looms large. Among the largest gay production companies, condom use has long been standard practice. On the other hand, in mainstream porn, condoms are almost never used, despite the fact that one in four performers test positive for a sexually transmitted disease each year.

In February of 2011, the crisis of disease in the industry took on a mystical quality when about two hundred attendees of a charity fund-raiser at the Playboy Mansion were suddenly struck with a mysterious illness. Symptoms included fever, chills, and malaise. The whole episode brought to mind the biblical plagues of Egypt.

Around the same time, the industry-run STD testing clinic closed abruptly after yet another actor tested positive for HIV. In Los Angeles—the epicenter of the porn industry—city officials finally proposed a new ordinance that would require the use of condoms on all sets. It is remarkable that it took more than three dozen HIV cases in just a little over a decade for the government to intervene.

I think the way porn companies exploit performers is deplorable. But part of me wants to say: If performers willingly take such risks, then who am I to stop them? However, there is collateral damage to consider in the form of the young people who watch porn and learn from it. Porn production companies shouldn't be allowed to increase the risk to kids by profiting from condom-free sex. The statistics for HIV and other STDs in the porn industry are deeply troubling. But there is one statistic that neither the Adult Industry Medical Health Care Foundation nor the Los Angeles Health Department can produce: No one knows how many young people end up with a sexually transmitted disease each year because they imitate what they have learned by watching condom-free porn.

That is just the point "the prude," Buck Angel, made during the Yale symposium. Buck surprised the other porn producers and actors on the panel by turning to ask them directly, "Do you feel it is irresponsible, as a pornographer, to show films without using condoms? I do."

This question produced a barrage of evasive responses: "I always have them on the set as an option," said one producer. "It's a Pandora's box of issues. . . . We'll be out of work," another panelist advised. "It's a decision you have to make as a director" and "I feel pretty safe." The chorus of voices answered everything but yes or no to Buck's question.

Buck didn't let up. "Don't you feel it's important for people who are watching our films to see us using condoms? Because people are kind of stupid sometimes, and they just think that it's totally okay if they see us [without them]."

I think the other panelists were fed up with Buck by this point. Onstage, there was a lot of throat clearing and shifting in the seats. The tension was palpable. But none of those porn producers had a good answer for Buck's question.

The next day, Sasha Grey was scheduled to make an appearance by herself. She was riding high on a wave of newly found fame at the time. And she had started to cross over from simply being big in the porn world to having some notoriety in mainstream pop culture. She had a book coming out. She had appeared in music videos for the Smashing Pumpkins and the Roots. *Rolling Stone* had recently done a big spread on her. The film director Steven Soderbergh had cast her in a mainstream film, albeit as a call girl. Many girls get into porn hoping to transition into mainstream Hollywood film. Almost none find anything like the fame and fortune they hope for. There are many thousands of porn performers, only a handful of porn "stars." Grey's success is truly an exception.

It's fifteen minutes after the scheduled start time and Sasha is running late. A student gets up and announces, "Sasha is about to come over, so get excited! She's even more beautiful in person!"

At this lecture, unlike most others at Yale, everyone seems to be sitting toward the front of the room. There are definitely more guys than girls in the audience. Some are geeks; some are jocks; others are just ordinary dudes. I browse the event's written program and it says something about Sasha's keen intelligence. Somehow I don't think that is what most of these guys will see in her. Most of them will be too busy thinking about the last time they saw her in one of her films.

Tonight the female body will almost certainly overwhelm the

female mind as a focus of student interest. It begs the question, What does Yale want from women? Does it want their breasts, their vulvas, their Lip Tricks? Or does it want their brains? How can a university that presents sex workers as leading authorities on sexuality, with no other real counterexamples, be the same one that repeatedly affirms its commitment to achieving gender parity on the university faculty?

Sasha arrives wearing black pants and shoes, and a little white button-down sweater. She looks very much like any of the girls in the audience. At twenty-one years of age, she is actually younger than many of the students present. That's what strikes me. She has been working in porn since she turned eighteen, and has performed in hundreds of scenes. She is a veteran in the business and perhaps its biggest star. Yet she is so young.

Sasha gained notoriety, partly, by pushing porn to more aggressive extremes. Millions watch her on film. Yet, here on this little stage, she looks nervous. She tells us how she was very conservative about sex as a teenager, and was almost seventeen before she became sexually active. In the course of a relationship with an older boyfriend, she got involved in BDSM (bondage, domination, sadism, and masochism). Eventually, she moved to L.A. and got into porn, with the intention of "breaking stereotypes, [and] breaking molds."

Most of the talk unfolds in a Q&A format. The moderator chooses from a stack of questions students turned in on note cards. One student asks if she considers herself a feminist. Answer: Sasha feels that the meaning of feminism has become too broad and watered down.

Another student asks if there is anything she wouldn't do on camera? Answer: She draws the line at pedophilia, bestiality, and scat.

A third student asks her about her views on nuclear weapons. "At heart," she answers, "I'm a hippie pacifist." Students applaud, then fall silent. "But it sucks because some people don't want to back down. . . . It's hard to tell blue-blooded Americans to stay home." She's referring to America's wars in the Middle East now. "I'm proud to be an American. I'm proud that I can have sex on camera, that I can do those things and not be stoned, and not be killed. And I have almost equal rights with men."

A couple of students have written in asking if she wants to have children someday. Sasha replies that she does. "I obviously will not be performing in adult films then. I will not perform on camera for a year to make sure my body is healthy." Without being prompted directly, she answers the question that must have been on the minds of those who asked the original question: Has she thought about how her career will affect her kids someday? "I don't know," she says. "No, I haven't fully thought it out because I don't know, honestly." She talks about how she envisions her life in five years. She wants to leave L.A., get a dog, find time for traveling and writing, make a normal life for herself, and start a family.

Many of the sex industry speakers who had given talks at Yale had struck me as disingenuous. But I didn't feel that way about Sasha. Listening to her describe this idyllic life she dreamed of, with the house, the two kids, and the dog, I felt nothing but a kind of sadness for her. And I wasn't really even sure why. Maybe it was because she seemed like she could have been just another student in the room, like she could have been one of my friends or classmates. Maybe it was because I doubted her domestic dream would ever really come true. And although she willingly chose to be in the kind of work she was in, and she had been unusually successful financially, I couldn't help feeling that the cost to her, years from now, would be far more than she could now reckon.

After the talk I met Sasha onstage for a brief interview. I asked her what she hoped students would take away from her talk. She thought for a moment. "It's about freedom and confidence," she answered. "People my age are uncomfortable with their sexuality and I want to change that. Ignorance breeds fear. The more you learn, the more you're aware of yourself. If we had better sex ed in this country there would be less teen pregnancy and a lower STD rate."

She knew how to do PR, that's for sure. Despite the rote, public-service-announcement-style answer she had given me, I wasn't annoyed. I was still too busy feeling sad for her.

I thanked her for her time, shook her hand, and wished her luck. I was struck in that moment by how petite she was. Her hand was tiny. For someone with such a fierce and extreme reputation in porn, she was altogether unimposing in person. At six three I towered over her. She couldn't have weighed more than a hundred pounds. She spoke to me with the same kind of gentle awkwardness I might expect from any of my female classmates upon meeting for the first time. Up close she looked even younger than she had before—like a teenager, really.

About a year later, she announced she was retiring from the porn business. Nevertheless, images last forever. I wonder if she'll ever really be able to leave her past life behind.

I hope Sasha gets that house someday, away from L.A., with the dog, and with something like a happy ending.

The event is over. I look around the great hall once more. A porn star has lectured students in this room for the second time in as many days. High on the walls above me hang rows of old, dark, faded paintings—portraits of the white-haired princes of Yale's distant past. The old portraits are cased in heavy, leafy, golden frames. The canvases are sagging and rippled by humidity and age. Who are these men? Old forgotten professors. There was a time when Yale professors were considered important enough to have their portraits painted. Now their faded and wrinkled faces gaze down through years of dirt, grime, and neglect. Next to the paintings, giant scarlet drapes extend toward the floor like the dead professors' tattered raiment.

The old Yale men have faded away. And the Yale they knew has faded with them. They must have considered themselves intelligent, progressive men. But progress went places they never envisioned. Would this university be recognizable to them now?

Above me I see a muraled ceiling depicting what looks like four men rowing a boat. I can make out a lion and a tree and lots of ornate patterns, all quite faded—more signs of humidity, neglect, time. What is the purpose of a grand hall like this one, if not to remind students of their connection to a long, grand history of human learning? Students are supposed to walk into halls like these and be awed—to realize that the past holds lessons that should not be forgotten. But today, the university is increasingly unmoored from the past, and from its responsibility to preserve and seek truth. Divorced from itself, from its history. A room like this no longer has any meaning here.

One hundred years ago, Yale was just stepping into a new age of science and progressivism. Facts trumped values. The facts—the concrete knowledge of the material world—were supposed to lead us toward a kinder, more enlightened, and more equitable future. Shedding the restraints of "primitive religion" and "superstition," we were supposed to have progress. And here at last we have our progress.

The old guard conceived of Yale as a temple of human reason. They never saw Sasha Grey coming. Through the veil of their dilapidated portraits, these men sit in perpetual torment, looking down on the Yale they created. They are a cloud of witnesses to all that Yale has become. They had faith in an enlightened tomorrow, resplendent with the fruits of man's innate goodness. They saw the great potential of unfettered man. But they were naïve. When mankind became unfettered, the base things of the world flourished, and spoiled their bright Hegelian tomorrow. The beautiful, orderly future they hoped for was replaced by the stench and stain of feces and semen on the face of a young girl. A XXX peep show came alive within the very walls of the temple they built.

Today Yale gives equal weight to seemingly any form of expression, no matter how base or juvenile. There was a time when pornified sex education would have been considered irrelevant to or even counter to the mission of the university. Where is that sense of mission now?

I look around the auditorium one last time. The question of why we are here is so hard to answer.

14

THE NAKED PROFESSOR

Aboard an eastbound transcontinental plane we have Flash
Gordon, Yale graduate and world-renowned polo player . . .
— *Flash Gordon*, inaugural comic strip,
January 7, 1934

Yale is perhaps the only university in the world where you can show up to class and find your instructor naked. These days, professors often complain how hard it is to get students to pay attention. Students come to class with all kinds of electronic gizmos: portable music players, laptop computers, iPads, smart phones, and any number of other gadgets to keep them distracted. So if you are a professor, you've got to be pretty exciting to keep students tuned in to the lecture. This must be why someone came up with the idea of lecturing in the nude. There's nothing like live nudity to pull students away from their Twittering and Facebooking, I say.

But let me back up for a moment. Back in the 1990s politicians were obsessed with the idea of getting "a computer in every classroom." Billions and billions of dollars later, every six-year-old Tom, Dick, and Jane had a dusty beige box in the corner where the chalkboard, the abacus, and the pencil sharpener used to be.

It was a bad idea.

Now we've got millions of kids who can text, e-mail, and update their social network status at lightning speed; but none of them can spell. And forget about adding double digits without the aid of a calculator. Elementary students show up at school with Internet-enabled phones and they are buzzing and flashing all through class, and no one even knows what the teacher is saying.

On the other hand, if you can at least teach kids to read and give them a basic knowledge of mathematics, technology can be very useful in the educational environment. For instance, I've always had terrible handwriting. In college, I started out taking lecture notes on paper. I had stacks of spiral-bound notebooks, with indecipherable ballpoint scrawl littering every page. I would open them up at the end of the term when it came time to study for a final exam, and it was a lucky day if ever I could read a single one of the great insights I had written down in class weeks before. Then, during my last couple of years, I switched to typing notes on a laptop computer. At last, I could actually read my notes. On the downside, I then discovered that most of my lecture notes were not all that insightful.

Once I started bringing a computer to class, I made some rules for myself. I tried to avoid checking the home page of the *New York Times* during class. I also tried to avoid checking my e-mail, because I found it very distracting to receive opportunities in broken English from troubled members of the Nigerian royal family, promising quick riches if only I would help them out, when at that moment I was actually supposed to be learning something about the Peloponnesian War or the absolute magnitude of pulsars. Studies have shown that when students study with laptops or e-readers, rather than old-fashioned textbooks, they comprehend less. I often recall looking out over a large lecture hall and beholding a sea of blue-and-white Facebook pages on the computer screens of my fellow students. I suppose they were typing status updates like: *OMG! Pericles for the win!!*

Enter the naked lecture! With all the distractions young people have today, I guess it was only a matter of time before someone tried showing a little skin in order to get students' attention. It makes sense. Professors have to compete with the Internet, which we all know is littered with porn. It may seem like a desperate measure. But when instructors go nude it just shows that much more commitment to teaching. Baring it all for the sake of education—it implies a certain noble abandonment to the cause.

As far as I know, Yale has no official policy either for or against lecturing au naturel. Most Yale professors wear what you might call "business casual" attire—slacks, polo shirts, tweed sport coats, loafers. Others have a habit of dressing sloppily in jeans, T-shirts, or even sandals. (For some reason science professors seem to be the sloppiest.) On the other end of the spectrum, I had a few professors who never showed up for class without a coat and tie. With very few exceptions, I would have found it extraordinarily unpleasant to see any of my teachers unclothed. But times are changing, and the exigencies of education are changing along with the times. For this fast-blinking, eye-twitching, buzzed-out, Twittered, cloud-computing, ADD- and ADHD-afflicted, and Ritalin-juiced generation, live nudity is the final educational frontier. As the final days of Sex Week at Yale 2010 approached, I was about to witness what I believe was the very first naked lecture in the history of Yale University.

It sounds like the opening scene of a low-budget porn movie: The teacher saunters up to the blackboard. Next she calls for a few student "volunteers," and puts them in handcuffs. Then the teacher decides she needs to "get more comfortable," so she slips off her tights, and before you know it she is standing bare-chested in front of the entire class.[1]

But this story isn't fiction.

The teacher, in this case, was a redheaded porn star from San Francisco who goes by the name Madison Young. Young made several appearances that week. Just the day before, she had put on an erotic "rope bondage" performance with the help of another porn star. It involved her being tied up and suspended upside down by her feet while a lot of swooning music played in the background. It wasn't by any means the most extreme event of the week. But, for some reason, this was the one event that Yale officials would not allow to be held on campus. At the last minute it was moved to a frat house one block away.

A crowd of students gathered in the yard, along with a few curious bystanders, to watch. Young's partner tied her up and suspended her over the front porch, and she hung there, dangling in her underwear. Across the street an alarmed passerby shouted, "Why are you doing that!?" The pendulous Ms. Young shouted back, "Because I liiiiiiiiiike it!"

Pretty soon the cops arrived. They were kind enough to wait for a break in the performance to go up and make sure Ms. Young was not being bound against her will. Then they stepped back and enjoyed the rest of the show.

It's very hard to stay outside for a lengthy period of time in one's underwear in New Haven in the dead of a February winter. Ms. Young later reported that she lost feeling in all her appendages during the performance. As her limbs grew gradually more blue and lifeless, she must have sensed the crowd's growing concern. She kept shouting, "I'm having fun!" at random intervals.

The next day, Ms. Young was scheduled to give a lecture called BDSM 101. As I entered the classroom where the event was to be held, I passed a table of free condoms by the door. There was also a pile of brightly colored boxers and panties, free for the taking, courtesy of Sex Week at Yale's corporate partnership with the American Apparel clothing company. (American Apparel has been in trouble several times over running ads featuring scantily clad girls who appear to be underage.) One student held up a pair of briefs that were neon orange. It looked like something you would wear around a nudist colony during hunting season.

I passed on the free underwear (I don't look good in orange) and took a seat near the back. I noticed the president of the Yale Political Union in the row in front of me, along with a couple other students I knew.

Room WLH 207 was familiar to me. I had once attended a class on international relations in that very room. But I was about to receive instruction in relations of a very different kind.

I look up to see our speaker is about to begin her talk. The first thing Ms. Young does when she reaches the podium is ask all of us to shed our coats and extra layers. "I want you to be comfortable," she says. "BDSM is very much about feeling comfortable in your own body." She takes off her shoes and starts doing a yogalike breathing exercise. The class does the exercise along with her, raising and lowering their arms with each breath. Suddenly Ms. Young lets out a screeching, catlike meow, which startles everyone in the room.

She is here to instruct us in the BDSM basics, and she wastes no time getting started. "The B stands for bondage. It can be hand-cuffs. It can be zip ties. It can be rope—anything that's restraining you. It can be neckties.

"The D is for discipline and dominance. . . . Dominance is more about power.

"S stands for submissive, often associated with service—dominant and slave, a teacher and a schoolboy.

"S&M stands for sadism and masochism. Sadists give sensation, or what might be referred to as pain.

"Is everyone in here eighteen or over?" It is an important question because she's about fire up the video projector. "If you are not over eighteen, would you please raise your hand?"

When the video turns on I see an image of Ms. Young herself, completely naked and bound with chains. A man on-screen begins lashing her with a whip. Red welts are visible across Young's torso. And I have to avert my eyes as the man continues to beat her. In between blows I hear him taunting her and hurling insults. He orders her to repeat the insults while he beats her; and she does.

Suddenly, Ms. Young speaks up. "The first couple of minutes are the most painful," she informs us.

When the video is over, she asks for a volunteer. A female student comes up, and Ms. Young binds her hands with a zip tie. She begins to lead the girl around the room, her hands still bound. Students applaud. "If you want to make it a little more difficult, you can tie the hands around the back," she adds.

She explains how to integrate various household items into BDSM. "Clothespins are good. I've had like twenty-five on my face before. You'll soon start to drool, which can be very humiliating."

She pauses for a moment in the front of the room, and bends over to remove her tights. She puts on one of the pairs of underwear that had been sitting by the door when I entered the room. Next, she sits up on a desk and begins to pin clothespins on her thighs. "These are also great labia clamps," she adds.

She calls for more assistants. A male student comes up, and, following Ms. Young's instructions, he begins to fasten the pins on her inner thighs. "You want to find the fleshy area of the thigh."

She gets the whole room involved. "Pass them around. Maybe you want to put them on your arm and test out the sensation. Maybe put them on the person next to you. . . . And I guess we are allowed to show nipples so feel free."

I notice a few people taking pictures. Meanwhile, the student volunteer is standing between Ms. Young's legs, attempting to fasten the clothespins. At first, he is too tentative. "Put it on with an intention," she tells him.

The clothespins are fastened up and down both thighs and attached to lay strings. And she asks a pair of students to take a string each. She takes a deep breath and raises her hands. The students wait for her direction. At her prompting they yank the strings and tear away the clothespins from her body. She exhales and smiles. "That was wonderful."

Once the volunteers return to their seats, Ms. Young removes the straps of her dress, revealing her naked breasts to the class. Immediately, she begins attaching the strings and pinching devices to her breasts and nipples.

I never saw who ended up tearing the clothespins from her breasts. At that point I decided to take my leave.

Young remained topless for a full twenty minutes after I left, I later learned. One can only guess what other demonstrations she carried out with students during that time.

Next door, in room 207, a very different event is already under way. It is a talk called "A Philosophical Defense of the Sexual Counterrevolution," sponsored by the Anscombe Society at Yale, a group of conservative undergraduates, most of them, that was active on campus at the time.

The society's goal is to promote premarital abstinence on purely rational, nonreligious grounds, and, more generally, to defend against some of the excesses of the sexual culture on campus. This kind of thing is a hard sell at Yale. I find only about a dozen students in attendance.

The speaker, David Schaengold, starts with an anecdote from Tom Wolfe's book *I Am Charlotte Simmons* about an unhappy girl who gets caught up in the loveless sexual culture at an elite university. Schaengold argues that after the sexual revolution, consent became the sole measure of what is moral. But he claims the consent-based system isn't working for women. "One in four women will experience what they call 'not quite consensual sex' in college. We used to call it rape."

If we want to improve our sexual culture, Schaengold argues, we need to do more than just talk about consent. "Can we move from saying what is permissible to saying what is right and what is good?" he asks. "Some kinds of sexual acts are incompatible with human dignity."

At that very moment, the beating, binding and pinching, and live nudity continue on the other side of the classroom wall.

I'm struck by the irony of my situation. Here I am, listening to a talk on chastity and "human dignity." Meanwhile, only a few feet away, on the other side of the wall, Madison Young is standing naked before a roomful of Yale students, while volunteers inflict pain on her for the instructional benefit of the class.*

The office of Yale's president is directly across the street, a couple hundred feet away, almost close enough to hear the lashes and the blows.

In the fall of 2009, after an e-mail circulated among students entitled "Preseason Scouting Report," which included photographs of newly admitted freshman girls, and ranked them on the basis of their sexual desirability, Mary Miller, the dean of Yale College, published a letter to students calling the incident an "assault on our community values."

Given the Yale administration's outspoken disapproval of such incidents, one would think Yale's "community values" would be affronted by images of women being stripped, chained, and sexually brutalized by men. But it isn't the case. I know because I asked Dean Miller myself.

In an e-mail message, I asked Dean Miller whether she thought Sex Week received adequate oversight from the university administration. I also asked her whether she felt it was appropriate for students to participate in sadomasochistic exercises with guest lecturers in Yale classrooms. Finally, I asked whether she was concerned that such episodes might send the wrong message to students about Yale's attitude toward sexual violence.

I received the following boilerplate response through a university spokesman:

---

* Nude photos from this event are now available on a pay-per-view porn Web site. Thus university administrators have unwittingly allowed a Yale classroom to become the functional equivalent of a commercial porn photography studio. Classy, isn't it?

Sex Week At Yale (SWAY) is a student organized and student produced series of events. SWAY is not a registered student organization and is not sponsored, sanctioned or funded by Yale College or Yale University. While the administration may find aspects of SWAY distasteful or offensive, Yale's policies on free expression permit students to invite the widest range of speakers, politicians, writers and performers to campus.[2]

In other words, live sadomasochistic performances and the screening of violent pornography fall under the university's definition of "free expression."

Sex Week at Yale was largely funded by corporate sponsors. However, the university's claim that it provided no funding for Sex Week isn't entirely accurate. A student who served as the executive director for Sex Week 2010 told me that Yale provided grant funds to publish printed materials for the week's events. Furthermore, I would argue that providing free classroom space, as well as paying to keep the heat and the lights on, amounts to a kind of sponsorship.

The university has lent its resources, its name, and its legitimacy to corporate interests in the sex industry. By doing so, Yale has cultivated a sexually degrading environment for women. Administrators may call it academic freedom; I call it academic negligence.

University administrators have sought to distance themselves publicly from Sex Week's content. Harvey Kliman, a faculty member in the medical school, told me the university preferred faculty members not to be linked to Sex Week in any official way, although he said he maintained an unofficial advisory role. With respect to Sex Week's controversial content, he described the attitude of senior administrators as "don't ask, don't tell."

Yale administrators pretended they weren't involved. Meanwhile, they officially approved the use of Yale classrooms for each individual event. In the case of at least one event on the schedule—the bondage suspension performance—I learned that Dean Miller was personally involved in the decision to deny access to Yale facilities. Every other talk, presentation, and performance that took place on campus during Sex Week, including Madison Young's nude S&M lecture, received prior approval from the university.

I don't think it's good enough for Yale's leaders to claim ignorance, or to justify themselves by citing free expression. If students tried to organize a "We hate black people week" or an "Asians are idiots week," the university would never allow it; and that's as it should be. Why, then, would they host the equivalent of "Women are sex objects week" without reservation?

After my magazine story on Sex Week was published, the university took a lot of heat from concerned alumni, especially older alumni who had no idea about what had been going on at Yale in recent years. They had been sending in their annual donations to the university for decades, never suspecting that they were paying to keep the lights on for Darlinda's deep-throating extravaganza. I have a feeling that when the next round of solicitations went out, some of those alumni dropped the letters into the trash unopened.

Like most universities, Yale is always asking its graduates for money. In addition to mailings, they sometimes hold special fundraising soirees at swanky hotels, and the president of the university shows up and shakes hands with alumni, and butters them up for more donations. I heard that at one of these events, a concerned alumnus who had read the article confronted President Levin about what he had read was taking place in Yale's classrooms. I was told that the president's response was something to the effect of: Kids will be kids.

I disagree with President Levin. Madison Young is no kid. However, she does enjoy playing games with her students.

While many students embrace Sex Week, others resent the hypersexualized atmosphere it promotes on campus. I asked my classmate Margaret, a Yale senior at the time, what she thought about it. "It is just pretty degrading," she told me. "It just seems to rob many things of dignity. Obviously as a woman in particular, objectification is more prevalent this week. . . . The whole week seems to just demystify everything and dereverence everything."

Margaret also said she thinks Sex Week promotes unhealthy views of women. "Just having this message bombarded: 'This is how you get it; this is how you should get it'—that naturally makes women feel more like an object. And if you know that all the guys are going to these talks just to learn how they can get pleasure, then you know that that's how they're going to look at you in a relationship."

Yale is not simply being permissive; it is pushing a specific sexual agenda. Another female friend of mine put it this way: "It's not Sex Week," she said. "It's *Have* Sex Week." I think it could just as easily be called "Sexism Week."

Over the past decade, university administrators have played willing host to the biennial pornification of Yale. Yale hasn't merely allowed the screening of porn. Yale has played host to the promotion and distribution of porn—not in the dorm room, but in the classroom itself. In both 2008 and 2010, I witnessed volunteers, guest lecturers, and, in a few cases, even professors passing out vibrators and pornographic DVDs to students.

While some students are comfortable with that agenda, others, like Margaret, feel marginalized by Yale's tacit endorsement of representations of women and sex that they find deeply degrading.

I wondered why Yale's leaders were so tone-deaf to the predicament of young women on campus. After I e-mailed the dean, I also e-mailed about half a dozen female Yale professors, most of them well-known feminists, and asked them whether they thought it was appropriate for the university to allow porn to be marketed and distributed at campus events. Not one of them chose to answer my question. Instead, one of them alerted the public affairs office, and warned them that I was asking questions. Even the reputed feminists on the Yale faculty seemed indifferent to the effects that graphic depictions of sexual violence against women might have on students and on the campus culture. How could this be?

I happen to believe that many of Yale's faculty members are, in fact, troubled by some of the extreme sexual material appearing in Yale's classrooms. Perhaps some senior administrators, such as Dean Miller, are as well. But they seem to believe that their commitment to academic freedom prevents them from setting ethical standards when it comes to sexual material in the classroom. They wouldn't tolerate racism. But sexism gets a free pass so long as it comes packaged in an edgy, kinky guise.

I suppose it's theoretically possible that all of Yale's senior administrators are secret bondage and kink enthusiasts, that they all have sex dungeons in their basements stocked full of leather and chains, and that they are collectively conspiring to indoctrinate Yale students into some weird sex cult. But, on the whole, they just don't strike me as, well—edgy enough for such things. Instead, they simply strike me as permissive to a fault.

Academic freedom is a wonderful and necessary thing. But it has its limits. If a professor decides to defecate on his desk during class, is that protected by academic freedom? If he wants to spend the whole term showing students television reruns of *The Fresh Prince of Bel-Air* instead of teaching what he is being paid to teach, is that also protected by academic freedom? Of course not. With freedom comes responsibility.

Not every idea, image, or expression is worthy of the university's sanction. Either Yale's leaders have been afraid to speak up when academic standards aren't being met, or else they actually believe that live sex acts fall within the bounds of acceptable classroom behavior. I honestly don't know for certain which category they fall into. But either way, it's a sad state of affairs.

PART FIVE

The Moral Void: *How I*

came to understand Yale's decline

as an inevitable consequence

of its abandonment of higher purpose

15

YALE WITHOUT GOD

I was rather literary in college—one year I wrote a series of very solemn and obvious editorials for the "Yale News."— and now I was going to bring back all such things into my life and become again that most limited of all specialists, the "well-rounded man."

—Nick Carraway (*The Great Gatsby*)

You enter Yale overawed by the place. You leave feeling like you own the place. I walked the halls at Yale as a senior, a veteran, knowing every inch, every sound, every smell. I had mastered the place. At any moment, anywhere on campus, I knew where to find the nearest quiet spot to read, where to go to find the printers that wouldn't jam, or even where I could likely get a free lunch swipe in the cafeteria if I had wanted to. I moved busily from one class to the next, nodding to friends along the way, always with an agenda, a task at hand, a purpose, and a goal. I had a Yale degree to earn.

After the experience is over, you realize how extraordinary it was. You got to spend years doing nothing but reading books and sitting down in rooms full of other young people talking about ideas. You had few responsibilities of any kind. Others cooked for you, and even cleaned for you. You lived like a prince. Your sole purpose was to bask in the pleasures of the mind. And you got to do it all side by side with friends.

All the while, you foolishly thought of nothing but the day when you would graduate and it would all be over.

Each year, during spring semester, I would notice a change in all my friends who were seniors. They would acquire a certain anxious look—a low-grade panic would set in. It was as if they suddenly realized that all they had lived for thus far in their lives—the great educational task in which they had striven and excelled since they were five years old—was coming to a conclusion. And the great question—What next?—hung like the sword of Damocles above their heads.

As I neared the end, I wanted to make sense of all that I had worked so hard to achieve. The worth of that Yale degree seemed unquestionable to me in the beginning as I struggled to gain admission. It seemed self-evident. The joy of being accepted, and the powerful sense of validation I felt after getting into Yale, were like waves that carried me through years of sleep-deprived study. I never questioned if it was worth it.

Somewhere inside, I think, I had been driven by a need to prove—to myself and others—that I belonged among the best. Only, now I knew all too well that not all Yalies are admitted because they are "the best." To be sure, Yale students are, on average, extremely intelligent. But, on the margins, some get in because their parents or grandparents are alumni, or because a family member gave a big donation to the school, or because they had some political connection, or simply because one of their parents is famous. Many of our nation's brightest students choose colleges that are less renowned, and yet come away with equally good educations. Today, I look back with suspicion on our national obsession with prestigious colleges, knowing full well that I participated heart and soul in that obsession.

At the end, I was in a much more objective state of mind. It seemed implausible to me that anything like Yale—with its fourteen dining halls—even existed on a planet where more than half the people struggle to feed themselves on a given day. It seemed incredible that Yale had a library system with more than 13 million books, when a fourth of the world cannot even read. Yale was an extraordinary experience in so many ways. I had given years of my life just to have a chance to have that experience. On the days when Yale was at its best, I never stopped to ask why.

But there were other times when the question was unavoidable. Every blow-job seminar, every masturbation how-to session, every tip I heard on how to stimulate the anus—each of these seemed to be mocking the greatest achievement of my life up to that point, which was that somehow I, a homeschooled dropout with a GED, had clawed and scratched and fought my way into Yale. I had come out with a degree that said what? That I'm a reasonably smart guy, ambitious, a winner?

Yale had been like some kind of drug. It was a blast, and then I came down with a crash. On a personal level, I began to wonder why I had so obsessively pursued the goal of that Yale degree with such unquestioning fervor. What was the meaning of all that toil? Of that diploma that now hung on my wall? It was a piece of paper, with Latin inscriptions I couldn't even read surrounding my name, encased in a $15 frame from Walmart.

Yet, at the same time, that paper still feels precious to me, even now. I love much of what Yale stands for. I love its beauty. I love the feeling of being linked to a long line of influential people—the makers of America's history. I loved being surrounded by so many extraordinary and bright young fellow students—the makers of America's future. For all it has meant to me from the day I won a place among its ranks, I owe a debt of gratitude to Yale. For the rest of my life, my identity will be bound up in it. I will always consider myself a Yale man. Nevertheless, I experienced many things that were unworthy of the place. The ambivalence I feel toward the education I received at Yale is a reflection of the moral ambivalence of those who run the place today.

People sometimes ask me what it was like at Yale, if I would choose it all over again, or if I would recommend it to another.

The truth is, the place was magical. But in order to experience the magic you have to swallow the occasional poison pill. Hopefully it won't kill you. Hopefully it won't corrupt your soul.

To navigate Yale successfully, one must glean pearls from the mire. In this way it's not unlike any other university. Only the pearls are more lovely, and the mire more vile. I've seen some who wade through the ideological sludge and come out all the stronger for it. But the big moral vacuum at Yale sucks many others right up. Its leaders are afflicted with ethical apathy. They have allowed sleaze peddlers to stand in a place where, by right, great poets, scientists, and statesmen should be. A distinguished university like Yale shouldn't be so morally hollow. By all rights, it ought to be an altogether uplifting place. Out of my great love for Yale flows a desire to expose the flagrant educational irresponsibility I found there.

Despite Yale's present-day shortcomings, I look up at that diploma on the wall—$15 frame and all—and smile. Yale may be a messed-up place, but it's my place. As it turns out, the occasion on which I received that diploma—graduation weekend—got me thinking a lot about how Yale arrived at such a place of moral emptiness to begin with. There were several VIPs on campus that weekend. One in particular surprised me. I had expected to see some celebrities and big-name politicians hanging around. Yale being Yale, it's full of privileged and well-connected people. But the last person I expected to show up at graduation was God.

Graduation at Yale is an elaborate three-day affair. It's a nonstop parade of nostalgia. There are ceremonies, soirees, dinners, and speeches to attend. It was all terrific—even the speeches. Under normal circumstances, commencement speeches have to be right up there with funeral wakes among the most boring activities known to man. But mine was an exception. The author Christopher Buckley did the honors on my big day, and, to my great surprise, he managed to be genuinely funny and touching.

Buckley's best-known book is his novel *Thank You for Smoking*.

It was an appropriate theme for the occasion. Normally, smoking is frowned upon at Yale, and the tobacco industry is widely considered to be evil. But, during commencement weekend, things are different. Traditionally, the university gives every graduating student a clay pipe and a bag full of smoking tobacco. At the end of Class Day exercises, you light up your pipe, smoke a little bit, then smash your pipe on the ground. Thereby you symbolically say good-bye to your youth forever.

Other than the good speech, and the aromatic tobacco, I was surprised most of all by the religious elements that were part of graduation. Yale isn't exactly a hotbed of religious fundamentalism. Normally, overt expressions of faith are quite rare. But graduation weekend began with a baccalaureate service, which included scripture readings and several prayers. I almost fell out of my chair when we began singing a hymn to God in the middle of the main ceremony on commencement day, with the president of the university standing right up there onstage. The song we sang was called "Thy Praise Alone." It was first featured in Yale commencement ceremonies in the year 1718, and it has been sung in every century since. The verses read thus:

Thy praise alone, O Lord, doth reign
In Zion thine own hill:
Their vows to thee they do maintain,
And evermore fulfill.

For that thou dost their pray'rs still hear
And dost thereto agree:
Thy people all both far and near
With trust shall come to thee.

Of thy great justice hear, O God,
Our health of thee doth rise;
The hope of all the earth abroad,
And the sea-coasts likewise.

We dedicate our lives anew that
Light and truth will shine
Throughout the world, O God, we pray,
To all of humankind.

I enjoyed the hymn. But I began to wonder if I had accidentally
shown up at Bob Jones University that morning. As the song came
to a close, I started to panic. Then I looked down into my graduation packet and found an environmentalist pamphlet called the
"Green Graduates Guide," which Yale had distributed to all its
graduates. At Yale, environmentalism functions as the unofficial
religion for the nonreligious majority. Only when I saw those reassuring words about "living sustainably" across the front of the
bright green pamphlet was I able to rest assured that—yes—I really
was at Yale.

The religious element of commencement is, for the most part,
simply a ceremonial gesture, a wink and nod to tradition. Nothing
serious. Still, if you had experienced how nonreligious and even
antireligious Yale is most of the time, you would understand why
the hymns and prayers came as such a shock to me. As a twenty-
first-century student, I entered Yale expecting a secular education.
And that's what I got. But there is tension between Yale's love of
tradition and its prevailing secularism. Even in terms of its architecture, Yale has not shed the aesthetic trappings of its religious past.
The old chapel buildings, the old mottoes, the old commencement
songs, they all serve as little reminders of Yale's religious lineage.

The slogan For God, for Country, and for Yale is etched in stone
in one of the most visible locations on campus, above a massive
arched gate facing Old Campus next to the iconic Harkness Tower.
In one sense, the slogan describes a set of ideals—the high and
noble purposes Yale aspires to fulfill. In another, unintended sense,
the slogan describes a historical progression—Yale's transformation
from a religious institution, to an institution defined by public service, to, finally, an institution that seems no longer aware of any
higher purpose other than advancing its own growth and prestige.

The key to understanding how Yale got where it is today is to first examine how its educational mission has changed over the course of its history. The sexual crisis currently raging at Yale is, ultimately, a symptom of two underlying problems. The first is Yale's loss of a sense of purpose. The second is Yale's profound moral aimlessness. Yale was founded as a religious seminary. Later, it evolved into a training ground for America's political and cultural elite. To some degree it still fulfills this latter purpose. But these days, faith and patriotism are not widely viewed as virtues at Yale. Instead, it is fashionable to scoff at the very values that defined Yale for its first two and a half centuries. Yale continues to train leaders, but it has no clear sense of what it should be teaching them. It has no real sense of why it exists anymore. This is the essence of what is wrong with Yale today. There came to be a void of purpose, and the carnival of sleaze I have described in previous chapters rose up to fill the emptiness.

If you went back in time, way back to the years immediately following Yale's founding in 1701, you would discover a fledgling seminary—no more than a few small buildings huddled together, housing a couple dozen students. Despite the college's small size, its leaders already had far-reaching ambitions. Their goal was to train up young missionaries to preach to rural communities throughout the colonies. From the very beginning, Yale was designed to be an institution of great societal influence.

In those days, if you traveled 150 miles up the northern fork of the old Boston post road, through rural Connecticut and on into Massachusetts, you could eventually find your way to another small college on the banks of the Charles River. Like Yale, Harvard began, essentially, as a missionary-training seminary. It was a very conservative place. Over time, however, the theology at Harvard drifted from its conservative religious roots. Eventually, a group of Harvard men became disgruntled with the direction Harvard was taking. They decided the colonies needed a new college that would teach more faithful doctrine. So they came down to Connecticut and founded Yale. Harvard's ousted president, Increase Mather, whose rigorous theology had placed him at odds with the more liberal Harvard faculty, was an important early supporter. The founders took Harvard's motto, *Veritas*—Latin for "Truth"—and upped the ante to *Lux et Veritas*—"Light and Truth." Ironically, it is possible to trace the fierce Harvard-Yale rivalry back to the religious roots of both universities. That's how the bad blood got started—it all began with Yale's founding quest to be holier than Harvard.

For a while, it seemed to be working. Yale's most famous child prodigy, Jonathan Edwards, entered Yale in 1716 at age thirteen and graduated four years later as valedictorian. Edwards went on to become president of Princeton and a nationally known preacher. His famous sermon entitled "Sinners in the Hands of an Angry God" includes the image of a spider hanging by a thread above hell's raging fire. The image is disturbing. But the spider metaphor went on to inspire a lovable eight-legged college mascot, which now hangs in a Yale dining hall. Hundreds of Yalies today live in a residential complex named after Edwards.

Spider mascots notwithstanding, Yale today is nothing like the Congregationalist seminary it started out to be. As recently as a hundred years ago, however, it still carried a strong sense of its religious past. In Woolsey Hall, alongside the marble-engraved names of Yale's deceased war veterans, there are several stone memorials honoring Yale graduates who were killed while serving as Christian missionaries abroad, including one plaque erected in honor of the Reverend Horace Pitkin, Yale class of 1892, killed in China's Boxer Rebellion. It's very hard to imagine a plaque like that being erected today.

While mainstream culture at Yale is thoroughly secular these days, as I walked around campus, I would encounter daily reminders of the school's religious past in the slogans and emblems carved on its buildings. Most were quite serious, while others, like the Jonathan Edwards spider, were rather comical. There are two churches built into Yale's Old Campus Quad, though only one is used for religious services anymore. The town of New Haven itself is dotted with scores of old church buildings. And, of course, there is some irony in the fact that while the statement of dedication For God, for Country, and for Yale is something students walk past every day, most Yale students aren't very religious. Yet, I think most nonreligious students accept that religion is part of Yale's past, even if they don't want it to be part of Yale's present.

The most conspicuous evidence of Yale's religious heritage is the presence of the Yale Divinity School. Out on the far north end of campus, far beyond where most undergraduates venture in the course of their day-to-day activities, the old brick structure stands— a lonely island—as distant physically as it is metaphorically from the rest of the intellectual life on campus. Two long wings stretch out from a central hall, facing inward upon themselves, as if to re-inforce, architecturally, the sense of the school's isolation from the rest of the university. I once had to retrieve a book from the divinity school library. That was the only time I ever set foot inside, and it was one visit more than most Yale undergraduates ever pay to the place. By way of contrast, the law school and the graduate school of arts and sciences are much more integrated into the undergraduate experience. With special permission, undergrads can supplement their course load with courses from the graduate and professional schools. But the divinity school just doesn't get much attention.

To be frank, many students and faculty members from other parts of the university don't take the divinity school seriously. From time to time, some have suggested that it should be spun off into a separate institution, as Princeton did with its theological seminary years ago. These critics suggest that a seminary with a religious agenda has no place within a secular university. In this way, some of the same people who condemn religious dogma while promot-ing the idea of "free academic inquiry" turn out to be unwilling to extend that free inquiry to religious ideas they don't agree with. Their brand of secularism becomes just another form of repressive dogma.

The atheists on campus have become positively evangelical. The Yale Society of Humanists holds weekly churchlike meetings and passes out tracts. They are very fervent in their nonbelief. I'm perplexed by the emergence of proselytizing atheists who aggressively evangelize *against* faith. Once, a controversial evangelical speaker was invited to speak on campus by a group of Christian students. His visit prompted a protest by students who didn't want the guy to appear. It was a group of people who, paradoxically, wanted to exclude a particular religious viewpoint because they thought that viewpoint was not inclusive enough.

The role religion plays in the Yale academic experience differs depending on which religion you happen to be talking about. Christianity, which played such a prominent role in Yale's history, seems to get added scrutiny. I once took a class in the Religious Studies Department, which is part of the main school of arts and sciences, not the divinity school. One day I was talking to the professor after class, and I remember him telling me with great passion how he wished that he could just get his religious students to stop believing that the Bible is divinely inspired—his hands waving in the air dramatically to emphasize his point. This professor actually had a seminary degree, yet I wasn't surprised by his lack of appreciation for his students' religious beliefs. I've observed the following paradox in the Religious Studies Department: Professors who teach about Christianity get hired only if they don't believe in it. Meanwhile, the standards are different for professors who teach about Hinduism, Buddhism, or Islam—any of the non-Western religions. They tend to be actual believers of what they teach.

It's as if the university believes that devout faith is a mark of cultural authenticity for those—and only those—who teach about non-Western religions. It enhances their intellectual credibility. On the other hand, devout faith would count as a mark against the credibility of someone who teaches about Christianity, which, as a religion integral to the development of Western civilization, lacks the multicultural value of the non-Western faiths. I had a visiting lecturer in one class who told me, in all seriousness, that he believed that a Hindu shaman could survive being buried alive for forty-five days. A few years ago, the university hired a Muslim named Dawood Yasin to teach in the Arabic Department and serve as a chaplain to the Muslim student association—this in spite of the fact that Yasin didn't even have a college degree. His only qualification seemed to be that he spent five years living in Syria after "embracing Islam."[1] It's very hard for me to imagine the university extending a teaching job or chaplain position to such an underqualified candidate if he had been a Christian instead. Maybe the double standard is, in part, an overreaction on the part of Yale administrators who feel uneasy about Yale's Christian past and are uncertain of how to reconcile that past with Yale's secular present.

Today Yale views its Christian past like a recovering alcoholic views his former life of boozing; Yale doesn't deny where it came from, but it's doing its best to move on. In the classroom context, religious belief is usually treated as intellectually unserious. If you put aside the multicultural fascination Yale has with devotees of Eastern religions, the presumption of religious skepticism is pervasive among the faculty. And students take note of it. I took many courses at Yale that incorporated religion, politics, philosophy, or ethics into the subject matter. Yet I never once saw a religious student open up about his faith in class. The assumption is that your grades may well suffer if you do.

A great university is supposed to be a haven for the free exchange of ideas. But in the academic world there is a sense of antagonism between reason and religion—as if one cannot embrace one without abandoning the other. In reality, religion is a fundamental part of human society, just as it has been throughout human history. If you consider world affairs, it's clear that religion continues to animate much of the geopolitical drama of our time. Clearly, therefore, religion should play a role in intellectual life if a university wishes to be relevant to the times. And by "play a role" I mean people of faith should be treated seriously, not dismissively. I don't think Yale needs to return to its days as a colonial seminary in order to be relevant, but I think religion should have a fair place at the table. If the climate of religious skepticism remains so overwhelming that religious students feel pressure to keep quiet, Yale will be a poorer place for it.

It's odd, isn't it? An institution founded for the sole purpose of spreading religious faith has now become a place where certain kinds of faith are intellectually stigmatized. In a turn of events about ten years ago that seems almost poetically symbolic, the university announced that it was going to tear down the divinity school building, which had fallen into disrepair. The divinity building is widely considered to have great historical importance. And the administration's announcement produced a swell of protests from architects and historical preservationists. Vincent Scully, one of the world's most famous art historians, who started teaching at the university in 1947 and was still going strong more than sixty years later when I was a student, threatened to resign if the university followed through with its plans. The public backlash prompted the administration to change its plans and actually repair the building.

Even within the walls of the divinity school—the one place on campus where you would assume religious faith would be considered compatible with serious intellectual study—there are signs that the climate of skepticism is taking hold. I read an article in the *Yale Daily News* profiling a number of students studying at the divinity school who described themselves as agnostic, atheistic, or even Hindu—this despite the fact that the express purpose of the school is to train up Christian ministers. When one reads about atheists taking classes with titles such as "Introduction to Pastoral Care," one begins to wonder if the divinity school is on its way to becoming just another place on campus for disinterested study about religion rather than a place where people of genuine faith engage in serious academic study.

There is a tremendous climate of intellectual conformity at Yale. In keeping with that sense of conformity there is a popular acceptance of the notion that, at the end of the day, smart people just aren't religious, and religious people, well, most of them just aren't very smart. While there are still plenty of religious people at Yale, they constitute a clear minority. And there is no sense on campus that university-wide standards of conduct ought to be informed by religion, since that would require nonbelieving students to abide by principles they do not accept as valid.

So where does that leave Yale when it comes time to address moral issues? Is it enough to simply say "To each his own"? There are many who would say so. But, in fact, Yale's leaders don't really believe in pure moral relativism. They take strong moral stances on issues related to the environment and race relations. They love to promote sustainable food and fluorescent lightbulbs. On a couple of occasions when I was a student, graffiti containing the n-word or a swastika was found on campus, and the administration reacted forcefully. Politically, it's very safe to take a moral stand on racial equality or the environment. Everyone agrees that racism is bad and that we should recycle aluminum cans. Those aren't bold moral positions. One might as well take a stand against kicking puppies or knocking down old ladies as they cross the street. Beyond the boilerplate, Miss America pageant–style ethical issues, the administration gets gun-shy.

What happens when moral questions get complicated? Pluralism may allow for a maximum sense of academic freedom; but, on the downside, Yale lacks the cohesive moral framework religion once provided. When faced with more complicated moral dilemmas, leaders at Yale have no agreed-upon basis for saying what should and shouldn't be advanced in the classroom. For instance, when it comes to a clash between sexual behavior and gender equality, they are unprepared to weigh those competing claims and take a stand— even if they observe things they don't approve of personally.

The tension that arises when pornography is introduced into the Yale classroom is, at a fundamental level, a tension between freedom of expression and women's equality. Freedom of expression is, at a basic level, a private good. It applies a benefit to an individual.

Meanwhile, women's equality could best be described as a public good. It applies a benefit to a larger population. When religion disappeared as an accepted standard for governing public mores, the emphasis switched to the conscience of the individual—the guiding principle became the idea that no one should impose his views upon another. And therein lies the problem. How can Yale administrators draw up rules to protect the public good when their moral framework does not extend beyond the realm of private conscience?

Liberty of conscience certainly does qualify as an important moral good. But what are the limits of morality governed by conscience alone? We arrive at those limits when liberty of conscience is used to justify an action that assaults the rights of others. This begs the additional question: From what source do humans derive their rights? How do we even determine there is such a thing as human rights? And this is where the puzzle begins to fall apart.

Not so long ago, perhaps as recently as the 1950s, many of Yale's leaders would have pointed to a divine source. They would have said that humans are worthy of dignity because they are made in the image of God. However, in a postreligious intellectual world, it becomes increasingly difficult to answer the question of why humans are worthy of being treated with dignity, or why there is any such thing as human rights.

We hold these truths to be self-evident, that all men are created equal, that they are endowed by their Creator with certain unalienable Rights . . . Those words made sense to our nation's most learned men more than two centuries ago. Today, however, we are living in the age of scientific materialism, the age of empiricism and reductionism. Science has nothing to say about morality, no insight into the issue of human rights. Science can do many wonderful things; but it cannot answer the greatest questions of human existence—how we should live and love. If you think of women as nothing more than the sum of their cells, how do you even know that they are worthy of equal treatment under the law? How do you know it is wrong to brutalize women sexually? Likewise, if man has no soul, what is the source of his dignity? Why should he seek to rise above his most brutal animalistic urges? Questions of human rights are, ultimately, moral questions. At its most basic level, the moral crisis at Yale is a crisis of lost faith. There is no cohesive moral framework in place to replace the one that was abandoned when God fell out of fashion.

How then should Yale answer moral questions? I have no tidy postreligious moral framework to offer in these pages because I don't think there is one. I've studied everything from natural law to Benthamite utilitarianism and just about every other ethical system in between, and none of them seemed to me like anything other than an elaborate attempt to intellectualize the prior-held feelings of a particular philosopher's own conscience. Philosophy helps man rationalize the predilections of conscience—I can choose any system of belief that feels good to me, and find a way to explain that system logically. But religion has the power to actually transform the conscience because it points to a standard higher than one's own will. I think man's dignity really does emanate from his being created by God, and I can't make sense of the notion of human rights or morality under any other pretext.

A critic of this view might ask this: How can a secular university operate under a premise that man is created by God? Wouldn't this amount to imposing a religious doctrine on nonbelieving students? My answer is this: I don't think acknowledging a source of human dignity rooted in a higher power amounts to an ideological imposition at all, unless, that is, one actually wants to violate others' dignity or rights. Nor do I think there is any way to logically justify a defense of one person's human rights against the whims of another individual by any other means—although, to be sure, many brilliant philosophers have tried to do just that. A rule that governs man must ultimately have a source of legitimacy higher than man. Otherwise a rule is nothing more than an arbitrary imposition of one man's will over another, or the will of one group over another. For this reason, we, as Americans, do not operate under simple majority rule. We have certain inalienable rights that, under law, none can violate, no matter how powerful or great in number they may be. The right to speak freely, the right to assemble peacefully, the right to exercise self-government—these rights are sacred. Yale is a secular university that imposes no specific religious orthodoxy on its students or faculty. But it must go at least this far—it must acknowledge mankind's God-given dignity as the basis of human rights. Otherwise it cannot defend those rights.

The various moral arguments I make in this book can be reduced, in large part, to a single argument against institutionalized sexism. The case against sexism has to have some coherent moral grounding. I believe that moral grounding must be derived from an acknowledgment of the fundamental dignity of humanity. When our God-given dignity is denied, the basis for human rights disappears. This is what is happening at Yale, and the consequences speak for themselves.

Yale is a place where one can find people expressing almost every imaginable viewpoint and belief system. But here is the unanswerable question: How does a secular university judge between the competing moral claims of its members when those claims breach the private sphere and enter the public realm? The irony is that every one of Yale's leaders would agree with the basic proposition that women have fundamental human rights and should be treated with dignity. But most of them couldn't articulate where those rights come from. All they know is that they "feel" that women deserve equal treatment and respect. But what if someone else does not feel that way? It becomes a question of one person's conscience against another's. Without the rationale for human dignity that religion once provided, morality is reduced to a consensus of feelings. When that consensus breaks down, there is no objective standard to appeal to. And nihilism knocks at the door.

Nihilism is, ultimately, where Yale is headed. Yale was built in order to nurture ideas that would elevate the soul and advance human understanding, but it now has no governing moral principle. As a result, the knowledge generated there is divorced from any larger human purpose. Apart from a kind of vague appreciation of certain concepts like tolerance and diversity, Yale is a moral vacuum. Therefore, almost anything goes. Yale is among a dwindling number of institutions that provide a classical liberal education, focusing on the great books of the Western canon—topped off with porn in HD. As I observed, within its walls, images of women being beaten and humiliated for no other reason than the pleasure and profit of others, I became aware that I was witnessing much more than the decline of a great university. I was witnessing nothing less than a prophetic vision of America's descent into an abyss of moral aimlessness, at the hands of those now charged with educating its future leaders.

16

YALE WITHOUT PATRIOTISM

Why! That canine has the proud bearing and glossy fur coat
of a Yale man . . . Smithers, I believe this dog was in Skull
and Bones.

—C. Montgomery Burns (*The Simpsons*)

In the bowels of an obscure building on the perimeter of Yale's campus, there is a vast collection of antique furniture that could keep the garage sale appraisers on PBS's *Antiques Roadshow* busy for a year. I was stunned when I saw the size of the collection. There were rows upon rows of chairs, dressers, chests, desks, and wardrobes. There were tables of every shape and size, lamps, bureaus, and nightstands stretching on as far as I could see. I held priceless silver platters and pitchers forged by the hands of Paul Revere. I was told that Yale students were allowed to drink ginger ale out of those priceless pitchers as recently as the 1970s.

What is all that furniture and silver doing down there? Not much of anything anymore. It belongs to another time in Yale's history—a time when Yale graduates were expected to have a gentleman's knowledge of antique furniture. A refined man of some means in those days would have been expected to know the difference between a Chinese-style Chippendale chair and a George III Mayhew and Ince. Yale built such a vast collection of antiques in order to serve a specific purpose. That purpose was to train up WASPy, wealthy, northeastern young men, and turn them into gentlemen. Where it had once been focused on training up God's "elect," Yale now turned its attentions to training up America's "elite." Students wore ties to class back then. But that all changed in the 1960s. In that decade Yale began to expand the racial and economic diversity of its student body on a large scale. Training WASPy, wealthy young men may no longer a suitable purpose for Yale, but the accoutrements of the old gentlemen's club are still around. And if you are looking for a two-hundred-year-old armoire, I know where you can find one.

In addition to its role as a curator of elite culture, Yale also enjoys a strong tradition of educating American political leaders. Over the course of its first two hundred years, as Yale's spiritual mission faded slowly into the background, a political purpose emerged as a new defining agenda. Serving country became a proxy for serving God. A patriotic purpose replaced a spiritual one. It was assumed for a long time that the interests of America were, by extension, Yale's interests as well. A large percentage of Yale graduates enrolled in the military immediately following graduation. And, of course, many went on to hold high political office.

The diversity that came to Yale in the sixties was a good thing. Other changes were less positive. In the late 1960s, Yale's patriotic ethos disintegrated in the face of pressures from the radical new left. The old-guard liberals, who had long governed the university, were replaced by a new, younger set. The old-guard liberals were in the mold of Jack Kennedy—they were New Deal liberals who were sympathetic to religion and proud of their country. They were traditionalists. The new leftists, on the other hand, wanted radical social transformation. They wanted to challenge the old moral assumptions and revolutionize the economic system. Empowered by the backlash against the Vietnam War, and a sanctimonious belief in the justness of their cause, students rose up and violently took over the agenda of the American left. Members of the Students for a Democratic Society and other radical progressive groups staged uprisings at many of America's leading college campuses, including well-publicized instances at Cornell and Columbia. At Yale, students took over buildings and held university workers hostage. In the spring of 1970, members of the Black Panthers were put on trial for murder in New Haven. Protests in support of the Black Panthers overwhelmed the campus. A university building was bombed. In the face of this new, aggressive strain of radicalism, the old liberal guard backed down. The president of the university, Kingman Brewster, made classes optional for students, and ordered that students be graded on a pass/fail basis rather than with the normal letter grades. Administrators didn't expel the violent disrupters; instead, they gave in to their demands. About this same time, the patriotic purpose that had defined the university for two hundred years disappeared. The faculty had voted the year before to revoke academic credit for ROTC courses. Later, Yale moved to restrict military recruiters' access to students. With the destruction of Yale's patriotic ethos, the last remaining sense of Yale having any higher educational purpose in service of the nation went out the door.

That isn't to say that Yale ceased being political. But from that point onward, Yale's political agenda was no longer tied to American interests. In fact, Yale's political climate came to be defined more and more by anti-Americanism. Economic theories in opposition to free markets became prevalent. Identity politics and interest-group politics began to take over academic life, endangering free speech in the name of cultural sensitivity, and ushering in a new era of suffocating political correctness.

The shift happened quickly. Only a couple of decades before, during World War II, faculty sentiment had been united against America's enemies in Nazi Germany and Fascist Italy. Now, if the topic of international affairs happened to be raised in the faculty lounge, it had become fashionable to speak of America as the bad guy. Saying nice things about America's enemies became a mark of intellectual sophistication—of rising above mindless nationalism.

Patriotism, like religion, had become a mark of low intelligence, an anachronism.

Among academics who work, eat, and socialize together, the pressure to conform to the prevailing political ideology is, apparently, irresistible. Today, the political balance at Yale is almost comically one-sided. Between the two major candidates in the 2004 presidential election cycle, 98 percent of the faculty's political donations went to the Democratic side, only 2 percent to the Republican side.

The first time I ever set foot on Yale's campus I was greeted by an anti-Bush sticker. A professor, whose office sat right next to Phelps Gate, the main entrance to the college, had stuck it up in his window. It was a play on the dairy industry's old "Got Milk?" marketing campaign. There was an image of George W. Bush with a piece of tape across his mouth, with the words "Got Tape?" written above. It stayed up for years, and I don't think it came down until after Obama was sworn into office. It's no secret that Yale is politically liberal. That little sticker, displayed so prominently in the main gateway, where hundreds of students enter the college on the first day of freshman year, and where tens of thousands of tourists every year start their tours through the university, served as a fitting reminder of where the university's allegiances lie.

If students were warned right away that they were entering a one-sided political atmosphere, it was probably for the best. I remember on election eve in 2008, a professor e-mailed my friend Brandon, along with the rest of the students in his class. The e-mail contained a slide show full of pictures of Barack Obama, admonishing Brandon to go vote for "change." Brandon, who leans Republican, was less than thrilled by his professor's blatant political advocacy. Political bias is inevitable, so long as there is such extreme political imbalance among the faculty. It comes with the territory, and right-leaning students learn to expect it. In some cases I think they actually feed off the sense of adversity.

On the night Obama won the presidency, hundreds of students rushed spontaneously onto the lawn on Yale's Old Campus. It turned into a spectacle not seen since the hashish-fueled choruses of "Kumbaya" filled the air at Yale in 1969, among the hostage-taking SDS crowd. Students poured onto the quad, gathered in a giant circle, and held hands. Someone began to sing the national anthem, and soon the mass of students was belting out "The Star-Spangled Banner" in unison—a midnight performance that served, I think, as something of catharsis for liberal-minded Yalies after eight years of Bush. In hindsight, I'm not sure Obama quite lived up to their messianic expectations. But, at the time, it was a touching scene, if for nothing more than the bit of honest patriotism it evoked. Regardless of whether one supported Obama or not, it was a great thing to see a black man elected president in America. I simply felt proud that such a thing was possible.

That night, when Yale's old patriotic ethos returned, if only briefly, to campus, the monster of identity politics threatened to rear its ugly head. As students were gathering to celebrate, the African American students' association discussed the idea of marching into Old Campus singing something called the "Black National Anthem." I didn't even know black Americans had their own anthem. Fortunately, someone spoke up and suggested that such a move might spoil the sense of unity and racial harmony that the night otherwise held. It's just one small example of how, in day-to-day life at Yale, identity politics often leads to divisiveness and political myopia. Multicultural fragmentation hinders students from appreciating the common stake we all have in America.

The American system isn't perfect, of course. But, in this nation, the kinds of things most academics say they value—freedom of speech, freedom of religion, and the promise of racial and gender equality—are protected under law. That just isn't the case in much of the world. For this reason, the patriotic purpose Yale long served should be viewed as a moral necessity. If the American system fails, the academic enterprise itself is compromised. The idea that we all hold a common stake in preserving America, and the unique liberties its political system affords, used to be taken for granted at Yale. No longer. Now it is not uncommon for Yale to hire professors who openly oppose America and who show little regard for our basic political liberties.

In the previous chapter I mentioned Dawood Yasin, the man who "embraced Islam" and managed to get hired to teach at Yale without any college degree. His story raises some important political questions. I recall reading how Yasin led a group of forty students to visit a local mosque in New Haven, where he also happened to serve as imam. In order to enter the mosque, female students were required to wear headscarves. I find that terribly ironic. Anyone who wants to wear a headscarf should have the right to do so, but the reality is that there are a number of countries where women can be punished as criminals if they dare to go outside without one. In this case, the embrace of the demands of fundamentalist Islam in the name of multiculturalism begins to look like the embrace of sexism. To put this story in context, would any white professor dare to take his students to visit an organization that actively practices apartheid, and then instruct Yale's black students to sit in the back of the bus and avoid drinking out of the white man's water fountain? Just so students could gain a nice multicultural understanding of apartheid society? It would never happen, nor should it. Why then, when it comes to a field trip to a mosque, is a symbol of women's political oppression adopted without question? It is because multiculturalism has supplanted more fundamental American principles—such as women's equality—on the scale of political importance at Yale.

In addition to its sense of responsibility to the nation, Yale needs to understand its responsibility to preserve the intellectual history of the West. We live in an age in which cultural relativism is very popular. We are told to believe that no single set of cultural beliefs and attitudes is superior to any other. While that sounds nice and open-minded, it simply isn't true. Not all cultures and belief systems are equal.

Does Yale have the moral courage, as an institution, to state emphatically that a culture that suppresses women is morally inferior? I'm not sure that it does. These days, Yale is too busy trying to avoid being judgmental to take such a stand.

Looking at the geopolitical landscape right now, you would think that Yale leaders would understand the cultural and moral issues that are at stake, and that they would realize that treating all political ideologies—even repressive ones—as morally equal is self-defeating. It leads to absurd contradictions. For instance, you can't logically call for the suppression of academic freedom, and do so in the name of academic freedom. But that's just what one member of the Yale faculty did.

One of the parties at Yale responsible for hiring the degreeless imam, Dawood Yasim, was a man named Bassam Frangieh, a senior Yale Arabic instructor. In 2006, during the height of that year's military conflict in Lebanon between Israel and Hezbollah, Frangieh signed his name to an anti-Israeli petition calling on "free-thinking intellectuals the world over" to boycott Israeli academic and scientific institutions.[1] The petition condemned the "Zionist state" and praised the "heroic operation carried out by HizbAllah."

Set aside for a moment the fact that Hezbollah is officially classified as a terrorist organization by the United States and many other nations, and that it has been linked to the murders of hundreds of innocent civilians in the last few decades in the course of waging jihad on Western civilization. Just think of Frangieh's outrageous suggestion that "free-thinking intellectuals" ought to boycott Israeli academic institutions as a gesture of solidarity with a group that seeks to enforce a repressive fundamentalist Islamic agenda. The letter promotes tyranny in the name of freedom. As Frangieh's career at Yale exemplifies, multiculturalism, which is supposed to be about embracing racial and cultural diversity, has become the justification for hiring people at Yale who seek to suppress others.

In various interviews given to the Arab press around the same time, including one to a Web site called Al Jabha, or "the Front," Frangieh praised Hamas—another group officially classified as a terrorist organization—saying that he viewed the group's rise "with great pleasure."[2] He signed documents that made references to "Zionist plots," "Zionist masters," and "the Zionist killing machine." In an essay Frangieh wrote earlier in his career at Yale, entitled "Modern Arabic Poetry: Vision and Reality," he appears to openly advocate violence:

> Even if the best one hundred Arab poets loaded themselves with dynamite and exploded in the streets of Arab capitals, it would not be enough. For real change to come about, thousands of people will have to die; thousands must martyr themselves. It appears that only massive revolution will succeed in overturning the corrupt regimes of the Arab world. Only then can significant and radical change take place.[3]

Frangieh is certainly entitled to his views, however heinous they may be. But does that mean that a university such as Yale, which is tasked with training America's future leaders, should have employed such a man?

In an interview, Frangieh told the Arab press of his strong desire to leave America: "Life in America has no taste and no life. It is suffocating," he said. "I am amazed by those who have a place to go and yet stay here. If I had a place, I would go there and stay there happily, and would not stay one more day here."[4] Considering Frangieh's obvious contempt for America, his expressed enthusiasm for terrorist organizations, and his belief in the necessity of suicide bombing as a means of political reform, it is remarkable that he found a home teaching at Yale—the cradle of American presidents—in this, the post-9/11 era.

In its blind pursuit of a radical multiculturalist agenda, Yale has clearly abandoned its sense of responsibility to the nation. But the evidence doesn't stop with Frangieh. In 2005, Yale invited a former diplomat-at-large for the Taliban, Sayed Rahmatullah Hashemi, to come study at the university. Now, put aside for a moment the fact that America was at war with the Taliban at the time. And just think about what the Taliban stand for from a moral perspective. They were known for, among other things, hauling off infidels into soccer fields and chopping their heads off, torturing and mutilating women, and denying women the right to an education.

Hashemi's presence at Yale created a media firestorm. After the media picked up on his story he told the *New York Times,* "I could have ended up in Guantanamo Bay. Instead, I ended up at Yale." A protest movement developed among alumni. Instead of financial contributions, many of them started sending in envelopes full of fake fingernails in order to protest his presence. (The Taliban used to torture people by pulling out their fingernails.)

I'm sure Yale administrators thought they were being very forward-thinking by inviting Hashemi to Yale. Think of the diversity he brought to the classroom! But did they stop to think about the moral implications of his presence on campus? Did they consider how it would make the university appear indifferent to the suffering of Afghani women and men?

There are many decent Muslim students who attend Yale. These students are not actively involved in human rights abuses and have not held official positions in the governments of America's enemies. One would think these students adequately satisfy the university's need for cultural diversity from the Muslim perspective. No need to have brought in the Taliban to fulfill that mission.

I had a class with Hashemi in international relations, and I ended up sitting next to him during the final exam. Meanwhile, American troops were fighting his comrades in the mountains of Afghanistan. We sat side by side for two hours, but we didn't speak a word. What could I say? It was an awful situation. Hashemi knew that many considered his presence at Yale unacceptable. I almost felt sorry for him. The greater blame for his presence, in my mind, belonged to the Yale administrators who invited him to study there in the first place. Because they should have known better.

After the exam, I never saw Hashemi again. The heat of controversy surrounding his presence at the university had gotten very intense. A few weeks later he left Yale and never came back.

After the Hashemi debacle, I thought I had seen the worst of Yale's cowardly political behavior. Then, a couple of years later, Yale lecturer Hillary Leverett took her class on a trip to New York to meet privately with Iran's despotic leader, Mahmoud Ahmadinejad, while the latter was in town to attend a United Nations assembly. This is the same man who has openly called for Israel to be "wiped off the map." The meeting had the flavor of a propaganda event. Students posed for a smiling photo-op, which was later published by Iran's state-controlled news agency. But no one challenged Ahmadinejad on his record of killing and violently oppressing thousands of Iranians who have dared to oppose his regime. Ahmadinejad told students that there is no hard scientific evidence that the Holocaust happened.[5] Afterward, Leverett said the meeting with students showed that Ahmadinejad "was probably not the stereotype of a crazy irrational figure. . . . He has a strategy for Iran."[6] It was a friendly, lighthearted interview, full of the kind of deferential, unquestioning multicultural posturing that has become all too common at Yale.

While we're on the topic of a notorious anti-Semite like Ahmadinejad, it's worth noting that in the summer of 2011, Yale announced that it was shutting down the Yale Initiative for the Interdisciplinary Study of Antisemitism because, a university representative explained, the institute failed to "serve the research and teaching interests of some significant group of Yale faculty."[7] Evidence later emerged that the university had come under pressure to shut down the YIISA because of the institute's special focus on Islamic anti-Semitism. An official representative of the Palestine Liberation Organization, Maen Rashid Areikat, was one of the people who contacted President Levin to complain about the YIISA's activities in the months prior to its dissolution. After catching a lot of heat in the news media and from alumni who were outraged that the university had pulled the plug on the YIISA, Yale responded by creating a new, watered-down replacement program called the Yale

Program for the Study of Anti-Semitism. The program's new director, Maurice Samuels, emphasized that it would focus on anti-Semitism in "many countries and cultures," rather than focusing on those dominated politically by Islamic extremism as the YIISA had done.

Yale has gone from cosseting oppressive tyrants, educating their ambassadors, and hiring their apologists to finally participating in some of that oppression itself. In 2005, the Danish newspaper *Jyllands-Posten* famously published a dozen cartoons depicting the prophet Muhammad. It was a controversial move because rendering the image of Muhammad is forbidden under fundamentalist Islamic law. The cartoons elicited a worldwide backlash from Muslim extremists, who bombed the Danish embassy in Pakistan and set fire to the embassies in Syria, Lebanon, and Iran. The Danish newspaper editors and cartoonists received numerous death threats, and at least one cartoonist was targeted in an assassination attempt. All because of a few measly sketches. If devout Muslims don't want to draw or look at pictures of Muhammad, that's up to them. But whenever extremists start throwing firebombs because of a few cartoons, I can't help wondering how devout they really are. When adherents of a religion find their faith so easily threatened that a dozen Danish doodles incite them into a murderous frenzy, I consider it evidence that their faith is as precarious as it is pathological.

Fast-forward to 2009, and Yale University Press was set to publish a scholarly book called *The Cartoons That Shook the World,* by Professor Jytte Klausen, which was to include reprints of the infamous cartoons. At the last minute, however, the university declined to publish the images because it feared that doing so would provoke the wrath of the extremists. So much for free academic expression. In the face of a violent and oppressive ideology, Yale backed down and became a passive participant in the suppression of speech—a move that will surely embolden the enemies of free speech.

In spring of 2011, Yale entered voluntarily into a joint venture with an oppressive regime by agreeing to a first-of-its-kind partnership with the National University of Singapore. Under terms of the agreement, Yale agreed to lend its name and prestige to create a new college called Yale-NUS, which will be funded and ultimately governed by the Singaporean government. Singapore, a one-party authoritarian state, which, according to Human Rights Watch, lacks "meaningful access to free speech, association, and assembly,"[8] will now be free to suppress speech and academic freedom directly under the banner of Yale University. And the absurdity doesn't end there. In past years American citizens visiting Singapore have been forced to submit to brutal cane lashings courtesy of the Singaporean penal system—this for such minor offenses as stealing a car radio or overstaying a travel visa. Here's hoping that future students of the Yale-NUS college can avoid thirty-nine lashes at the hands of a martial arts master, and remember to get their passports stamped properly.

Yale has lost touch with its sense of responsibility for upholding American liberties and values in the world. If it abandons the principles of American liberty in its engagement with the world, it will inevitably end up being a partner in oppression. Shadows of that oppression have already reached New Haven in the form of a band of female students being instructed to don the *hijab* on a class field trip to a local mosque.

In similar fashion, up at Harvard, they have lately discovered something called Muslim night at the gym. Question: How do burka-wearing ladies keep their svelte figures while heeding Islam's injunctions against girls wearing jogging shorts? Answer: Lobby the university to ban men from the gym during special Muslim hours. That's the problem with extreme multiculturalism: In order to extend tolerance to one group, oftentimes you must deny it to another. Turns out, strict Sharia law isn't really compatible with liberal democratic society unless you are willing to cut out a few "liberties" here and there.

Try as it may to accommodate every belief system, a university must ultimately decide on certain basic principles that will govern its campus. It cannot remain politically or morally neutral in all matters. Why didn't Yale know that educating a former Taliban official falls outside the university's moral purpose? It's because Yale's administrators failed to realize that cultural relativism, when taken to an extreme, will cannibalize the academic freedom that enables it to take hold in the first place. It's because they failed to realize that academic freedom cannot include the advancing of agendas that restrict freedom without becoming nonsensical and self-defeating. It's because they failed to realize that Yale's ability to function freely is premised upon "certain unalienable rights," and they forgot where those rights come from.

When you first enter Yale, one of the first things you are likely to see is the statue of Nathan Hale, which stands outside Connecticut Hall. For many years, that statue has represented the idea that Yale is dedicated to the service of the nation. In 1776, a new institutional calling emerged at Yale. Patriotism became a guiding ethos. Yale took pride in its role as a training ground for generations of the country's most prominent military and political leaders. Over the years, memorials were erected all over campus in honor of Yale's military heroes.

A few generations ago, it was assumed that most Yale graduates would join the military after graduation. Today, I think there are more Yale students who want to be president of the United States than want to be military officers. Over time, Yale has retained its sense of ambition but lost its sense of responsibility to the nation. It needs to get it back. Perhaps, with the recently announced return of the ROTC to campus, there is some hope for a renewal of the ethos of national service.

What kind of graduate should Yale seek to turn out into the world? There used to be definite meaning behind the idea of the Yale Man. At first he was a preacher; then he was a patriot and a gentleman. Today, the Yale Man is harder to define. Yale is no longer a seminary, and no longer a finishing school for privileged young white men. Today, it is humanistic, co-ed, and multiracial.

So who is today's Yale Man?

He is, above all, a leader.

Yale graduates, very often, become powerful people later in life. Yale students are incredibly well connected. During a recent experiment related to technology and privacy in one class, a freshman student allowed his classmates access to all of his personal electronic information. On his cell phone, they found the personal phone numbers for Ernesto Zedillo and Eduardo Medina Mora, respectively a former president and a former attorney general of Mexico, and for Eliot Spitzer, the former governor of New York.[9] And this kid was just a freshman. Those are the kinds of connections that allow many Yale students to become unusually successful and influential. The fact that Yale is training leaders means it has a special responsibility to train thoughtful, ethical, responsible graduates who will use their power and influence for the good of society.

Today, Yale remains a pathway to success and power, but does it prepare its students to use that power for good? In my experience, many Yale graduates tend to focus too much on getting rich, and not enough on finding a worthy purpose in life. Wealth and power are great, but only if they serve a noble end. Yale needs to foster a sense of social responsibility in its privileged and gifted students so that they will take all the advantages they have in life and use them for the good of others, not just themselves. Service to the nation is a good place to start. Apart from the military, there are many ways to serve one's country. There are the foreign service, the intelligence service, the Peace Corps. By renewing the call to service, Yale can renew its own sense of purpose as an institution.

Getting that sense of purpose back is critical. The intellectual tradition of the West produced technological progress and unprecedented economic prosperity, pulling mankind out of the barbarism of the Dark Ages and into a more prosperous and humane state of being. As Tocqueville illustrated so powerfully in his tome

Democracy in America, religion, and Protestant Christianity in particular, played a powerful role in that intellectual history, and in the emergence of the unprecedented liberties of self-government that America's founding brought forth into the world. Yale cannot preserve and further progress so long as it adheres to an extreme form of moral relativism, because the intellectual history that carried man into the modern age was built upon a particular moral order—the idea that there is such a thing as right and wrong, such a thing as noble and base, such a thing as worthy and unworthy.

The extreme sexual material detailed in this book is meant to serve as a measure of sorts—a way to illustrate the extent to which Yale has forsaken its guiding purposes and lost touch with all common sense. When it comes to sex, there seems to be no topic so degrading that it isn't worth teaching and promoting. Likewise, there seems to be no political agenda so oppressive that it isn't worth advancing. When a member of the Taliban comes knocking, Yale's leaders aren't sure why they shouldn't let him in, so they do.

What sort of moral leadership can we expect from future Yale-educated presidents and CEOs, given the depravity they are exposed to as part of their education? Will Aliza the abortion artist be leading the National Endowment for the Arts in twenty years? Will some future Yale-educated president be practicing the moves he learned from Darlinda in the closet of the Oval Office? If tyrants tell little Afghani girls they aren't allowed to go to school, will a Yale-educated Taliban emissary be the one to deliver the message?

Across the wide scope of human political history, liberty is the rare exception, not the rule. It's naïve to think that liberty will prevail if we refuse to defend it against the idea that all cultures and ideologies are equally valid. To advance the principles of liberty and human rights, Yale must reclaim its lost sense of duty and rededicate itself to the furtherance of America's highest political ideals.

17

NAKED PARTIES AND ELITISM
AS TRANSCENDENCE

Yale is at once a tradition, a company of scholars, and a society of friends.

—Yale historian George W. Pierson

One day in the late seventies, high up in one of Yale's Gothic stone towers, a lone maintenance worker stumbled upon an old musty storage room. The room had been kept locked for years. Unbeknownst to him, hidden inside that dark room were certain remnants from Yale's past—things university administrators would rather have forgotten about. Things they would rather had never existed.

The worker approached one of the many dusty old boxes lying about the room. He opened the lid. He stood for a moment, frozen in disbelief, disturbed by what he saw. He ran immediately to find his supervisor. Soon, inquiries were made, quietly, to higher authorities. Everyone agreed. The evidence in the boxes had to be destroyed.

Photographs. Thousands of them.

A private company was called in to shred every last one, and then to incinerate the entire heap. Yes, burn them. All of them had to be destroyed. It was vital. What if they were leaked or stolen? Unthinkable. What if the faces were recognized? The bodies?

—Did we get them all?
—All of them.
—You're certain?
—Every last one.
—Good. Now it's over.

But they didn't get them all. And it wasn't over.

Thousands of nude photographs—full body shots taken from the front and rear, and in profile—were burned that day. On each body, hideous four-inch pins protruded from the spine at regular intervals, like the work of a sadistic alien acupuncturist. Each young face stared blankly at the camera like a ghost from a dark era of Yale's past—a time when it handed its young students over to the machinations of a practitioner of a long-discredited pseudoscience, like so many guinea pigs in a laboratory cage.

What could it mean?

If you happened to enter Yale as a freshman anytime from the forties through the late sixties, during part of your orientation week, you were likely ushered into a windowless room atop Yale's Payne Whitney Gymnasium. There you were told to remove all your clothes. Men in white frocks attached metal pins to your back, positioned you in front of stark white lights, and then photographed you naked from several angles.

Yale officials called it a "posture photo" in those days. Experts would examine the position of the pins along your spine. You were told that if the curvature of your spine proved irregular, you would be given some sort of corrective physical therapy. But you weren't told the truth. In fact, these "posture photos" were actually part of a much larger physiognomic study, with intellectual links going back to the progressive eugenics movement as well as the selective breeding efforts employed by the Nazis in their attempt to create a master race.

In a letter published in the *New York Times* back in the early nineties, Yale professor George Hersey explained the rationale behind the project:

> [The photos] had nothing to do with posture . . . that is only what we were told. . . . The reigning school of the time, presided over by E. A. Hooton of Harvard and W. H. Sheldon, held that a person's body, measured and analyzed, could tell much about intelligence, temperament, moral worth and probable future achievement. The inspiration came from the founder of social Darwinism, Francis Galton, who proposed such a photo archive for the British population. . . . The Nazis compiled similar archives analyzing the photos for racial as well as characterological content.[1]

Hersey went on to explain how the Nazis often used photographs from American high school yearbooks for their sordid studies. American investigators continued in the same ugly intellectual tradition, planning to amass an archive that would match each student's bodily configuration or "somatotype" with his or her later life history.

W. H. Sheldon, the man behind the photographs, was an intellectual phony and a racist. He once wrote an essay entitled "The Intelligence of Mexican Children," in which he stated that "negro intelligence" comes to a "standstill at about the 10th year," while Mexicans continue to gain intelligence until only about the 12th year.[2] Sheldon's equally well-initialed colleague in physiognomic studies, the illustrious E. A. Hooton, Ph.D., of Harvard, believed that studies derived from the posture photos would eventually lead to proposals to "control and limit the production of inferior and useless organisms." By "organisms," of course, Hooton meant humans, the lesser examples of whom he hoped the government would forcibly sterilize. These are the kinds of low-life scholars on whose behalf Yale eagerly forced its students to pose in the nude year after year. Sheldon personally took many of the photographs.

There was almost no actual science behind what he was doing. By the time Sheldon died he had seen his work fully discredited, although he continued to hold fast, to the very end, to the idea that the body reveals the inner character of man—and woman.

Although Sheldon collected mostly photographs of male students, he also photographed young women at several of the elite "Seven Sisters" colleges in the Northeast. In the sixties, there were constant rumors at Yale (still all-male at the time) about a batch of stolen posture photos from Vassar or—depending on which version of the rumor you heard—one of the other elite Seven Sisters schools. Fortunately for those young women, the rumored stolen photographs never materialized.

Still, I can scarcely imagine what it must have been like for a young woman of eighteen, reared in a proper upper-class family in the reserved cultural climate of the fifties or early sixties, to be sent off to an elite women's college, away from home for perhaps the first time, where she is told that the first thing she must do is strip completely naked and allow herself to be photographed from multiple angles while onlookers peer and scratch at their notebooks.

Yale allowed other controversial experiments to be carried out on its students from time to time. One of the most notorious was designed by Stanley Milgram, a Yale psychologist who, with assistance from a fake electric shock machine and voice recordings of what sounded like people screaming in excruciating pain, made students believe that they were torturing and shocking an unseen individual to death in the course of the experiment. Milgram's methods came under intense scrutiny from the American Psychological Association. To this day critics argue that the experiments risked inflicting undue harm on those who participated in the experiment. Milgram has plenty of defenders. But, in my view, his work is representative of a prior era in Yale history, when Yale's leaders were far too willing to offer students up as guinea pigs without their proper informed consent. Remarkably, in the course of their self-assured march toward scientific knowledge and the greater good, Yale authorities never stopped to wonder if participating in these kinds experiments might harm the students involved. Instead, they exhibited a kind of elitist, "we know better than they do" attitude, and were willing to risk students' well-being.

At issue is a certain brand of intellectual elitism—elitism that believes its own intentions are self-justifying and is willing to run roughshod over the rights of others in the name of the "greater good." It's no accident that the posture photo studies were carried out, almost exclusively, among a small group of elite colleges. The fact that Yale, along with a few other (supposedly) sophisticated schools, would subject its students to this strange, scientifically baseless, and potentially humiliating experimentation is truly astonishing in hindsight. It is doubly astonishing because so many of these students would go on to assume positions among the nation's cultural and political elite. Former president George H. W. Bush, former New York governor George Pataki, and journalist Bob Woodward are just a few of the prominent Yale graduates who had posture photos taken. The actress Meryl Streep was photographed at Vassar, Diane Sawyer and Hillary Clinton at Wellesley.[3] For such people, it would obviously be very damaging if the images went public. It must be a horrific feeling for them to know that scandalous photographs could be floating around out there, just waiting for someone to upload them to the Internet or sell them to *Hustler* magazine.

Like Yale, most of the colleges involved destroyed their posture photo collections during the seventies and eighties. But for decades among the collected research papers of W. H. Sheldon, which are stored in the archives of the Smithsonian, more than twenty-five thousand naked posture photographs remained.[4] Nine thousand of them were of Yale students. Only about ten years ago were those remaining images finally destroyed.

* * *

It's been many years since Yale undergraduates stripped down by the thousands on behalf of W. H. Sheldon. But in the decades since, Yalies have carried on the naked tradition on their own. Only now, they have taken the nudity out of the hidden room at the top of the gymnasium and into the classrooms, the libraries, the courtyards, and quads. Yalies, it must be said, have a passion for public nudity. They revel in its infinite manifestations.

Yale is famous for, among other things, its naked parties. It's just what it sounds like, except these tend to be quieter events than you might imagine, with a lot of guys and girls standing around, casually conversing about the weather and their potential course selections for the next semester. Only they are naked.

There are unwritten rules to Yale naked parties. Rule number one: *Don't look down.* There is a lot of intense eye contact at these parties, since allowing one's eyes to drift below the shoulders causes one to appear like an oafish ogler. Typically, clothed parties at Yale involve a lot of dancing, bumping, and grinding. On the other hand, at the naked parties, there is generally no dancing going on, no scented oils or fanning palm fronds, no orgies. It's actually quite reserved. Or so I hear.

I never actually made it out to a naked party. Personally, I prefer to carry on casual conversations with my clothes on. Nudity can be very distracting when you are trying to meet new people. And, come to think of it, the idea of willfully desexualizing a lot of naked young women just doesn't sound very—sexy. Leave me a little mystery. Please.

It's true, I missed out on one of Yale's core social experiences, but I wasn't alone. There were other defiantly clothed students in my company. We formed a conspicuously clad counterculture.

Casual, disinterested nudity is the order of the day at the naked parties. But, occasionally, a Yale man is unable to live up to the platonic code of naked party conduct. Try as he may to stop it, occasionally a guy will get a little excited. In such cases he may be asked to go outside until he calms down. Sounds like a terrible punishment. I can't think of much worse than standing around in the cold in close proximity to a bunch of drunken, excited dudes.

Other universities experience a little streaking now and then. Harvard kids traditionally streak when it comes time for finals. Tufts students used to do it too, until recently, when multiple hospitalizations caused the president of the university to cancel the annual naked fun run. (Seems too many drunken naked people were falling down and breaking arms and legs.) I have heard that they have begun having naked gatherings of some kind at Brown. If you know anything about Brown, you won't be surprised to learn that they've taken up the practice.

One must distinguish between good old-fashioned streaking, on the one hand, and a Yale naked party on the other. They are very different things. Streaking happens, at least occasionally, at most any university. It is a matter of young people letting off a little steam, being rebellious and wild for a moment. Picture Will Ferrell running down the vacant streets of a college town in the movie *Old School*, yelling, "We're going streeeeaking!" Yale students do this kind of spontaneous streaking from time to time as well. Each year, on Parent's Day, groups of students go streaking through libraries, courtyards—anywhere visiting, red-faced parents might be found. Typically, there's a lot of shouting and whooping and laughing going on.

Yale's naked parties aren't like that. The naked parties are typically held indoors. They are quiet, studied events where whooping and prancing are severely frowned upon. Furthermore, these events are not done on the spur of the drunken moment. Yalies are highly organized about their naked parties, and they have well-planned events throughout the year, although they do often end up drunk.

You have to understand that naked parties are a mainstream social activity at Yale. This is not the pastime of a few odd or scandalous students. A large percentage of students attend such events at least a time or two during their Yale careers. Possibly this is one reason why so many Yale graduates become investment bankers on

Wall Street, where, I hear, it is customary to conduct financial business after hours at various Manhattan strip clubs. Under the pulsing lights of New York's unofficial stock exchange, cocaine-fueled speculations over derivatives and credit default swaps inevitably drive stock prices higher and higher. The unavoidable result is a bubble, a crash, and financial ruin for us all. The recent collapse of the global financial system, therefore, may be indirectly linked to the irregular customs of conversation developed in so many late-night get-togethers among groups of Yale students wearing no clothes.

The Yale Women's Center sponsors the occasional all-female naked party. For some reason, I received an e-mail invitation to these on a few occasions. One time, the e-mail included a photo of about two dozen naked women huddled together in what looked like a giant bathtub, their arms merrily upraised in gestures of liberated revelry. "E-mail . . . if you care to know the time and place," it read. To be sure, the image advertising the all-woman naked party did look a lot more festive than the rather grave co-ed events I had heard so much about. Not that it mattered, of course, since my own particular anatomy wasn't invited.

Or was it? In fact, many of the students involved with the Yale Women's Center believe that gender is merely a social construction. I was a bit tempted to attend their naked party, if for no other reason than to test the limits of their attachment to this theory. But, alas, I thought it best not to sully the Venusian purity of the gathering, since that was obviously what they were aiming for.

Barbara Bush (W's daughter) attended Yale a little before my time. She reportedly attended at least one naked party during her college career, a decision which, if true, probably wasn't the wisest thing in the world for the daughter of a sitting president to do, especially in an age where cell phone cameras are abundant. I expect she may have begun to regret her attendance when, a short time later, Larry Flynt, the publisher of *Hustler* magazine and a major donor to the Democratic Party, offered a million dollars to anyone who could produce a nude photo of the Republican president's daughter.

* * *

Even if you choose not to join in with the naked parties, you cannot avoid public nudity at Yale. An acquaintance of mine recounted the experience of a newly admitted freshman girl about a year ago. The girl attended a preorientation camping trip sponsored by the university. On the first night, she and other newly admitted students were gathered around a campfire, and she was shocked when a male student counselor—her guide and mentor on the trip—pranced out in front of the group completely naked. Welcome to Yale, honey.

The Pundits, a group of campus pranksters active at Yale for decades, are known to start stripping down in the middle of various classes and campus events. The Finals Fairies sweep through the library in the buff each semester on the night before finals begin, passing out candy and reviving the spirits of languishing student scholars on the brink of academic exhaustion. Metaphorically, security guards and staff at the library look the other way, even though certain of their number, understandably, remain visually fixated on the spectacle.

These staff members, maintenance workers, janitors, security guards, and the like are all local residents. (Yale is the largest employer in New Haven.) Many of the locals who work at Yale come from modest economic backgrounds. They lack fancy educations. They have no experience with the sweet tastes and privileges of wealth, or all the wonders of refined culture. What do they think of the spectacle of so many wealthy sons and daughters cavorting around the library in nothing but their own skin? Do they begin to wonder if the whole of America's upper class lives a kind of alternative naked lifestyle, wheeling around to operas and cocktail parties in plush gowns and overcoats, only to tear them off once they get inside?

There is a connection between the elitism of Yale and the ease with which its students transgress social norms. If you take a trip some evening down to your local community college, you won't find any bacchanalian revelries under way. And I note with some annoyance that no matter how comfortable Yale students may be being naked with each other, they would never invite a poor, uneducated, working-class Joe from the surrounding neighborhood to join in the party. They wouldn't want him standing there with a fruity vodka drink, maintaining intense eye contact and talking about his job bagging groceries at the local supermarket. I have heard Yale students talk about how nudity is a great equalizer, how nakedness removes all the trappings of social status from the body. But the equality Yale students claim to see in each other's naked bodies is not something they would ever extend to others outside the privileged Yale bubble.

All college kids go a bit wild on the weekends. But there is something unique, something disturbingly premeditated, about the "wildness" happening at Yale. It's not actually wild; it's not even spontaneous. Many Yale students are self-conscious about their own attempts at subversiveness. They see themselves as forward-thinking transgressors of cultural norms. These students aspire to be people to whom the normal rules don't apply. And that's why naked parties provide such an important insight into Yale culture.

While students at other universities may not be so quick to disrobe in front of dozens of their classmates for the purpose of casual chitchat, I think some Yale students engage in such behavior in a conscious attempt to move beyond the petty constraints suffered by those whom they view as less enlightened. The willingness to bare all at Yale is a mark of election into a club of moral sophisticates.

Elitism amounts to a kind of faith system at Yale. Elitism governs the moral order. It would not be a stretch to say that public nudity amounts to a kind of existential, or even spiritual, experience for students who engage in it—giving them a feeling of distinction and meaning in the midst of lives that are often noticeably empty of spiritual purpose. In this way, naked parties at Yale function as proxy religious rituals in an age of moral relativism. It's transgression as transcendence. Many ancient pagan religions incorporated ritualized nudity. Ironically, in these sophisticated, modern times, nudity has reemerged as a sacred rite at a university that has largely abandoned its religious past.

When it comes to the faculty and the senior administration, many of them suffer from a similar sense of supreme self-exceptionalism. Thus, while some universities may shy away from live sadomasochism in the classroom, Yale believes that it is big enough and enlightened enough to absorb this behavior in stride. It's like the guy who parks his Maserati across two spaces in the parking lot. He doesn't give a tinker's damn if you can't find a spot. He has a better car than anyone around, so he doesn't feel like he has to follow the same rules as everyone else. It's not about pushing boundaries; it's about pushing your weight around, seeing how much you can get away with. It's almost as if the mere act of transgression increases his sense of importance and self-worth.

To point to some extreme examples, Hollywood celebrities sometimes act like fools after living for years with everyone worshipping them and telling them how wonderful they are. They start trashing hotels and throwing tantrums on airplanes. Many Yalies, likewise, have grown up deriving their sense of self-worth from being just a little smarter than everyone else in the room. For some, it goes to their head; and it affects their behavior, occasionally, for the worse.

I think that most of the outrageous behavior I witnessed during my years at Yale boils down to an assertion of ego. I understand it to a point. Most anybody who obtains an enviable position in life finds it difficult to keep his ego in check. The fact is, people are born with varying abilities. And that's okay. I'm in favor of rewarding and celebrating excellence. But there is a great difference between simply *doing* something better, on the one hand, and believing that you *are* better than someone else, on the other. When you start down that latter road, you soon begin to believe that you are capable of living on an entirely different plane of cultural norms than the rest of society. And maybe, just maybe, you will be willing to stand around naked with a hundred friends and strangers just to prove it.

Let me give you lowlier example: When I first got to New Haven, I decided to take one of the guided tours offered by the visitors' office. I figured I would get the lay of the land around campus and learn some interesting historical facts along the way. Tens of thousands of tourists visit Yale each year. I was with a group of perhaps twenty that day. We were standing outside one of the residential buildings, listening to the tour guide, when suddenly a student barged into our midst, trailing a suitcase behind him, calling sharply at all of us to clear out of his way. He began to physically push people out of the way. He laid into me so hard that he nearly knocked me to the ground before lunging though the locked gate beyond and slamming it in our faces.

For about two weeks after that I fantasized about punching that guy. The thing is, I don't think he would knowingly have pushed a fellow Yale student that way. Part of the reason he did what he did was that he saw our little tour group as a group of outsiders. Consequently, he felt entitled to transgress the boundaries of civility. Happily, that kind of foul behavior is truly rare at Yale. Most Yalies would never want to come across as pretentious. Nonetheless, after students have been steeped in a culture of elitism for four years, an attitude of superiority does start to rub off on even some of the best of them.

Most Yalies are extremely pleasant, conscientious people—really. But the tide of elitism on campus sometimes sweeps away even the most well-intentioned Yalie—out to the distant prehistoric jungle lands where the uneducated, unrefined, uncultured heathen tribes of the world established the custom of casual nudity long before Yale students ever prided themselves on the innovation.

A friend of mine named Ryan once paid a visit to Yale. He was on the debate team for the University of Chicago, which was set to compete against Yale. He was sitting down, minding his business, trying to prepare for the big debate. All of a sudden he noticed a guy from Yale standing next to him. He also noticed the guy's penis dangling mere inches away. Standing there in all his flaccid wonder, the naked guy wore a vacant, senseless grin. But Ryan wasn't smiling, and you can bet he was wishing that he was not seated at that moment and therefore so odiously positioned near the fellow's waist level.

Welcome to Yale.

"I thought this was supposed to be some kind of elite institution," Ryan said after telling me the story. Ryan was shocked. But I had to smile at the irony of the tale. Properly understood, that fellow's nudity was actually evidence of the very elitism Ryan had expected to find at Yale.

Try as Yalies may to desexualize public nudity and introduce things like breasts and penises into polite society, things do occasionally get out of hand. Recently the Pundits, those rascally pranksters so famous for baring it all, came under fire for some very unfunny activity that took place at one of their initiation ceremonies for new recruits.

A number of major news outlets picked up the story after police began investigating a possible sexual assault. About fifty students had gathered for the invitation-only event. Midway through the evening, after everyone was good and drunk, leaders of the Pundits ordered the gathered students to strip. News accounts said that students were force-fed more alcohol. Five students—three of whom were underage—ended up being hospitalized due to excessive alcohol consumption. Police received an anonymous tip that there had been a sexual assault as part of the hazing activities. Once the gathered students were extremely drunk, they were forced to kiss one another. One student allegedly had his face forced into another's penis. Ultimately, police were unable to gather enough evidence to press charges on the assault allegations.[5]

The Pundits alone hold as many as a dozen naked parties each year. Considering how many other groups host them, it's difficult to say how many take place at Yale in a given year in total. The various naked parties all have one thing in common—there is normally lots of drinking. Apparently, many students require a heavy dose of liquid courage before they bare it all. Reports of sexual assaults at these events are rare. Then again, studies have shown that most sexual assaults on college campuses go unreported. Inevitably, alcohol lowers inhibitions, impairs judgment, and muddies the lines of consent. I think the story above shows that putting a lot of naked students in a room and getting them drunk out of their minds is a recipe for disaster.

In addition to naked parties of the ordinary variety, there are other, strange or more mysterious kinds of naked gatherings. One of the a cappella groups on campus, appropriately named the Society of Orpheus and Bacchus—the SOB's for short—hosts occasional naked sing-alongs.

There is also the issue of secret-society nudity, which I know much less about due to the fact that it is, as the name implies, secret. There are twelve secret societies at Yale, with enigmatic names like Book and Snake, Berzelius, Scroll and Key, and Wolf's Head. They meet in eerie-looking templelike structures scattered around campus. These buildings are normally closed to all but their own members. However, these groups are all quite small—normally consisting of only a dozen or so students at a time—and therefore they constitute a relatively minor part of the social scene on campus. Out of about five thousand undergraduates, only a couple hundred students are tapped to join one of the societies each year.

The most famous of the secret societies is, of course, Skull and Bones, which has gained quite an ominous reputation among conspiracy theorists due the remarkable career success of its members, for whom it seems to be rather common to be elected president of the United States. William Howard Taft and George H.W. Bush were members. And during the 2004 campaign, Senator John Kerry, Skull and Bones class of '66, went head-to-head with George W. Bush, Skull and Bones class of '67. I watched very closely during the televised debate to see if the two shared any secret handshakes or mumbled incantations. But all I remember was how uncomfortable

Bush looked in front of the camera, and how immovable Kerry's Botoxed brow remained.

Among students, the prestige of Skull and Bones has waned over the years. But conspiracy theorists can't get enough of it. In 2001, ABC News broadcast a video some students shot of the group's secret initiation rites. It showed a bunch of kids wrapped in sheets, kissing a skull and acting out mock killings, trying to frighten the new recruits. But it may actually get weirder once you're in the group. The oddest rumor I ever heard about Skull and Bones was that, at their meetings, it is customary for members to sit in a circle and share intimate details of their sexual histories. Some may find the political power and influence of the small, secretive group frightening, as they meet year after year in their dark, windowless temple to collude, incant, and conspire. But, to me, the most frightening thing about it is the idea of George Bush Sr. wiping away tears and dribbling into a handkerchief while sharing the intimate details of his sexual history.

When you're in college, and your mother comes to visit, the last thing you want is to see the odd-looking guy who sits behind you in chem class running down the hall, giving your mother a dose of the full monty. Thankfully, this never happened to me. My mother, being as I have indicated before, a person of humble means, could afford to visit me only once—and that was for my graduation. It was not only her first time at Yale; it was also her first time in New England. I took her on a long private tour, showing her all the architectural wonders the campus had to offer. The Finals Fairies did not streak on that day, and I didn't take her to any naked parties. However, there was one close call.

We were visiting one of the most incredible buildings at Yale—the Beinecke Rare Book and Manuscript Library. It looks like a hideous cyborg beehive from the outside. But, inside, it is nothing short of a wonder. The entire building is sheathed in translucent marble, allowing small amounts of refracted sunlight to filter in straight through the stone walls. In the center of the structure is a mighty glass tower, filled with thousands upon thousands of the oldest and rarest books known to man.

The Beinecke is a treasure, the kind of resource that made me feel so lucky to be at Yale. The books there are so valuable that no one is allowed to bring a bag or backpack into the underground reading area. The security guards take their jobs very seriously, and I always got the feeling that, had they been armed, they would gladly have shot me on sight if I had made any false moves. When you reach the underground reading area, special librarians, wearing white gloves, retrieve the books out of the sealed, climate-controlled glass chamber. I had the opportunity to read with my own eyes a first-edition copy of Sir Isaac Newton's *Principia Mathematica* from 1687,* a first-edition copy of Copernicus's *De Revolutionibus Orbium Caelestium* from the year 1543, and a 1641 copy of *Meditationes de Prima Philosophia*, hand-signed by Descartes.

I was beaming with pride as I showed my mother around the library, telling her all about the ancient books around us. Then I showed her a copy of the Gutenberg Bible on display in a glass case nearby. Copies of the original Gutenberg Bible, published in 1454, are housed in some of the greatest museums in the world. Only twenty-one complete copies remain in existence. Yale has two of them.

The Gutenberg, of course, is famous as the first book ever printed on a movable-type printing press, which made books widely available to both rich and poor for the first time. Its publication, arguably, marks the most important moment in modern intellectual history, the key that unlocked the chains of ignorance and brutality, the match that lit the flame of mankind's untapped potential, extending the possibility of literacy to the masses and lifting us out of the Dark Ages and into the age of Enlightenment. As my mother and I stood, gazing awestruck upon this historic and

---

* Yale keeps a second-edition copy, just a few years newer, sitting on the shelf in the stacks at the main library, as if it were just another ordinary book.

celebrated object, I noticed something out of the corner of my eye. It was a naked man.

There upon the wall, in another glass display case, was a series of photographs, showing, I believe, various penises and other naked body parts, along with a plaque, indicating that what I was seeing was some sort of art project. What those images had to do with rare books, I wasn't sure. But, knowing my mother and her modest disposition, all I could think about at that moment was how to get her across the room and to the exit without spoiling her positive impression of the place. I have a feeling I was unsuccessful in my mission. But I suppose I will never know for sure. As we passed by the final naked man, and out into the courtyard, she made no mention of the strange gallery of photographs surrounding the Gutenberg Bible, and neither did I.

And, truth be told, I had reason to be thankful. While taking my mother around the library that day, we had encountered only pictures of naked men; but, being at Yale, we might just as easily have encountered the real thing.

If elitism is Yale's proxy religion—its governing moral principle— then going to a naked party is like going to church. It marks you as one of the enlightened ones, one of the elect in a kingdom of sophisticated, postmoral relativists. And that leads to the following irony: At Yale, public nudity is no longer distinctive. It's been done so much that it no longer even feels particularly rebellious to most students. Instead, celibacy has emerged as the new mode of campus radicalism. My friend Margaret, a devout Catholic, led a group on campus called, simply, Greatness, which sought to promote the idea of premarital chastity. Among students, the group raised more than a few snickers. When held up against the prevailing culture, where sex is often considered no more serious than a handshake, and casual public nudity is considered both cool and progressive, the group's agenda seemed radical. And the name of the group—Greatness— makes me chuckle even now for its unprecedented combination of vagueness and ambitious swagger. I like people who swim against the stream and do it in style.

I've always thought it's a good thing if leaders of the chastity movement look like they are chaste because they want to be, not because they have to be. According to these standards, Margaret was a great ambassador for the cause. She was a pretty blonde with brilliant, impossibly big eyes. Her moral convictions, I am sure, disappointed the hopes of more than a few young men on campus who met her. I always admired her for being so bold and outspoken about her beliefs, however unpopular they might have been.

I was curious about what motivated Margaret to practice such a countercultural way of life, and especially what motivated her to be so outspoken about it. I can tell you that the majority of students and faculty on campus viewed her belief system with total incomprehension, as if she had entered our realm from another galaxy. But I wanted to understand better why she and those in her group thought the way they did.

At a local restaurant once, I asked her about her group, what it was about, and what it stood for. For Margaret, abstinence was a religious decision, first and foremost. But she also said that she thought there were basic emotional and relational reasons not to participate in casual hookups. She argued that the divorce of sex and love deprives students of lasting happiness.

In the late sixties, free love was considered edgy and rebellious. Casual sex became, in some circles, a kind of political act, a way to fight the racist, sexist, capitalist system, maybe even a way to protest the war in Vietnam. For others, it was a way to cast off the moral restraints of religion.

It has been forty years; and how things have changed. The relationship between sex and God at Yale has been reversed. Margaret and her friends are the new campus radicals. They move among other students as social outsiders, seeking with their bodies to reestablish a religious lifestyle that long ago fell out of fashion. It's not easy to be different. Margaret may not have changed many minds, but she didn't just try to fit in either. She set her own standards, and lived, for four years, so far as I could tell, according to her own set of beliefs.

Even for those who do not necessarily share her moral ideas or religious beliefs, Margaret and her friends in the Greatness group provide a fascinating point of reference, against which it becomes startlingly clear how extreme the sexual climate at Yale has become, replete with expert classes on sadomasochism, blow jobs, and sex toys, topped off with evenings of somber (but definitely not sober) group nudity.

18

SEX WITH PROFESSORS: THE FINAL FRONTIER

Eros in the true sense is at the heart of the pedagogical rela-
tionship.

—William Deresiewicz,
former Yale professor of English

Even while I was at Yale, my music career never really slowed down. I had a couple of gigs per week going throughout much of my time there. I played often in New Haven and in the surrounding area. It was better than working in the cafeteria or reshelving books in the library. At one point, I was pulling down about a thousand bucks a month with part-time gigs. It was great money, and a lovely way to take a break from the books.

During my senior year I played a weekly gig at the Lansdowne, an Irish pub on Crown Street, just a couple of blocks from campus. Just me, my guitar, and a microphone, and, usually, a mostly empty room. Sometimes a group of Chinese businessmen would come in and order buckets full of Budweiser, and that's when things would get exciting. Once, they even came up onstage to do a little live ka-raoke. Apparently, John Denver's "Take Me Home, Country Roads" is something of a national pop-culture anthem in China.

On one occasion, during a break between sets, my buddy Brandon and I were having a beer at one of the tables near the bar, and he began to talk about a well-known Yale professor.

"Yeah, one of these girls I know had sex with him," Brandon said.

"Are you serious?"

"Yeah, she used to go over to his house sometimes. You know what he said after they were done?" Brandon chuckled.

"I can't imagine."

"He rolled over and said, 'You've beached a whale, my dear.'"

This particular professor had a reputation for being flirtatious with female students and, I had heard, for getting on intimate terms with them. I had no way of knowing whether it was true, but Brandon's tale didn't surprise me. Still, the story grossed me out, especially because the professor was in his seventies, and the idea of a young student cavorting around naked with his wrinkled body was just about enough to make me lose what I'd been drinking.

Among students, it's no secret that professors at Yale sometimes indulge in sexual relations with undergraduates. It's like doping at the Tour de France—there are rules against it, but everybody knows it goes on anyway. While these relationships are rare, certain professors gain reputations for them. Most often, it's a male professor involved with a female student. There is nothing illegal about these relationships, so long as they are consensual. And until recently, Yale had no policy against faculty sex with undergraduates. In 2010, after years of debate over the issue, the university finally instituted a ban. However, unless the administrators plan to install hidden cameras in everyone's bedrooms, I'm not sure how they hope to enforce it.

Students are, legally, adults. Some argue that they should be free to engage in whatever relationships they wish with faculty. But the unequal power dynamic between professors and students makes such relationships problematic. Professors hold tremendous power over their students. They can pass them or fail them in a course. They can destroy their grade point average with the stroke of a pen. They can advance their careers with letters of recommendation, which are critical for students as they try to find jobs or gain entrance to top graduate schools. When professors get sexually involved with their students there is a tremendous potential for academic integrity to be compromised. In particular, if the course in question is graded on a curve, it has the potential to negatively affect everyone in the class.

All too often, these kinds of relationships take on the appearance of quid pro quo exchanges. You have, on the one hand, cases of *the girl who would do anything for an A*. And, on the other hand, you have cases of *the professor who would give any grade to a girl who would do anything for an A*. There are even instances when a professor threatens to damage his student's prospects if she doesn't comply with his wishes, as was the case with one alleged example I will give shortly.

Some people like to say that any sex between two consenting adults is okay. But professors shouldn't be having sex with students under their tutelage for the same reasons bosses shouldn't be having sex with subordinate employees. Whether there is coercion involved, or mutual consent, there are lots of potential problems either way.

"My dears, depending on how one reads him, one could say that Shakespeare was either heterosexual, homosexual, or asexual." This was one of Harold Bloom's favorite things to say about Shakespeare. Bloom is, unquestionably, the most famous professor at Yale. He holds the rank of Sterling Professor, the highest bestowed by the university. As a literary critic and scholar he has stood atop his field for six decades, garnering perhaps as many critics as admirers along the way. Through lectures around the world, television appearances, numerous articles, dozens of books of his own, even his own publishing imprint, Bloom has transcended academia and become something of cultural celebrity.

Best known for his devotion to the classic works of the Western literary canon, he has taken controversial stands against more recent fashions in literary criticism such as poststructuralist, feminist, and Marxist literary theory. Bloom is devoted to the old masters, and, most of all, to Shakespeare. He once told me, in all seriousness, "Shakespeare is my god, if there is a god."

Because of his fame, Bloom enjoys tremendous deference from the administration. He is very well paid, and enjoys lots of other perks. During the semester I studied with him, a financial aid student (on university payroll) acted as Bloom's personal assistant and chauffeur for the entire semester, bringing him his mail, running errands, and driving him back and forth in a black BMW between the campus and his home. Bloom holds an appointment in the English Department but never attends faculty meetings there. Instead, his classes are listed under Yale's interdisciplinary Humanities Program, giving Bloom the freedom to, in effect, act as a department unto himself. During fall of my senior year I decided I wanted to take his class on Shakespeare.

You don't take Harold Bloom to learn about Shakespeare. You take Harold Bloom to experience Harold Bloom. He is one of the most eccentric personalities on the Yale faculty. Like some vestige of Yale's distant past, he would walk into the small classroom, hobbling on a cane, pale as ghost, and gazing out mournfully from under billowing white eyebrows. Old, entitled, opinionated. He sipped constantly from a black thermos throughout the two-hour class. (I always wondered what was in that thermos.) And he talked incessantly of his poor health, stopping only occasionally to comment on the attractiveness of the young ladies in the room. It was a strange experience. But, yes, he did know his Shakespeare.

It is not easy to get into a Harold Bloom course. There were only fifteen spaces available in the class, but more than sixty students showed up on the first day, so we had to compete for a spot; he asked each of us to write a forty-five-minute impromptu essay explaining why we wanted to study Shakespeare. Whatever I wrote had the desired effect. Several days later a list of admitted students was taped to his office door. My name was on the list.

On a personal level, Bloom struck me as a bit narcissistic. And it didn't help that so many students openly groveled for his attention and affirmation. On an intellectual level, however, I think his fame is deserved. He is a brilliant and charismatic scholar. His insight into texts is deep. And his passion for literature is infectious. He clearly loves to teach, or at least to be listened to. On a couple of occasions, during breaks in the class, he and I ended up hitting the restroom at the same time. As a rule, men don't usually talk to one another while they pee. It's kind of an unwritten code. But, standing side by side at the urinals, Bloom would keep talking about language or etymology. I figured, what the heck? So I chatted right back.

Near the end of the semester, as we prepared our term papers, Bloom met with each student one-on-one. I was writing about *Twelfth Night,* but during our meeting we ended up talking as much about Stevie Ray Vaughn and Texas blues guitar as we did about Feste and Malvolio. I decided maybe Bloom wasn't so disagreeable a character after all.

Bloom has his detractors. Around this time I discovered a controversial article that had been published in *New York* magazine a few years before. In it, Naomi Wolf, an author and well-known Yale alumna, accused Harold Bloom of physically encroaching upon her on an alcohol-fueled night more than two decades earlier. It was a dramatic account: "I moved back and took the manuscript and turned it around so he could read. The next thing I knew, his heavy, boneless hand was hot on my thigh," and so on.[1] Naomi Wolf's accusation is among the most well-known student/professor misconduct allegations in Yale history. Unfortunately, it may also be one of the least credible. There are a couple of problems with Wolf's account. First of all, the details are not consistent with a prior account she gave in a book years earlier.[2] Second, she was twenty years too late in speaking out. Last, the magazine gave Bloom no chance to defend himself in the article or to dispute Wolf's claims, even though it had been many years since the alleged events took place. Bloom denied her accusations, but within hours of the article's appearance, Bloom opened his door to find live CNN cameras clamoring for his response.

If what Wolf claims happened really did happen, then that's really sad. But to bring all it up publicly for the first time, decades after the fact, without giving him a chance to respond within the article, seems rather pointless. To me, the more relevant part of her article is when she describes a host of other cases of faculty sexual misconduct at Yale in recent decades. Most of these latter cases struck me as far more serious. They include the following:

- In the mideighties, Deborah Amory, an undergraduate, was touched on the inner thigh by a drunken professor. She filed an official complaint. The university's report made no mention of professional consequences for the offending professor.
- In 1992 a law student, Cynthia Powell, was invited back to a professor's apartment for a glass of wine. The professor made advances. She resisted. She blacked out. When she regained consciousness, she found that the professor had removed her clothes and penetrated her. After she filed a complaint, Powell claims, the university wanted to "quietly" push the professor out. "They said he'd been 'careless,' 'reckless.' They didn't want to use the word rape." A few months later the professor resigned and got hired right away by another university.
- In 1996, the university learned that math professor Jay Jorgenson had had consensual sex with a freshman, one whom he was responsible for teaching and grading. A disciplinary board advised that Jorgenson should be prohibited from teaching undergraduates for the rest of the term. But he was allowed to go on teaching anyway. The dean of the undergraduate college told the *Yale Daily News* that he "didn't think it would be possible to find a replacement that quickly."

Wolf notes that it was at this point, when the university was on the receiving end of a wave of negative publicity over the Jorgenson case, that Yale moved to formally forbid sex between faculty and students over whom they had direct supervisory responsibility. Up until that point, such relationships had simply been discouraged.

She goes on to describe other cases of alleged sexual misconduct, and leaves the impression that the university is evasive and secretive about how it handles disciplinary cases, and ultimately seems to spend more energy guarding against legal and financial liability than it does looking after the interests of students.

Wolf points out, rightly, that one incident of harassment doesn't make a professor "a monster." Human passion is unruly. People make mistakes. They can be redeemed. Her greater point in the article is that Yale has a responsibility to make sure that when such incidents do occur, consequences are "both clear and real." If sexual misconduct goes unpunished, or if no one ever hears what the punishment is, it sends the message that there aren't any real consequences. Soon enough minor offenses turn into major ones. Students are more likely to suffer harm, and less likely to report it. On this point, Wolf is dead on.

We live in postfeminist age, when it is hard to believe that any institution would do less than jump over backward to avoid accusations of sexism or sexual harassment. For any university, such cases inevitably arise. But Yale's fear of landing in court has actually made it less responsive. Wolf's article revealed to me that Yale has a long history of protecting its own legal interests above all else, and of failing to respond sternly and openly in cases of sexual wrongdoing. It's a hard thing for a student to report sexual misconduct. Doing so can involve shame, embarrassment, and fear of reprisal. Accordingly, the university should do all it can to make the process simple, transparent, and effective.

Sadly, the antagonistic sexual environment that some women encountered in the eighties and nineties has, I think, only gotten worse with time. Not only has the administration allowed depictions of violent sexual behavior in the classroom, but by the time I got to Yale, the administration had so mangled the process by which students could get help if they were actually harassed or assaulted, so filled it with mazes of lawyers and committees and secretive disciplinary bodies, that students could almost feel harassed simply by the sheer incomprehensibility of the grievance system.

Every time Yale gets some bad publicity over sexual misconduct on campus, it has a very simple response: It creates a new committee. Yale has something called the Executive Committee, commonly referred to as "Excomm," which functions as the university's main disciplinary body. There was also the *Women's Faculty Forum Report*, which was based on an earlier *Report on Sexual Harassment and Assault Prevention Education*.[3] The official Sexual Misconduct Committee created another report that led to the creation of something called a Universitywide Committee to handle sexual misconduct complaints. If you are sexually assaulted at Yale, good luck figuring out whom to report it to and what, if anything, is actually being done about it.

The impenetrability of the grievance system is equally apparent in cases of student-to-student misconduct. A girl in my residential college was raped by a fellow student in the college the year before I got there. I've heard several girls talk about how their friends were assaulted by fellow classmates and the university did nothing. The result was that, in some cases, they had to endure continuing to go to class side by side with the guys that assaulted them. Many of these girls did not go to the police. Rule number one, in my book, if you are sexually assaulted: Go to the police first, not some pencil pusher in the dean's office. Rape is a crime, not an academic infraction. Sadly, studies have shown that up to 60 percent of sexual assaults are never reported to law enforcement. All the more reason why it is the university's responsibility to be clear and transparent about its own disciplinary actions.

I also heard more than one girl claim that the university discouraged her from reporting an alleged assault to law enforcement. I can hardly believe such a thing is true, but if it is, it could only be because the university is so obsessed with guarding itself against legal and financial liability.

* * *

The university's secrecy about sexual misconduct on campus is, at times, mind numbing. In February 1999, Yale geophysicist Antonio Lasaga abruptly resigned after the FBI informed him that he was under investigation for possessing child pornography. Eventually more than 150,000 pornographic images of children were confiscated from his home and office computers. Lasaga was not only a respected geophysicist and a popular teacher; he was also the resident master of Saybrook, one of Yale's residential colleges. As master, he was responsible for directing the social lives of about four hundred undergraduates.

After Lasaga's sudden resignation, Dean Richard Brodhead* held an emergency meeting in the Saybrook dining hall and told students only that Lasaga had resigned for "personal reasons."[4] It would take weeks for the gruesome details of Lasaga's crimes to come to light. Among the 150,000 confiscated images, investigators found two videotapes that Lasaga had made of himself raping an eleven-year-old boy. He shot one of the videos in a Yale laboratory and another in the master's house at Saybrook—right in the midst of student residences.[5] He had met the boy through a local mentorship program for underprivileged youth, and abused him for five years.

Lasaga is currently serving a twenty-year sentence in federal prison. In addition, a judge awarded the victim $16.5 million in personal damages. The victim eventually sued Yale as well, alleging that an assistant professor in the Geology Department had once walked in on Lasaga as he was standing over the victim while he was seated on a classroom desk. But instead of reporting the incident to authorities, as required by law, the other professor allegedly closed the door and walked away.

I desperately hope that this final wrinkle in the despicable saga

---

* Brodhead eventually left Yale to become the president of Duke University. There, in 2006, he famously came under fire after he canceled the Duke lacrosse team's season on the basis of sexual assault charges that ultimately proved false.

is untrue. But it's not impossible for me to imagine, in particular if the younger professor didn't get a good enough look at the victim to see that he was a minor. Perhaps he assumed the victim was just another Yale student "doing anything for an A." If the young victim was presumed to be a somewhat older student, then I think the observation of a professor in some state of sexual entanglement with him might well go unreported at Yale.

Flagrant cases of faculty sexual misconduct, such as the ones I've mentioned above, are rare. More often, what I observed was a weird willingness, on the part of certain professors, to overstep normal bounds of decency around young students. During Sex Week 2008, they were handing out free goodies during one session. I saw Harvey Kliman, a gynecologist and research scientist at the Yale hospital, who also teaches undergraduates, pass a vibrating Trojan cock ring to a sophomore girl I knew, while organizers distributed them to other students in attendance. He was laughing and asked her, "Are you happy?" The girl blushed, and was visibly uncomfortable. And who wouldn't be? Handing a vibrating cock ring to a student seems like a weird thing for a teacher at a prestigious university to do.

Then there's the case of William Summers, M.D., Ph.D., professor of theoretical radiology, biophysics, and radiation, who in recent years taught a course called "The Biology of Gender and Sexuality," commonly known among students as "Porn in the Morn." It was held in a massive lecture hall. More than 10 percent of the student body was enrolled in the class in the spring of 2005.[6] It was for several years the most popular course in the entire university. You could actually fulfill your "science" distributional requirement at Yale by spending the semester doing work that included differentiating between the clitoral orgasm and the G-spot orgasm.

I picked up the student paper one day and read a story titled "The Very Intimate Professor." It was an account of Professor Summers on a little field trip to a local sex shop with a female student reporter named Danielle.

The story begins with Professor Summers and the student driving to a local sex shop called Very Intimate Pleasures. They browse the aisles of the establishment together, and Danielle offers a detailed account of all the items they pick up and discuss. They start with the "Erotic Love Piggy," an inflatable farm animal. "See, animals are a big thing," Professor Summers comments. He goes on to explain to Danielle why a lot of women like to wear leather and rubber.

Danielle writes about how, in addition to covering various sex-toy issues, Professor Summers likes to consider the sociological implications of sex, asking his students, "What is intergenerational sex?" and "What is it about Anna Nicole Smith that so interests people? Why was she with a 95-year-old man? What does she see in him?"

As we peruse the vibrator aisle these seem appropriate questions, as a friendly female staff member offers, "If you want to know how anything works, I'm happy to put batteries in it for you . . ."

Undeterred, Summers resumes his explanation of the store's wares. "See, they come in all colors and sizes," he says, gesturing to the Crystal Ice, the Top Stud, the Shock Wave, the Cyclone. "This one lights up. Like you can see it down there anyway."

The employee in the article seems to approach Danielle and the professor as if they were a couple. The whole situation is just so strange, isn't it? The rest of the article recounts Summers's musings over a batch of "pleasure pearls," and tells of a penetrating inquiry into the purpose of what looks like a can of Dr Pepper.[7]

Professor Summers is a highly paid, very well-known member of the faculty. Was he embarrassed to see his name attached to this story? I don't know. He certainly knew Danielle was acting as a reporter when he agreed to accompany her to the sex shop. All I know is this: Traveling to the local sex shop with a young female student seems like a weird thing for a professor at a prestigious university to do.

Yale likes to invite porn stars in for this kind of instruction. But in the absence of buxom babes, there appears to be no shortage of tenured professors who are willing to do the job. Commonsense understanding of the boundaries between professional behavior and what is crass and puerile has obviously been lost. I want to emphasize that these professors aren't hiding these activities; they are participating in them openly. And that, to me, is telling. Reading something like this, one begins to wonder: What are the standards for appropriate conduct between professors and students at Yale? There really aren't any. Almost anything goes.

Yale's undergraduate population is divided into twelve residential "colleges," modeled after the old Oxford/Cambridge system. Each residential college is like a dorm on steroids, with an inner courtyard, a dining hall, a game room, and a library, and a unique architectural style. Each serves as home to about four hundred students. The colleges have old English-sounding names like Berkeley, Trumbull, Silliman, and Davenport. As a student, in addition to your loyalty to Yale, you tend to develop a fierce loyalty to your residential college. (I'm a Berkeleyite forever.) This system provides an intimate college-within-a-college atmosphere, and it's one of the best features of undergraduate life at Yale.

Each college at Yale has a master—normally a highly respected member of the faculty—who lives in a special residence right alongside the undergraduate dorms. The college masters are very involved with students and are responsible for setting the tone of social life within each residential college. Throughout the year, they will invite various artists, writers, and intellectuals to give informal talks in the master's house, called "Master's Teas." Occasionally, they'll muster a Hollywood celebrity: Jodie Foster and Denzel Washington have appeared in recent years. Students are served tea and hors d'oeuvres. Attendance is normally limited to about two dozen.

On one such occasion I arrived at the Saybrook master's house to attend a Master's Tea with a guest of honor named Dr. Susan Block—an HBO late-night sex "educator" and hard-core-porn personality. Unlike similarly themed Sex Week events I described in earlier chapters, Block's event was organized directly by the college master. She was speaking that day as his guest and at his invitation.

I enter to find her sporting a broad-brimmed hat, lots of black sequins, and fishnet stockings. She begins by saying that Yale is a true pioneer in the art of XXX education. She praises Yale because its example has "inspired other colleges and universities" to incorporate boundary-pushing sexual material into the educational experience.

What a legacy.

Next to Block sits a pile of DVDs she has produced, which include the following titles: *Squirt Salon, The Bonobo Way,* and, with a patriotic touch, *Eros Day 10: An Orgy for Obama,* depicting an orgy she says she held in honor of Obama's presidential victory.

Her talk is full of advice for students on how to cultivate sexual fantasy. There is the "classic guy doing two women," she says before waxing poetic: "Double the pleasure, double the fun; two lovers are better than one." But that's not all. "Then there are those bisexual fantasies we all have—I think we all have."

She discusses teacher/student relationships. "Now, you can't have sex with your teacher. That's taboo. When I was in school it was different." (Block attended Yale in the seventies as an undergrad.) No need to worry, she assures us, because, through fantasy, you can safely violate any taboo. "You might have a fantasy that you want to kill your professor or have sex with them [*sic*]," she explains, as though either course of action would be equally valid.

Hey, whatever works for you!

She makes sure to mention submission and dominance. "Power is a rush," she says. "We know that. And submission is also a rush, if we have it in the right way. Feminism is beginning to accept that. . . . No one wants to be raped. But it's a popular fantasy because you are being raped by the perfect lover."

As the talk unfolds, Block begins passing out DVDs to students along with a number of "Dr. Johnson's Pocket Rockets." Professor Paul Hudak, the Saybrook master, is seated next to Block throughout the talk. He looks slightly embarrassed by all that is unfolding.

Nevertheless, he lends a hand in passing out the porn to the students. Block passes out more DVDs, more Dr. Johnson vibrators, and a few white thongs imprinted with the logo "Lust et Veritas"—a cheeky play on the university's official motto.

Block soon turns to talk of religion. Her take on monotheism: "You have to have one partner under this one-god system. We maintained that for two thousand years, but now we have a certain openness. We're coming up on a new pantheistic age. . . . I like all the gods and goddesses." A student speaks up and asks what Block would recommend if a priest asked how to use fantasy. Block pauses a moment to hike up her fishnet stockings. "We're all animal and angel," she says. "Nuns marry to Jesus, whether they masturbate or not; I mean, I think it wasn't as much of a big reach."

Block's intellectual interests are broad. In a flash she turns from theology ("I'm kind of a pantheist"), to zoology ("We are all primates"), to xenoarchaeology ("Fantasize about aliens—it's a divine experience"). She hands out still more of her DVDs and sex toys.

Mercifully, time expires. Master Hudak leads the room in a round of applause. "Dr. Block has been giving out a lot of things," he says. "I'd like to give her something." The college doesn't have any sex toys, he points out, so he settles for a pair of pajamas emblazoned with the Yale logo. Block reciprocates by giving the master one of her books, entitled, *Ethical Hedonism,* for him to add to the Saybrook library, along with one called *The Ten Commandments of Pleasure,* for his own personal collection.

Master Hudak seemed slightly uncomfortable during the whole Susan Block soiree. Nevertheless, he appeared to do his best to take it all in stride. He helped pass out the porn, and sat by and listened to all the mindless talk about alien sex fantasies, as if it were just another day on the job. In any event, as college master, he was the one responsible for inviting her to speak in the first place.

Hudak isn't a weirdo. Far from it. He is a respected computer scientist, and is well liked by students. But the lesson one should take away is just how normal passing out porn or vibrators is at Yale today. In fact, the previous master of Saybrook hosted a similar Master's Tea with Susan Block only two years earlier. That woman, Hudak's predecessor, happens to be Mary Miller. She was promoted not long after that event. Today she is the dean of Yale College.

So, you see, what Hudak was doing—indulging a lot of vile gibberish, personally distributing porn to students—might seem outrageous. But he was simply following the example set by one of Yale's most senior administrators. We are left with an unanswerable question: Why do Yale's top leaders think Susan Block is a person worthy of multiple invitations to speak to Yale students? It's senseless. Exactly how Block's rape fantasies and sex toys and porn fit within the educational goals of the university is something I would dearly love to hear Yale's leaders explain.

The sexual climate at Yale is clearly troubled. On the one hand, the university, through its perpetually defensive legal posture, has cultivated an environment of secrecy. On the other hand, with its wildly aggressive sex education agenda in recent years, it has sent a message to the community that almost anything goes. Inevitably, students have suffered as a result, and female students in particular. Here are some examples:

In 2006, a group of fraternity pledges gathered outside the Yale Women's Center and shouted, "No means yes, yes means anal."[8]

In 2007 a Yale student pleaded no contest to sexual assault against another student. The victim sued the university for failing to enforce underage drinking laws and failing to educate students about sexual assault. Later that year, a former secretary brought another lawsuit against the university. She claimed the university had failed to act on complaints that her boss, the chair of the Pharmacology Department at Yale Medical School, Joseph Schlessinger, was sexually harassing her. The case was settled out of court for an undisclosed sum.[9]

In October 2010, a group of pledges for the Delta Kappa Epsilon fraternity marched through Old Campus, where most freshmen live, shouting, once again, "No means yes, yes means anal!" Not very original, those guys.

Some of these incidents, taken by themselves, amount to little more than the crass adventures of rude frat boys in need of a good sobering up. For example, when fraternity pledges shouted, "No means yes," I don't think it was truly "an active call to sexual violence,"[10] as one member of the Yale Women's Center put it. But I do think it reflects an indifferent attitude toward women that poisons the social climate at Yale.

I see evidence of this indifference in the campus hookup culture. Quite a few men at Yale assume that women should be sexually available to them. They assume that like the eager women one sees in pornography, Yale women—albeit with a bit less eagerness—will be at their beck and call. And sometimes, in the heat of an alcohol-fueled Friday night, with its quick and easy hookups, it might seem like they are. But it isn't always the case. And alcohol, along with some guys' unrealistic sexual expectations, is at the root of many of the sexual assaults that occur between students.

Yale's leaders have done far more damage to Yale's sexual climate than any fraternity pledges have done. Indeed, by allowing the sex industry to have open access to the campus, Yale's leaders have helped create an environment where crass and aggressive sexual behavior around campus feels oddly normal. While some of these events, by themselves, seem relatively minor, taken together, the catalog of alleged sexual harassment incidents at Yale in recent years paints an ugly picture. I'm not surprised that many Yale women don't feel respected. I'm not surprised that some of them don't feel safe.

Nor was I particularly surprised when, in March of 2011, the Department of Education's Office for Civil Rights launched an investigation to review Yale's policies for dealing with sexual harassment and sexual assault in order to determine whether Yale is in violation of women's rights provisions under Title IX.

* * *

Christina Huffington, a Yale student and daughter of media mogul Arianna Huffington, broke the story in the *Yale Herald*. The official complaint, signed by sixteen current undergraduates and recent grads, alleged that by failing to properly address incidents of sexual harassment and sexual assault, Yale created a "hostile environment" for women. The complaint cited many of the incidents I mentioned above. But the most damning portion of the complaint came in the form of personal testimonies from girls who identified themselves as victims of sexual assault, and who complained that the university's resulting disciplinary actions against the perpetrators were weak and inadequate. The complaint also criticized the university for attempting to deal with sexual assault cases secretly and internally, thereby leaving it unclear to students what, if any, consequences were put into effect.[11]

The Title IX investigation immediately became national news, and it didn't do anything to burnish Yale's reputation. Hopefully the investigation has served as a wake-up call to senior administrators. Yale, so proud of its liberal concern for women's rights, has done precious little good on behalf of women in recent years—unless you consider porn star look-alike contests and how-to seminars on the binding and flogging of female "submissives" to be the kinds of events that promote positive views of women.

Yale's leaders are ultimately responsible for this disgraceful state of affairs. And their failure to uphold basic standards of decency and responsible sexual conduct could have serious long-term consequences for the university. Over the last few years, there have been severe budget cuts in the wake of the global financial crisis. The endowment suffered losses in the billions. And the university forecast a $68 million budget shortfall for the 2011–12 academic year.[12] If Yale were ever found to be in violation of Title IX statutes, it could lose all federal funding, currently more than half a billion dollars per year. Financially, it would bring the university to its knees almost overnight.

CONCLUSION

The dean of my residential college, Kevin Hicks, was one of my favorite people at Yale. He was loved and admired by students—an all-around great soul. He sent me an e-mail in the fall of my senior year. It was finals week and he was organizing an evening study break for students with pizza and soft drinks. As was always the case during finals, we students were under a lot of pressure. Hicks figured a bit of fun might help us make it through with our sanity intact. He asked another student and me to provide a little light-hearted musical entertainment, and he even helped select the set list. Characteristically, he went all out for the occasion and had a fog machine brought into the dining hall, along with a sound system. Eventually, I ended up gyrating on top of a coffee table with a microphone, leading my fellow students in a rousing rendition of Tommy Tutone's hit song "867-5309."

Jenny, I got your number . . .
I got your number on the wall;
For a good time call . . .

At Yale, students take their work seriously but still know how to have a good time.

After about an hour of hilarious, exuberant singing of inane eighties pop songs, everyone went back to the books, back to slaving away into the wee hours. I lingered behind. I remember collapsing on a couch, sweaty and exhausted from all that singing and gyrating. Dean Hicks came over and sat down. We started chatting about a paper I was working on. Within minutes, we were engrossed in a fascinating literary discussion of Dante's theology of desire, sweat still dripping from my forehead. It was the kind of poignant, beautifully eccentric experience that could happen only at Yale.

I cherish that memory, and many others like it.

My days at Yale passed like a dream—it was over all too quickly. It was a time full of great ideas, great challenges, and, above all, great people. It is—in the end—the talent, energy, creativity, and genius of its students that make Yale such an extraordinary place to study. When you're in the middle of finals, and you're on no sleep, and you're trying to finish that last big term paper, it can feel like torture. All you can think about is getting to the end. Graduating. Then, suddenly, the end overtakes you, and it's all too soon. You realize that you will soon have to leave behind the charmed life you've been living.

On the day I finished my last final exam at Yale, I walked out of Linsly-Chittenden Hall—something I had done hundreds of times before. On my way, I passed the small classroom where I had sat for my first class at Yale. Things had come full circle.

During the previous two hours, the morning's light snowfall had turned into a blizzard. The snow was shin-high on the ground, and still falling. I pressed my face against the driving snow. Gale-force winds blew against me, nearly knocking me over. I ducked under an archway to gain a moment's relief. I looked back. The two-hundred-foot-tall Harkness Tower loomed like a lonely giant over the deserted Old Campus quad. Everything was covered in white. I pulled out my cell phone and snapped a picture, just so I could remember the moment.

I felt a deep sense of relief and gratitude. All I had worked for was now nearly in hand. The odds had been against me. I had come from nothing, and had fought my way into Yale, and had received what is often described as the best undergraduate education in the world. The naïve hope that had sprung up in my heart years before as a boy, while flipping through my family's dusty encyclopedia, had now—most improbably—become reality. The knowledge that my life at Yale was drawing to a close brought an ache to my stomach. When I finally stepped out of my little archway and back into the quad, the fierce wind slowed my progress. It was as if nature were conspiring to delay my exit from Yale, and make the whole experience last just a little longer.

Given all I've written about, it may seem surprising that I harbor so many fond feelings for Yale. I suppose the good times tend to stand out in one's memory as time passes, and other memories fade. On the whole, my feelings about the experience are bittersweet. Altogether, I spent six terms at Yale—the equivalent of three academic years. During that time I experienced some of the vilest moments of my life. For every expression of what is high and noble and beautiful and true, there seemed to be another following close behind—of the lowest, basest, ugliest, and most cynical ideas the world has to offer. At times, I witnessed attitudes toward and depictions of women that could only be described by one word—evil.

I worked hard and sacrificed a great deal to get to Yale. Today, as I look at the diploma hanging on my wall, I realize that, years ago, I bought into a vision of what that diploma means that was, in part, a myth. I thought Yale would be a place where humanity's greatest ideas would be tested and debated by some of its greatest minds. But I found that the moral aimlessness of the place has caused many there to lose touch with what it means to be virtuously and compassionately human. It has caused them to ignore the ideas that made civilization great, and worth studying, to begin with. I had thought of Yale as a modern-day equivalent of the Athenian agora; but all too often, I found myself sitting in the equivalent of an intellectual whorehouse.

When I arrived at Yale, I expected to be in a liberal environment. But I didn't expect it to be a place where the dignity of women would constantly be undermined in the name of academic freedom. And I didn't know that Yale had moved beyond simply being permissive, to actively promoting a low-minded sexual agenda, which has no logical relation to Yale's purpose as a training ground for the world's intellectual, cultural, and political leaders.

Academic freedom is vital, just as freedom of conscience and individual liberty are vital. But a great university cannot use academic freedom as an excuse for ignoring the basic rights and human dignity of its members. In an attempt to avoid appearing moralistic, Yale's leaders have cultivated an atmosphere at odds with the equality they say they believe in. They say they are committed to equality for women. Then, in the name of academic freedom, they have welcomed the woman-objectifying porn industry with open arms. Afterward, they act surprised when young men on campus begin to display similar callousness and disrespect toward women. It's not a long trip from sadomasochistic porn screenings with glamorized violence toward women, to frat boys chanting "No means yes!" and "We love Yale sluts!" on the campus quad. But Yale's current leaders don't seem to make the connection. They don't seem able to see the hypocrisy of permitting the former, and then pretending horror at the latter. They fail to realize that by cultivating a selfish and exploitative sexual culture, they have harmed all students, and especially women.

The number of high-profile sexual assault and harassment cases on campus in recent years has been a huge source of embarrassment for the university. Yale's leaders can create all the disciplinary committees they want, but if they really want to change the sexual climate on campus, they ought to start by asking themselves why they have given an open door to the sex industry. They ought to ask themselves why they have repeatedly invited exploitative corporations to market their products directly to students. They ought to ask themselves why teaching students how to perform oral sex, or how to use anal plugs, is related to the mission of a great university. They ought to ask themselves how showing images of a man beating a naked woman with a whip fits into the university's goal of training the future leaders of the world.

These activities have not gone on in secret. The university has publicly welcomed the most extreme elements of the sex industry onto the campus. And Yale's leaders have done so unapologetically. Therefore, the responsibility for Yale's moral emptiness rests chiefly upon them. And they must accept some measure of responsibility for Yale's culture of inequality and hostility toward women—a problem for which the university has now come under federal investigation.

How did it come to this? The president, the provost, the dean of Yale College, and many of lower rank—they talk about lofty principles of academic freedom and gender equality, but they seem unaware of how their decisions affect the real lives of students.

Time to wake up.

The days of in loco parentis are over. What students choose to do on their own time is, for the most part, not the university's business. But the university has a legal and moral obligation to guard the public space from sexual harassment, intimidation, and denigration. In my judgment it has failed miserably.

There is a line between liberality and moral indifference; Yale crossed it long ago.

The moral crisis at Yale is really only an extreme example of what students are beginning to experience at universities nationwide. Most universities offer no guidance for students except to shove heaps of condoms at them and tell them to "be safe." University health "experts" give little thought to the emotional repercussions of sex. These repercussions apply to both sexes. However, studies show that female students are most often the ones who come out of college feeling cheated, dissatisfied, and, in some cases, struggling with low self-esteem. On top of the emotional toll, there is a physical toll to consider. Today, one in four teenage girls has a sexually transmitted disease.[1] One of the most common afflictions is gonorrhea of the throat.

If colleges can't do anything to help students, I wish they would at least stop actively doing them harm. I recall the Yale official who expressed the wish for all students to have "glorious" consensual sex, and all the bawdy how-to seminars I witnessed. I ask you this: What interest should Yale have in the details of students' sex lives? What interest should it have in making sure that students are having "really good sex" or "really kinky sex," or that girls know how to give guys really good blow jobs? Why is this a concern for Yale's leaders? What's their motivation?

I can only guess that the strange sexual agenda they are pushing is, at some level, a belligerent reaction against religious moralism and traditionalism—Yale's attempt to run from its own past. The more outrageous the debauchery, the more self-assured Yale's leaders become about the distance between themselves and the ghost of Jerry Falwell. Probably the worst thing you could do to a typical member of the Yale faculty would be to spread a rumor that he or she is secretly a right-winger, or a closet religious zealot. There is a deep fear in many academics that if they ever say, "This is right, and that is wrong," it would amount to imposing their beliefs on others. But their failure to uphold even limited moral standards is, ironically, the very thing that leads to impositions on women—whose equal treatment they say is a matter of moral right. You can't believe in both moral relativism and the equality of women. You have to choose one or the other.

I do think the radical sexual environment at Yale invites sexual assault and harassment. But, at a deeper level, I think it also robs students of the chance to begin experiencing real love. Students' future lives, and their future families, may someday be casualties of Yale's indifference.

CONCLUSION

Sex at Yale is radically divorced from love. Sex is presented to Yale students in the form of advice about getting what you want when you want it. But love entails both giving and receiving. Perfect love is a blend of both passion and compassion. But the sexual climate at Yale is about using others, not loving them. As students move on in their lives, I fear, the ways of relating they learned here will continue to make love elusive. Of all the negative consequences that result from Yale's appalling educational irresponsibility, that may be the worst, and most enduring, consequence of all.

In the early fifties, William F. Buckley wrote the famous book *God and Man at Yale,* in which he complained that Yale was promoting collectivist economics, and also that it had strayed from its religious roots. I had the opportunity to meet Bill Buckley not long before he passed away, at a small gathering at the house of one of my professors. Little did I know then that within a few years I would write a book of my own that, in some ways, serves as a continuation of the story he began to tell. In its time, Buckley's book caused quite a stir. Yet, more than sixty years later, his complaints look quaint alongside the hard-core realities of today's Yale.

By the end of my own journey through Yale, I had acquired a mixed bag of feelings. I both love and hate the things it stands for. I will always consider myself a Yalie. My appreciation for all the opportunities Yale has afforded me, as well as all it could—and should—be, as a great university, has not waned. In fact, my loyalty to Yale is what motivates me to expose the scandalous negligence of those entrusted with its care. I love much of what Yale offers. I love its beauty, its connection to history, and, most of all, its people. But I hate the way women are degraded there, the way humanity is itself degraded, and the way Yale's leaders seem determined to sexualize the campus and embrace every kind of lewdness and indecency— just, it seems, because they can. All with a wink and a nod that smacks of elitism and the arrogant belief that—somehow—really smart people should be considered immune to moral accountability.

For more than three hundred years, Yale has influenced the culture and politics of America and the world. To study at Yale was one of the great privileges of my life. Yale is still a great university. But it is afflicted with a profound lack of political vision and moral purpose. Reforming the culture there will require leadership from those who are not indifferent to the struggles of students in their charge.

Yale seeks to enroll the world's future leaders. Such a mission implies a special responsibility to educate responsibly. The bright and ambitious classmates I studied with will go on to positions of leadership in every aspect of society. They will own the businesses, chair the committees, and run the institutions that shape the culture we live in and the laws we live by. What is happening at Yale right now will affect life in America and the world beyond for decades to come. If you are concerned about women's equality, society's values, or just basic human decency and dignity, you may find that cause for alarm.

Over the last decade, Yale's national influence has proved to be as pervasive as it is perverse. Sex Week at Yale started as an educational novelty, a biennial Ivy League freak show. But the phenomenon has now spread to dozens of campuses around the country. Formerly vibrator-free schools are now following Yale's bawdy lead, hosting porn-riddled events such as "Sex Out Loud" at the University of Illinois, and "Sex on the Beach" at Indiana University Southeast, "Sex Fest" at the University of Wisconsin and Northwestern University's "Sex Week." At Brown University, porn companies are handing students free thirty-minute on-demand porn access cards to be used online.

We have Yale to thank for pioneering a curriculum of smut, to be copied by forward-thinking universities around the country. Now your children do not have to have a perfect score on the SATs in order to have a barebacking porn star teach them how to avoid STDs. What's happening at Yale is coming to a university near you.

ACKNOWLEDGMENTS

There are so many who helped make this book possible, either directly and indirectly. I want to thank my talented and extraordinary classmates: You inspired me with your vibrance and virtuosity; and you were what made Yale the extraordinary place it was. Also the professors who helped shape my educational journey in positive ways, especially Charles Kesler, Charles Hill, Kevin Hicks, and Virginia Jewiss. Some of you became more than great teachers; you became friends. I want to thank the editors and colleagues who gave me some of my first big breaks, and helped support my writing career in its earliest stages, including Robert, John, and Jonah at *NRO,* as well as Adam Bellow. To Bryan Norman, for your time and valuable advice. Special thanks to Jon Sternfeld for your early and persistent faith and vision—may it reward you many times over. To the bold and independent-minded folks at Thomas Dunne, especially my crack editor. Rob, it has been a pleasure: He who makes my writing better is my friend.

Special thanks to Bill Donner, an all-around rock and role-model, and a rare and true friend. Years ago, you saw a certain kind of promise in me, long before anyone else. Without your influence, I wouldn't be where I am. "A friend sticks closer than a brother." To Christopher Buckley, for your astonishing generosity, and for keeping me awake on Class Day.

All of you have my enduring gratitude.

NOTES

CHAPTER 1. SEX WEEK

1. Sara Bonisteel, "Sex Toys 101 and Other Lessons from Yale Sex Week," Foxnews.com, February 15, 2008, http://www.foxnews.com/story/0,2933,330812,00.html.
2. Associated Press, "Yale's Ivy League Education in . . . Sex," Foxnews.com, February 17, 2006.
3. Tom Randall, "Porn Stars, Dr. Ruth, 'Freaked' Parents: It's Sex Week at Yale," Bloomberg.com, February 15, 2008, http://www.bloomberg.com/apps/news?pid=20601109&refer=home&sid=aNB5lQm.eKlE.
4. Ibid.
5. Bonisteel.

CHAPTER 2. THE GREAT PORN DEBATE

1. http://www.yelp.com/biz/hula-hanks-new-haven#hrid:sKVjvn 1dGTgWe89Lb8MKHw, accessed April 17, 2011.
2. "Yale Student: 'I'm Here 'Cause I Love Porn,'" ABC News, February 19, 2008, http://abcnews.go.com/Health/story?id= 4245514&page=1.
3. "Yale's 'Nightlife' Class Brings Students to the Boom Boom Room for Field Trip," *New York Post,* November 24, 2011, http://www.foxnews.com/us/2011/11/24/yales-nightlife -class-brings-students-to-boom-boom-room-for-field-trip/ #ixzz1ekU43Ehj.

CHAPTER 3. THE BUSINESS OF SEX ED

1. Gina Piccalo, "Porn Actor's Struggles Began Long Before HIV," *Los Angeles Times,* May 5, 2004, http://articles.latimes. com/2004/may/05/entertainment/et-porn5?pg=1.
2. ABC News, "Young Women, Porn & Profits," *Primetime Live,* May 27, 2004.
3. Tristan Taormino, "Porn Faces Reality," *Village Voice,* April 27, 2004, http://www.villagevoice.com/content/printVersion/ 182946.
4. Rong-Gong Lin II, "Investigation of HIV in Porn Industry Hurt by 'Limited Cooperation' from Filmmakers, Report Says," *Los Angeles Times,* April 16, 2011. See also: Kim Yoshihno and Rong-Gong Lin II, "At Least 16 Previously Unpublicized HIV Cases in Porn Film Performers, Public Health Officials Say," LATimes.com, June 11, 2009; Gardiner Harris, "H.I.V Found in 22 Actors in Sex Films Since 2004," *New York Times,* June 12, 2009, http://www.nytimes.com/2009/06/13/health/ 13hiv.html.
5. John Rogers, "Porn Industry Promotes Record in Fighting HIV," *Ventura County Star,* June 11, 2009, http://www.ventura

countystar.com/news/2009/Jun/11/16-previously-confirmed
-hiv-cases-in-porn.

6. Taormino.

7. Associated Press, "Porn Industry Not Safe in Its Practices, More HIV Cases Reported," *New York Daily News,* June 13, 2009, http://www.nydailynews.com/gossip/2009/06/13/2009-06-13_porn_industry_not_safe_in_its_practices_hiv.html.

CHAPTER 4. ABORTION AS ART

1. Martine Powers, "For Senior, Abortion a Medium for Art, Political Discourse," *Yale Daily News,* April 17, 2008.

2. Samantha Broussard-Wilson, "Reaction to Shvarts: Outrage, Shock, Disgust," *Yale Daily News,* April 18, 2008.

3. Aliza Shvarts, "Shvarts Explains Her 'Repeated Self-Induced Miscarriages,'" *Yale Daily News,* April 18, 2008.

4. Catherine Donaldson-Evans, "Yale Officials Conclude Student's Shocking Claim of 'Abortion Art' Was 'Creative Fiction,'" FoxNews.com, April 17, 2008, http://www.foxnews.com/story/0,2933,351608,00.html.

5. Zachary Abrahamson, Thomas Kaplan, and Martine Powers, "Shvarts, Yale Clash Over Project," *Yale Daily News,* April 18, 2008.

6. Ambika Bhushan, "Experts Shed Doubt on Shvarts' Claims," *Yale Daily News,* April 23, 2008.

7. Zachary Abrahamson and Thomas Kaplan, "Shvarts to Present New Piece at Tate Modern," *Yale Daily News,* June 26, 2008.

CHAPTER 5. DIRTY LANGUAGE

1. Mark Schilling, "Pensioners Can Do 'Porn' Too," *Japan Times,* February 15, 2008.

2. Gail Dines, *Pornland: How Porn Has Hijacked our Sexuality* (Boston: Beacon Press, 2010), p. 124.
3. Ben Beitler, "'Pink' Soft-Core Films Screened at Whitney," *Yale Daily News,* January 29, 2008.

CHAPTER 7. FINDING MY CHAKRA AT YALE

1. B.K.S. Iyengar, John J Evans, and Douglas Carlton Abrams, *Light on Life: The Yoga Journey to Wholeness, Inner Peace, and Ultimate Freedom* (Emmaus, PA: Rodale Books, 2005), pp. 54–61.

CHAPTER 8. PORN 'N' CHICKEN

1. "Back to a Time When Lawyers Watched Porn Together," *Yale Herald,* February 12, 2010, http://yaleherald.com/featured/back-to-a-time-when-lawyers-watched-porn-together/#respond.
2. Joel Stein, "The Chicken Was Delicious," *Time,* April 29, 2001 http://www.time.com/time/magazine/article/0,9171,110 1010507-107977,00.html.
3. Elaine Jarvik, "Utah No. 1 in Online Porn Subscriptions, Report Says," *Deseret News,* March 3, 2009, http://www.deseret news.com/article/705288350/Utah-No-1-in-online-porn-subscriptions-report-says.html.
4. Kelli Morgan, "No. 1 Nation in Sexy Web Searches? Call It Pornistan," FoxNews.com, July 13, 2010, http://www.foxnews.com/world/2010/07/12/data-shows-pakistan-googling-por nographic-material.
5. My description in this book of Gail Dines's *Pornland* is expanded upon in a longer review: Nathan Harden, "Feminism, Pornography, and Choice," *American Spectator,* August 24, 2010, http://spectator.org/archives/2010/08/24/feminism-pornography-and-choice.
6. BYU Women's Center, "National Pornography Statistics,"

http://wsr.byu.edu/content/national-pornography-statistics, accessed December 28, 2010; BYU Women's Services.

7. Jen Wieczner, "5 Fascinating Facts About Porn," MarieClaire .com, May 10, 2010, http://www.marieclaire.com/world-re ports/opinion/5-fascinating-facts-about-porn.

8. Jason Buchanan, "Biography of Linda Lovelace," NewYork Times.com, http://movies.nytimes.com/person/43452/Linda -Lovelace/biography, accessed December 29, 2010.

9. Samantha Broussard-Wilson, "Violent Porn Flick Prompts Apology," *Yale Daily News,* February 18, 2008.

CHAPTER 9. FEMINISM AND FOOTBALL

1. Zeta Psi Fraternity of North America, http://www.zetapsi.org.

2. Jon Charest, "Zeta Psi Apologizes for Its Members' 'Lack of Judgment,'" *Yale Daily News,* January 22, 2008, http://www .yaledailynews.com/articles/view/23058.

3. Thomas Kaplan, "Brief: Zeta Pledge: I Did Not Read 'Sluts' Sign," *Yale Daily News,* January 24, 2008, http://www.yale dailynews.com/articles/view/23105.

4. Lawrence Gipson, "A Year Later, Little Impact from 'Sluts' Controversy," *Yale Daily News,* February 16, 2009, http:// www.yaledailynews.com/articles/view/27753.

5. Seth Mydans, "In Pakistan, Rape Victims Are the 'Criminals,'" *The New York Times,* May 17, 2002, http://www.nytimes.com/ 2002/05/17/international/asia/17RAPE.html?scp=3& sq=raped%20stoned&st=cse.

6. Gipson.

7. Sean Alfano, "Poll: Women Strive to Find Balance," CBS News, May 14, 2006, http://www.cbsnews.com/stories/2006/05/ 14/opinion/polls/main1616577_page2.shtml?tag=content Main;contentBody.

8. Gipson.

9. I explored this point more fully in a previously published essay:

Nathan Harden, "The Girls I Knew at Yale," chapter in *Proud to Be Right: Voices of the Next Conservative Generation*, ed. Jonah Goldberg (New York: HarperCollins, 2010).

10. Chyng Sun, "Revisiting the Obscenity Debate," *Counterpunch*, January 31, 2005, http://www.counterpunch.org/sun0131 2005.html.

11. *The Harris Poll—No Consensus Among American Public on the Effects of Pornography on Adults or Children or What Government Should Do About It*, Harris Interactive, October 7, 2005, http://www.harrisinteractive.com/harris_poll/index.asp ?PID=606.

CHAPTER 10. HOOKING UP

1. For more on the hookup culture see Laura Sessions Stepp, *Unhooked: How Young Women Pursue Sex, Delay Love, and Lose at Both* (New York: Riverhead, 2007).

2. Tracy Clark-Flory, "The Sexual Cost of Female Success," Salon .com, January 19, 2011, http://mobile.salon.com/mwt/feature/ 2011/01/19/young_women_romance/index.html.

3. Natalie Kinsky, "Spit or Swallow? It's All About the Sauce," *Yale Daily News*, December 7, 2001.

4. Clark-Flory.

5. Catherine M. Grello, Deborah P. Welsh, and Melinda S. Harper, "No Strings Attached: The Nature of Casual Sex in College Students," *Journal of Sex Research* 43, issue 3 (August 1, 2001): p. 255.

6. Steven E. Rhoads, Laura Webber, and Diana Van Vleet, "The Emotional Costs of Hooking Up," *Chronicle of Higher Education*, June 20, 2010.

7. Marvin Olasky, "A Man's World," *World*, June 4, 2011.

8. Miranda, "Dean Gentry Reminds Yale Students That 'Consensual Sex Can Be Glorious,'" YaleHerald.com, October 27, 2010.

9. Claire Gordon, "Gordon: Glorious Consensual Sex Is Real?," *Yale Daily News,* November 6, 2009.

CHAPTER 11. DEFIANT DESIRES

1. Luke Harding, "Victim of Cannibal Agreed to Be Eaten," *Guardian* (London), December 4, 2003, http://www.guardian .co.uk/world/2003/dec/04/germany.lukeharding.

CHAPTER 12. ORAL EXAMINATIONS

1. http://store.babeland.com/eco-sex-toys.

CHAPTER 14. THE NAKED PROFESSOR

1. A shorter version of this account was reported in a previously published article: Nathan Harden, "Bawd and Man at Yale," *National Review,* April 5, 2010.
2. E-mail message from Thomas Conroy, Yale University press secretary, February 25, 2010.

CHAPTER 15. YALE WITHOUT GOD

1. Amanda Ruggeri, "Former Model Follows Spiritual Path at Yale," *Yale Daily News,* November 5, 2004.

CHAPTER 16. YALE WITHOUT PATRIOTISM

1. Charles C. Johnson, "Head of Middle East Studies Supports Terrorist Group," *Claremont Independent,* April 26, 2010.

2. Charles C. Johnson, "Middle East Studies Director Believes 'Zionist Plot' Behind Plan to Partition Iraq, Views Hamas 'with Great Pleasure,'" *Claremont Independent*, December 6, 2010.
3. Bassam Frangieh, "Modern Arabic Poetry: Vision and Reality," in *Tradition, Modernity, and Postmodernity in Arabic Literature: Essays in Honor of Professor Issa J. Boullata*, ed. Issa J. Boullata, Kamal Abdel-Malek, and Wael B. Hallaq (Leiden; Boston: Brill, 2000), p. 249.
4. Joel B. Pollak, "One Lone Student Against Terror at Claremont McKenna," BigPeace.com, March 15, 2011, http://bigpeace.com/jpollak/2011/03/15/one-lone-student-against-terror-at-claremont-mckenna.
5. Abby Wisse Schachter, "Yale's Latest Gift to Anti-Semitism," *New York Post*, June 7, 2011.
6. Sharif Vakili, "Vakili: Real Talks with Iran," *Yale Daily News*, September 29, 2010.
7. Schachter.
8. Human Rights Watch, "Singapore: UN Rights Body Should Press for Fundamental Freedoms," May 4, 2011, http://www.hrw.org/news/2011/05/04/singapore-un-rights-body-should-press-fundamental-freedoms.
9. Tapley Stephenson, "Yalie Allows Privacy to Be Violated for Class Project," *Yale Daily News*, May 14, 2011.

CHAPTER 17. NAKED PARTIES AND ELITISM AS TRANSCENDENCE

1. George L. Hersey, Letter to the Editor: "A Secret Lies Hidden in Vassar and Yale Nude 'Posture Photos,'" *New York Times*, June 16, 1992.
2. Ron Rosenbaum, "The Great Ivy League Nude Posture Photo Scandal," *New York Times*, January 15, 1995.
3. Ibid.
4. Ibid.

5. Everett Rosenfeld, "No Criminal Charges for Pundits," *Yale Daily News*, March 28, 2011.

CHAPTER 18. SEX WITH PROFESSORS: THE FINAL FRONTIER

1. Naomi Wolf, "The Silent Treatment," *New York*, March 1, 2004.
2. Rachel Donadio, "Naomi Wolf Makes Much Ado About Nuzzling at Yale," *New York Observer*, February 29, 2004.
3. Claire Gordon, "Title IX Complaint Against Yale Has a Case," *Huffington Post*, April 1, 2011.
4. Molly Ball, "The Mysterious Fall of Antonio Lasaga," *Yale Herald*, November 13, 1998.
5. Thomas Kaplan, "In Twist to Decade-Old Scandal, Lasaga's Victim Sues Yale," *Yale Daily News*, June 15, 2008.
6. Shahla Naimi, "'Porn in the Morn' Is No More," *Yale Daily News*, September 17, 2009.
7. Danielle La Rocco, "The Very Intimate Professor," *Yale Daily News Magazine* 25, issue 4 (February 2008).
8. Gordon.
9. Campus Clips, *Yale Alumni Magazine*, July-August 2007.
10. "News' View: The Right Kind of Feminism," *Yale Daily News*, October 18, 2010.
11. Christina Huffington, "Yale Students File Title IX Complaint Against University," *Yale Herald*, March 31, 2011.
12. Alison Griswold, "Yale Tries to Fill Budget Gap," *Yale Daily News*, January 21, 2011.

CONCLUSION

1. Associated Press, "1 in 4 Teen Girls Has Sexually Transmitted Disease," MSNBC.com, March 11, 2008.

DATE DUE